D1154597

THE MAUTHAUSEN TRIAL

THE MAUTHAUSEN TRIAL

American Military Justice in Germany

TOMAZ JARDIM

Harvard University Press
Cambridge, Massachusetts
London, England
2012

Library of Congress Cataloging-in-Publication Data

Jardim, Tomaz, 1974–
The Mauthausen trial : American military justice in
Germany / Tomaz Jardim.
 p. cm.
Includes bibliographical references and index.
ISBN 978-0-674-06157-6 (alk. paper)
1. War crime trials—Germany—Dachau. 2. Trials
(Genocide)—Germany—Dachau. 3. Mauthausen
(Concentration camp) 4. War crime trials—Germany—
Dachau. 5. World War, 1939–1945—Atrocities.
6. Holocaust, Jewish (1939–1945)—Austria. I. Title.

KK73.5.D32J37 2011
341.6'90268—dc22   2011011137

For my father

Contents

THE MAUTHAUSEN TRIAL

Introduction

Shortly after 9:00 A.M. on May 27, 1947, the first of forty-nine men condemned to death for war crimes at Mauthausen concentration camp mounted the gallows in the courtyard of Landsberg Prison near Munich. The mass execution that followed resulted from an American military trial conducted at Dachau in the spring of 1946—a trial that had lasted only thirty-six days and yet produced more death sentences than any other in American history. To be sure, the crimes of the condemned men had been monstrous, laying bare the murderous nature of Hitler's twelve-year Reich. Yet despite meting out punishment to a group of incontestably guilty men, the Mauthausen trial reveals a troubling and seldom-recognized face of American postwar justice—one characterized by rapid proceedings, lax rules of evidence, and questionable interrogations. This book tells the story of the Mauthausen trial and the investigation that preceded it.

Very little is known about the vast majority of war crimes cases tried by American authorities in the aftermath of the Second World War. Though the Trial of the Major War Criminals before the International Military Tribunal at Nuremberg (IMT) has received the benefit of extensive research, it represents only one of three distinct paths the United States followed in bringing Nazi perpetrators to justice at war's end. Under the jurisdiction of the London Charter signed by the United States, the Soviet Union, Great Britain, and France, the IMT heard the cases of twenty-two of the highest-ranking figures of the Third Reich for war crimes, crimes against peace, crimes against humanity, and participating in a common plan or conspiracy to commit any of these crimes. As a result of rapidly decaying relations between the United States and the Soviet Union, however, plans to bring other high-ranking Nazis before the IMT were shelved. Instead, the American administration decided to pursue further prosecutions at Nuremberg unilaterally. Known as the U.S. Nuremberg Military Tribunals (NMT), this second path saw the indictment of an additional 185 defendants representing the Schutzstaffel or SS, the military, the legal and medical professions, as well as various government ministries and industry. The IMT and NMT were exceptional, however, as they dealt with only a small fraction of the 1,885 Nazi war crimes suspects tried in the American zone of occupation between 1945 and 1949. The overwhelming majority of U.S. war crimes prosecutions were instead conducted by American military commission courts in 462 trials held on the grounds of the former concentration camp Dachau between mid-1945 and the end of 1947. Having little in common with the proceedings at Nuremberg, the Dachau trials used the preexisting mechanisms of military law to prosecute rapidly nearly 1,700 war crimes suspects. Because of the extraordinary number of defendants tried, the Dachau trials together remain the largest war crimes prosecution program ever undertaken in history.

The Mauthausen trial was among the biggest and most important of the Dachau trials, proceeding against sixty-one defendants, including camp personnel, prisoner functionaries, and civilian workers implicated in the atrocities committed there. Although Mauthausen has never had the notoriety of concentration camps like Auschwitz or Bergen-Belsen, the role it played in the Nazi system of incarceration and terror was no less critical. Located only twenty kilometers from Hitler's boyhood home of Linz, Mauthausen and the dozens of subcamps it spawned comprised the largest and most murderous penal institution in Austria. In the seven years it operated, some 100,000 political dissidents, Soviet POWs, Jews, Gypsies, and other "enemies" of the National Socialist state lost their lives there. Combining slave labor with systematized mass murder, Mauthausen had the infamous distinction of containing the last gas chamber to function during the Second World War. The overwhelming evidence of atrocities discovered at Mauthausen following its liberation by U.S. forces motivated American military prosecutors to seek the apprehension, conviction, and punishment of the camp's personnel with particular zeal.

Despite the centrality of Mauthausen to the history of the Nazi era, scholarship on the trial of its personnel remains undeveloped. Major works on Mauthausen have yet to draw on trial records in order to reconstruct the crimes at the camp, provide survivor testimony, or probe the motivations of the camp's most notorious perpetrators.[1] Aside from a few brief articles, the trial itself has not been the central theme of any publication.[2] To a large extent, therefore, the Mauthausen trial has remained an unexamined footnote, leaving the thousands of pages of Mauthausen trial documents, stored at the National Archives in Washington, D.C., largely unexplored. In part, the lack of scholarly attention paid either to the Mauthausen trial or to the broader Dachau trial program stems from the fact that the records of the trials were not released until many years after proceedings had concluded. Remarkably, some Dachau trial documents remained classified until the early 1990s.

In addition, historians have tended to focus on the Nuremberg trials because of the notoriety and rank of the defendants tried there. As some scholars have pointed out, the IMT helped convey the flawed perception that the Holocaust could be understood best by examining the high-level policies of Hitler and his leading henchman, rather than focusing on the intricacies of what appeared to be only the implementation of a preconceived master plan.[3] In recent years, however, the scholarly shift in Holocaust research toward examination of "ordinary" perpetrators has helped to illustrate how low-ranking operatives not only carried out but also served to shape the policies handed down from above.[4] Though still in its infancy, a growing interest in the Dachau trials as a whole, and in the lower-ranking perpetrators who stood trial there, is indicative of this shift.[5] As this book illustrates, the Mauthausen trial and the voluminous testimony presented there helps to shed further light on the motives, justifications, and worldviews of common concentration camp personnel.

The lack of attention paid to the Mauthausen trial has not been without its consequences. Critical aspects of the postwar pursuit and punishment of Nazi perpetrators have remained obscured. First, the crucial contribution of American military investigators who worked in concentration camps in the immediate wake of their liberation has gone unrecognized. As revealed in the following chapters, American investigators arrived at Mauthausen with little or no prior experience dealing with war crimes and only an anecdotal knowledge of the Nazi concentration camp system. Yet despite their inexperience, they succeeded in drawing together comprehensive reports that provided the basis for the indictment of dozens of Mauthausen personnel and that ultimately informed proceedings at Dachau. It was these investigators who lent shape to the vision of Nazi crimes ultimately presented in the courtroom. The in-depth study of the investigation process presented here—and generally absent from other scholarship dealing with postwar trials of Nazi perpetrators—therefore helps to illustrate how knowledge of concentration camp crimes first emerged in the immediate aftermath of the war.

Second, historians have seldom appreciated the central role of camp survivors in the investigation of Nazi crimes at war's end. Often portrayed as meek and helpless in the wake of their liberation, camp survivors appear in the following pages instead as key players in the punishment process. American investigators working at Mauthausen lacked resources and sufficient staff and therefore came to rely wholly on a group of survivors determined to play a role in bringing their former captors to justice. Army personnel put former inmates of Mauthausen to work as translators, clerks, personal assistants, and interrogators. Survivors wrote histories of the camp, identified perpetrators for arrest, and later helped choose defendants for trial. This remarkable and intimate working relationship forged between American military personnel and camp survivors allowed the former to assemble the Mauthausen case and the latter to emerge from powerlessness. As this book illustrates, one cannot understand the Mauthausen trial—and by extension, any other such trial—without first understanding the dynamics of the investigation.

In comparison with the eleven months of proceedings at the IMT, the Mauthausen trial itself was remarkably brief and reveals features of American postwar justice that challenge the dominant Nuremberg paradigm. Where the IMT and NMT were designed to produce an unimpeachable record of the evils of Nazism while providing defendants with a full and fair trial, Mauthausen trial proceedings were designed to mete out punishment in the most expeditious fashion the law would allow. Defendants appearing before Dachau courts were charged only with war crimes, as defined decades earlier by the Geneva and Hague conventions. Working within a narrow jurisdiction that prohibited both the use of the novel legal charges pursued at Nuremberg and the prosecution of crimes committed either prior to 1942 or against German nationals, military prosecutors reached back as far as the American Civil War for trial precedents. Prosecutors necessarily depicted the crimes at Mauthausen not as unprecedented acts that warranted new legal tools to indict, but instead as extreme manifestations of the excesses of war. Army guidelines greatly eased the burden on Mauthausen trial prosecutors, allowing them to work with relaxed rules of trial procedure and to make extensive use of hearsay evidence, practices not tolerated at either the IMT or NMT. Further, trial prosecutors alleged that the sixty-one defendants took part in a *common design* to commit war crimes—a stipulation similar to conspiracy, which added efficiency to the trial process. Accordingly, prosecutors contended that Mauthausen constituted a criminal enterprise and that each and every one of the defendants, regardless of rank, could be sent to the gallows for taking part in its maintenance.

By trial's end, the Dachau court had spent an average total of only four hours hearing each defendant's case. As the following chapters reveal, the efficiency of the Dachau trial system was achieved at the cost of introducing legally dubious strategies and procedures that prompted outcry in Germany and eventually led to a Senate subcommittee investigation back in the United States. Most troubling at the Mauthausen trial was defense counsel's insistence that signed confessions of the accused, used by the prosecution to great effect, had been extracted from the defendants through physical abuse, coercion, and deceit. Though discounted by the judges as unfounded, such accusations rippled through numerous Dachau trial proceedings and threatened to undermine the integrity of the program as a whole. In Germany, allegations of improprieties at Dachau allowed the general public to question the validity of the American trial program and to avoid any real reflection on responsibility for the crimes in question. During Senate hearings in the United States, Senator Joseph McCarthy used allegations of abuse at Dachau to criticize the Truman administration for the handling of war crimes prosecutions and to accuse American military authorities in Germany of using "Gestapo tactics" in pursuit of their cases.

Questionable as proceedings at Dachau may have been, however, they were not without their merits. The Mauthausen trial succeeded in punishing dozens of perpetrators involved in heinous atrocities—men who in all likelihood would otherwise have evaded prosecution. In addition, the Mauthausen trial granted victims of National Socialism a chance to play an active role in the prosecution process.

Unlike the trials at Nuremberg, where a preference for documentary evidence left little room for the voices of the victims of Nazism to be heard, Mauthausen trial prosecutors made survivor testimony the foundation of their case. This book therefore challenges the commonly held contention that the American postwar trial program failed to give voice to, or act on behalf of, Holocaust survivors. To the contrary, the Mauthausen trial provided a venue in which more than one hundred victims of Nazi persecution could both tell their stories and participate in the prosecution of their former oppressors.

As part of the Dachau trial program, the Mauthausen trial was emblematic of the fervor with which the American military in fact pursued concentration camp perpetrators in the immediate aftermath of the war. In total, more than one thousand camp personnel stood trial for war crimes before military commission courts at Dachau. Therefore, where the IMT and NMT may have kept Holocaust victims at arm's length, the Mauthausen trial reveals a very different story—one in which survivors stood front and center. In the chapters that follow, the voices of those survivors who stood up and faced their former SS captors and helped secure their convictions are heard once again. Despite the flaws of the Dachau trial system, this book asks whether the Mauthausen trial may nonetheless have rendered a measure of justice.

Contemplating the complex issues that arise from the Mauthausen trial has seldom been so critical. The Mauthausen trial represents an alternative approach to prosecuting state-sanctioned mass violence, an approach that has yet to be integrated into current debates concerning the establishment of international courts and the most effective ways of addressing war crimes and genocide in the courtroom. In light of recent attempts to prosecute the perpetrators of atrocities committed in the former Yugoslavia, in Rwanda, in Cambodia, and elsewhere, it is in fact remarkable that the Mauthausen trial has thus far escaped scrutiny. While the Mauthausen trial was part of a military justice system that may be viewed as legally inadequate, the deep involvement of survivors in the prosecution process as described here reveals one way that legal processes can empower victims of mass violence. Though the Nuremberg trials are often regarded as epitomizing American judicial ideals, the Mauthausen trial remains indicative of the most common—and yet least understood—approach to war crimes prosecution historically taken by the United States. As scandal envelopes American military commission court proceedings at Guantánamo Bay, Cuba, against "unlawful enemy combatants," the Mauthausen trial sheds much-needed light on the nature and function of this trial system, and on the successes and failures of one attempt to try foreign nationals for war crimes in a U.S. Army court.

Drawing upon the original Mauthausen trial transcript, investigative records, surrounding documentation, and interviews with key trial participants, this book reconstructs the full arc of the prosecution process. To provide background and context for the trial, I begin by charting the birth and distinct course of the U.S. Army's approach to war crimes prosecution and early attempts at trying mass atrocity and concentration camp cases. A brief history of Mauthausen follows, as does a detailed look at the American investigation of war crimes at the camp that took place there in the weeks after its liberation. I pay special attention to the ways in which investigators gathered and interpreted evidence, and how the voices of camp survivors influenced the vision of Nazi crimes these investigators presented in the reports they filed. I then assess the manner in which military prosecutors at Dachau drew together these reports and the accompanying evidentiary materials in order to forge an indictment. By looking also at the way in which defendants were selected for trial, I reveal the sometimes dubious interrogation methods used by American personnel to extract signed confessions from war crimes suspects.

The second part of the book explores the conduct of the trial itself and shows how the strategies of both the prosecution and defense played out in the courtroom and how survivor testimony gradually "conditioned" the court to fully grasp the depth of criminality within the Mauthausen camp system. My analysis of the court's final judgment accounts not only for the verdicts and resulting sentences handed down by the members of the court in a matter of hours, but also for the perception of Nazi crimes implicit in their ruling. I then scrutinize the subsequent review process, the reasoning behind the clemency extended to nine of the trial convicts, and the mass execution that awaited those who were less fortunate.

Finally, I conclude with an exploration of the aftermath of the Mauthausen trial. In the months following the trial's end, the U.S. Army initiated dozens of subsequent proceedings spawned by the main Mauthausen trial—proceedings that seldom provided defendants with more than a few hours of court time before judges announced both verdict and sentence. Soon, however, mounting political pressures ultimately brought the American judicial proceedings in Germany to an end, while an ensuing clemency program saw the premature release of the surviving Mauthausen trial convicts.

To assess the legacy of the trial, I ask a number of critical questions. Did the Mauthausen trial fulfill its designated purpose? Were the crimes in question accurately depicted and sufficiently understood in the courtroom? And most important of all: did the Mauthausen trial ultimately render justice?

CHAPTER 1

War Crimes Trials and the U.S. Army

At the end of October 1943, the foreign ministers of Great Britain, the Soviet Union, and the United States came together to discuss the issue of German atrocities and possible measures to be taken against the perpetrators. The resulting Moscow Declaration, released to the press on November 1, 1943, established two separate paths along which Nazi war criminals would be brought to justice once hostilities had ended. The first path, which led ultimately to both the International Military Tribunal and the U.S. Military Tribunals at Nuremberg, was reserved for the arch-criminals of the Third Reich. The second path, which culminated in a disparate array of military trials governed by laws and regulations wholly different from those in play at Nuremberg, led to the Mauthausen trial and many others like it. This latter story is not one of ambitious international cooperation, nor of lofty philosophical and legal concepts designed to make sense of unprecedented crimes. Rather, this is the story of an American trial system designed to meet the demands of pragmatism over ideology and capable of prosecuting thousands of lower-level Nazi perpetrators in the most expedient fashion the law would allow.

The Emergence of the War Crimes Issue

Allied attitudes toward the punishment of war criminals evolved continually throughout the course of the war and were shaped by a combination of diplomatic pressures, domestic demands from interest groups and government officials, and the changing realities of the conflict in Europe. It was not the United States, Great Britain, nor the other major Allied powers that first raised the war crimes issue during the Second World War, however, but rather the Polish government in exile. The Poles were the first to experience the brutality of German invasion and occupation and the first to sound the alarm. During 1940 and the first half of 1941, their impassioned pleas nonetheless fell largely on deaf ears. Although the invasion of the Soviet Union on June 22, 1941, drew greater attention to the barbarity of the German war machine, war crimes remained a low-priority issue for the British and the Americans. For the former, the tide of war had yet to turn in their favor, leaving little room for issues that were perceived as peripheral while bombs rained down on London and Coventry. For the latter, the official neutrality that the Americans maintained until the Japanese attack on Pearl Harbor freed them from any expectation to intercede. Further, once the United States entered the war, the wrath of the American administration in Washington, as well as the public at large, was aimed largely at the Japanese, and not at German forces operating in Europe.

Though scattered information concerning German atrocities had been available since the early months of the war, 1942 brought with it the first substantive reports regarding large-scale massacres of Jews and the horrors committed in the concentration camps.[1] For the first time, newspaper readers in the United States and Great Britain confronted headlines that described brutalities previously unknown in the history of war.[2] Though a sense of skepticism continued to prevail, the mounting evidence of the criminality of the

German foe became harder to ignore. Yet despite increasing pressure from various exiled governments, as well as from organizations such as the World Jewish Congress, the major Allied powers were wary of committing to any formal war crimes punishment policy. Not surprisingly, the first major international declaration to condemn Nazi war crimes was not made by the United States, Great Britain, or the Soviet Union but was rather issued by the nine governments in exile. Coming together in London on January 13, 1942, representatives from Poland, Czechoslovakia, and other conquered nations signed the Declaration of St. James, which stated that all signatory powers "place among their principal war aims the punishment, through the channels of organized justice, of those guilty of or responsible for [war] crimes."[3]

By the end of the year both mounting pressure and evidence of atrocity had made the silence of the major Allied powers on the war crimes issue conspicuous. Despite a continuing reluctance to agree upon any decisive action on war crimes, the United States, Great Britain, and the Soviet Union nevertheless issued a statement that directly addressed German lawlessness and threatened punishment for those involved. The Joint Declaration, released December 17, 1942, under the banner of the newly formed United Nations, confirmed that the victims of the Nazis included "many hundreds of thousands of entirely innocent men, women, and children."[4] The Allied nations further condemned "in the strongest possible terms the bestial policy of cold-blooded extermination" and vowed "to insure that those responsible for these crimes shall not escape retribution."[5] What form this retribution was to take, however, remained unclear. Although the declaration helped to confirm for skeptical observers the scope of German atrocities, the Allies remained uncertain of what they were to do about them.

The conflicting attitudes and impulses that defined the early Allied response to war crimes were illustrated most vividly with the establishment of the United Nations War Crimes Commission

(UNWCC) in October 1943. The new body, organized in London, was made up of representatives from the United States, Great Britain, China, Australia, and India, as well as the nine governments in exile, and was created for the express purpose of investigating and gathering evidence of war crimes. Though a promising development at the outset, it soon became clear that the UNWCC was politically weak, manned by representatives backed either by shadow governments, or reluctant ones. Though the investigation of war crimes was central to its mandate, the UNWCC was given no investigative staff of its own and could therefore only record cases brought to it by its member governments.[6] Further, the UNWCC had to rely entirely on Allied initiative to prosecute the various individuals and groups whose atrocities it had documented. It soon became evident that the major Allied powers, particularly Britain and the United States, remained ambivalent as to the best way to pursue the war crimes issue. The American State Department, as well as the British Foreign Office, apparently viewed the UNWCC largely as a tool to be exploited for political ends, particularly in keeping at bay the demands of the governments in exile.[7]

The reluctance of the United States and Britain to provide the UNWCC with investigative power stemmed from several anxieties. First, it was feared that if war criminals were pursued and punished during wartime, the Germans might retaliate with reprisals against American and British POWs under their control. Further, the Americans and British did not want to commit themselves to participating in a potentially huge number of war crimes trials once victory had been achieved. Rather than have the UNWCC blazing the trail for a comprehensive Allied war crimes initiative, the organization was to be a toothless technical committee.[8] Despite the desire to thwart its influence, however, the UNWCC did manage to become a repository of important evidence used later in numerous war crimes cases.

The anxieties that helped to limit the influence of the UNWCC still remained when the American, British, and Soviet foreign ministers met in Moscow at the end of October 1943 to discuss the issue of war crimes. Although the resulting declaration came on the heels of the creation of the UNWCC, it proved to be a turning point in Allied thinking and ultimately laid the groundwork for the emergence of the various postwar trial programs. The Big Three, speaking on behalf of the thirty-two United Nations, used the Moscow Declaration to once again confirm the horrific scope of Nazi barbarism and to repeat their warning that those responsible for atrocities would be sought out and punished. More important, however, the declaration distinguished between two groups of war criminals and detailed for the first time the nature of the justice each would face. The first group consisted of those whose crimes had "no particular geographic localization"—the most senior Nazi figures, who would be punished according to a future "joint decision of the Governments of the Allies."[9] The second group was by far the largest: those whose crimes had been committed within a specific geographic area. These offenders were to be returned to the nations where such atrocities occurred, in order that they be tried in courts under the jurisdiction of the countries in question. According to the declaration, such offenders should expect to be "brought back to the scene of their crimes and judged on the spot by the peoples whom they have outraged."[10]

The Moscow Declaration proved to be the only example of Allied agreement on the subject of war crimes prosecution reached before the end of the war. Though the declaration represented a significant step toward reaching consensus on a plan to punish those responsible for war crimes, it was not without its shortcomings. On the one hand, the declaration asserted the right of the Allies to prosecute enemy nationals for war crimes in accordance with established international law.[11] This assertion would be fundamental to the creation of military courts charged with the prosecution of lesser war criminals. On the other hand, the United States, Great Britain, and the Soviet Union had only agreed to agree on actions to be taken against the major figures of the Reich. As with the creation of the UNWCC, both the United States and Great Britain remained wary of any formal commitment to a prosecutorial plan.[12] The American and British governments were interested first and foremost in the capacity of the Moscow Declaration to deter further atrocities.[13] Such interest was not to be confused, however, with any commitment to hold trials to achieve similar ends. This became clear with the displeasure voiced by both nations when the Soviet Union used the declaration to justify the trial and execution of German war criminals in the Ukraine in December 1943.[14] Both the United States and Great Britain contended that the staging of trials prior to the end of hostilities would only prompt reprisals against Allied soldiers and civilians. The Russians, having experienced on their own soil the worst excesses of Nazi barbarism, did not share this perspective. They viewed wartime trials themselves as the best deterrent to such atrocities, and saw in them a way to cultivate greater sympathy for the Soviet people.[15] Though the Soviet Union, under Allied pressure, reluctantly agreed to suspend its wartime trial program, disagreements of this sort underscored the fact that some sort of prosecutorial plan would have to be agreed upon if Allied unity was to be maintained. By mid-1944, the United States had seized this initiative.

The Evolution of an American War Crimes Policy

By 1944, the issue of war crimes punishment had become a contentious topic of debate in Washington, particularly between the heads of the Treasury and War departments. The proposals put forth by each were the product of the fundamentally different worldviews of their creators. Both, however, would prove influential as President Roosevelt sought a solution palatable to his British and Russian counterparts. The proposal put forth by Henry Morgenthau of the Treasury Department did not recommend legal proceedings of any sort for the leading figures of the Third Reich. Rather, Morgenthau proposed their outright execution once their identities had been established. He further proposed the emasculation of Germany through a program of deindustrialization and pastoralization.[16] Competing with the Treasury Department for the ear of the president was Secretary of War Henry Stimson. In stark contrast to Morgenthau, Stimson insisted that the due process of law would have to be extended to the leaders of the Reich if America was to maintain the moral high ground in the postwar world. He further argued that postwar trials would help prevent the resurgence of Nazism by making the barbarism of the Third Reich known to all. Stimson feared that Morgenthau's punitive proposals would only sow the seeds of new discontent in Germany and pave the way for future conflicts, as he believed the Treaty of Versailles had done in 1919.[17]

Despite Stimson's warnings, Roosevelt initially favored Morgenthau's proposal. During a conference in Quebec City in September 1944, Roosevelt and Churchill initialed a plan to summarily execute the major Nazi war criminals, and planned to consult with Stalin on those to be included on the list. The process of selecting and executing war criminals was to follow the "Napoleonic precedent," in that parties deemed incontestably guilty would be punished by political decision rather than by trial.[18] Immediately following the conference, however, Morgenthau's proposal leaked to the press and was met with condemnation. Nazi propaganda minister Joseph Goebbels had seized on the plan as evidence that Germans had no option but to fight to the last man—a development that forced Roosevelt to distance himself from Morgenthau. As circumstances prompted Roosevelt to reconsider his approach to the war crimes issue, Stimson's ideas gained greater influence. In the months that followed, the War Department busied itself putting together proposals that would ultimately form the framework for the trials at Nuremberg.[19]

The United States Army and the War Crimes Issue

Even before Stimson's ideas concerning the punishment of the major Nazi war criminals had won out over Morgenthau's, rare consensus had emerged regarding the role of the U.S. Army in the investigation and trial of lesser war criminals. Due to the army's proximity to the crime scene in Europe, the State and Navy departments, as well as other relevant government agencies, agreed that it would be best placed to gather evidence and prepare cases for future trial.[20] In May 1944, therefore, Secretary of War Stimson handed the responsibility for the coordination and implementation of United States policy on war crimes punishment to the judicial arm of the U.S. Army—the Judge Advocate General's office.[21] In turn, the responsibility for both the gathering of evidence and the development of war crimes cases for trial fell upon the principal legal officer in the European theater of operations, the Theater Judge Advocate.[22] Thereby, policy-making power regarding the trial of lesser war criminals came to reside principally with the American forces in the European theater and later with the occupation regime—and not with Washington.[23]

The war crimes investigation and trial program overseen by the U.S. military developed continuously, adapting to the changing needs and realities of war and peace. The program would eventually evolve from a poorly organized, understaffed, and ill-defined operation to a centralized and efficient system of investigation, trial, and punishment. According to a lengthy report submitted by the Deputy Judge Advocate, the early months of the army's involvement with the war crimes program were "marked by a substantial lack of a national policy as to the punishment of those who committed war crimes, broad restrictions on trials of war criminals, and an almost complete lack of appreciation of the magnitude of the impending problem."[24]

Poor coordination caused chaos. While all military personnel were charged with the responsibility of reporting war crimes, no clear protocol existed for the processing of this information. Ultimately, the Supreme Headquarters Allied Expeditionary Force (SHAEF) assumed responsibility for handling all reports of war crimes and apprehending suspects. However, the officials in charge passed the task of investigating alleged atrocities to judge advocates, the inspector general, the assistant chiefs of staff, or various other agencies.[25] To make matters worse, the Deputy Judge Advocate reported that alongside these issues, the "cardinal impediment" in the early stages of the program was the "continuous shortage of qualified personnel."[26] Soldiers sent to investigate alleged war crimes generally had no legal training or proper direction, resulting in work that was often of little use.[27]

The numerous shortfalls of the program evident in 1944 derived from the fact that the army had yet to realize that war crimes had been committed on such a vast scale.[28] And so while political forces had helped give shape to the American war crimes investigation and trial program, events, more than individuals or agencies, would provide the main thrust for its further development. The first events that helped harden the resolve of the U.S. Army to aggressively pursue and punish war criminals were the increasingly common killings of downed American fliers. Although Germany had initially adhered to international law in dealing with captured airmen, murders and maltreatment of captured Americans in the spring and summer of 1944 revealed a clear deviation from this course.[29] In response to this disturbing development, SHAEF announced the establishment of a Court of Inquiry on August 20, 1944, to prepare cases against those involved in such crimes. The Court of Inquiry gathered evidence, as well as lists of suspects and witnesses, to be used in future trials. These investigations naturally focused almost exclusively on crimes committed against Americans and their allies. It was not until December 1944 that SHAEF finally directed subordinate commands to report all violations of the laws of war, regardless of the nationality of the victims.

Though atrocities committed against downed fliers spurred some important developments, no event or set of circumstances would ignite the passion of the U.S. Army for the war crimes issue as violently as the massacre of unarmed American POWs near the town of Malmédy, Belgium, during Hitler's Ardennes offensive (known to Americans as the Battle of the Bulge). On the afternoon of December 17, 1944, Kampfgruppe Peiper, leading the First SS Panzer Division Leibstandarte Adolf Hitler, captured 113 U.S. servicemen, including 90 men from the 285th Field Artillery Observation Battalion. Once disarmed, the men were assembled in a field and shot down in a barrage of machine-gun fire. Many of the bodies later recovered were found with their arms still raised above their heads. This event would mark a turning point in American thinking.[30]

The massacre at Malmédy prompted a number of developments that were crucial in transforming the American military war crimes program into a viable and functional system of prosecution. First, the Theater Judge Advocate was instructed to set up a dedicated war crimes office in Europe to coordinate the collection of evidence and to prepare cases for trial.[31] Headquartered in Paris and governed by the newly appointed Deputy Judge Advocate for War Crimes, the War Crimes Group brought much-needed coordination and centralization to the investigation process. Second, the Deputy Judge Advocate created dedicated war crimes investigation teams that were trained through the War Crimes Group. Despite these promising developments, however, it remained extremely difficult for the War Crimes Group, as well as the new investigation teams under its command, to obtain personnel and material.[32] Despite requests, the War Department in Washington took no effective steps to remedy this shortage. Once again, this can be credited to the fact that government officials in the United States still did not fully appreciate that war crimes had been committed on an unprecedented scale.[33] Further, there was great hesitancy to divert military personnel away from the war effort. As a result, only seven war crimes investigating teams could be organized prior to the end of hostilities in Europe.[34]

Taken together, the murder of American fliers and the massacre of unarmed soldiers at Malmédy helped to convince the army of the inherent criminality of the German war machine and of the need to punish those responsible. However, crimes against civilians, and especially the atrocities occurring in concentration camps, remained a peripheral issue almost until war's end. For this reason, the liberation of Ohrdruf by American forces on April 4, 1945, proved to be a watershed event that accelerated the evolution of the army's war crimes program. Ohrdruf, the first concentration camp to be liberated by soldiers from the United States, was a subcamp of Buchenwald, near the town of Gotha, Germany. On entering the camp, the Americans encountered horrifying scenes unlike anything they had seen before. The masses of corpses and flocks of starving inmates were so unbelievable that Generals Dwight D. Eisenhower, George S. Patton, and Omar Bradley all visited the camp personally to bear witness. General Patton insisted that immediate arrangements be made to force local residents to witness the scene and for residents to be brought also from the town of Weimar to the main camp of Buchenwald.[35] General Eisenhower exclaimed that every American soldier should visit the camp to be reminded of what he had been fighting for. "Up to that time," Eisenhower later recalled, "I had known about [such crimes] only generally or through secondary sources . . . I visited every nook and cranny of the camp because I felt it my duty to be in a position from then on to testify at first hand about these things."[36]

The outrage that the scenes at Ohrdruf inspired in Eisenhower prompted an immediate order to increase the size of the SHAEF war crimes operation. During May and June 1945, SHAEF organized, staffed, and deployed an additional twelve war crimes investigation teams. All efforts were made to acquire information from former POWs and other personnel who might have witnessed or been the victim of war crimes. The headquarters of the European theater of operations instructed the principal commands in regions under American control to screen all patients in hospitals, as well as all U.S. military or civilian personnel arriving at any assembly points, in order to gather information regarding war crimes. Such individuals were then to be interrogated under oath.[37] To facilitate and coordinate these actions, the Office of the Deputy Judge Advocate for War Crimes was relocated from Paris to Wiesbaden, Germany, in order to be closer to the field. The liberation of Ohrdruf and the public outrage that ensued were crucial catalysts in these developments, spurring those in command to acknowledge the extent of Nazi criminality and the necessary scope of any initiative aimed at thoroughly investigating and apprehending those responsible for such atrocities.

Despite advancements, the army's war crimes investigators still faced a central obstacle: the continuing ban on trials during wartime. On May 7, 1945, however, the need for this prohibition evaporated with the German surrender. On June 19, the Combined Chiefs of Staff therefore authorized theater commanders to move forward with cases against the thousands of suspects already in custody, "other than those who held high political, civil or military positions."[38] This latter group was to be dealt with through a future joint decision of the Allies, as spelled out in the Moscow Declaration. Joint Chiefs of Staff Directive 1023/10, issued July 8, 1945, clarified the type of crimes to be brought before military commission courts, while instructing war crimes investigators on the broad range of offenders to be taken into custody. Reflecting a new appreciation of the scope of Nazi criminality, military personnel were instructed to arrest and try those who had taken part in, been accessories to, or been members of organizations responsible for

(a) Atrocities and offenses against persons or property constituting violations of international law, including the laws, rules and customs of land and naval warfare.

(b) Initiation of invasions of other countries and of wars of aggression . . .

(c) Other atrocities and offenses, including atrocities and persecutions on racial, religious or political grounds, committed since January 30, 1933.[39]

The directive also provided a first glimpse into the sort of trials the army envisioned. The military commission courts were "to the greatest practicable extent" to adopt "simple and expeditious procedures designed to accomplish substantial justice without technicality."[40] The need for efficiency became the defining feature of the emergent trial program, owing largely to the fact that military planners recognized that they were tasked with a judicial undertaking "without parallel" in its magnitude.[41]

Owing also to the need to streamline the American war crimes investigation and trial program, military officials decided to centralize the entire operation on the grounds of the former concentration camp of Dachau. The choice of Dachau was at once practical and symbolic. The existing facilities at the camp easily held the 15,000 suspects and witnesses that the army had rounded up, though an intensive screening process eventually reduced this number to roughly 3,500 slated to be tried for war crimes.[42] In the War Crimes Enclosure at Dachau, former perpetrators took up residence in the very barracks that victims of National Socialism had inhabited only a few months earlier.

By the end of August 1945, the United States was committed to two distinct war crimes trial programs, one under American military jurisdiction alone and the other under the joint jurisdiction of the major Allied powers. As to the first, Eisenhower authorized the commanding generals of the Eastern and Western Military Districts to appoint military government courts for the trial of such war crimes cases as might be forwarded by the Judge Advocate.[43] The Judge Advocate, directly responsible for the investigation, preparation, prosecution, defense, and review of all cases brought before American military courts, received the responsibility of bringing to trial (a) those suspected of war crimes involving American nationals as victims, and (b) mass-atrocity cases committed in the American area of control, or in concentration camps overrun by American forces.[44]

As to the second trial group, negotiations in London in the summer of 1945 resulted in an agreement to establish an international tribunal at Nuremberg to try the major figures of the Third Reich. Robert H. Jackson, chief of counsel for the prosecution of Nazi war crimes at Nuremberg, was assigned the responsibility of bringing to trial "leaders of the European Axis powers and their principal agents and accessories" and "such members of groups or organizations . . . declared to be criminal by the International Military Tribunal."[45] Those appearing before the tribunal would be indicted on new legal charges created expressly for the Nuremberg court. Aside from war crimes, which was already a part of customary international law, prosecutors would charge the defendants with "crimes against peace," which criminalized the "planning, preparation or initiation of wars of aggression," and "crimes against humanity," which included "murder, extermination, enslavement, [and] deportation" and "persecution on racial, religious or political grounds."[46] Yet despite the innovation of the crimes against peace and crimes against humanity charges, designed to address the unprecedented nature of Nazi atrocity, these new legal concepts would play no part in the American military trial program, which was already functioning when the Nuremberg Charter was adopted on August 8, 1945. The Allied introduction of Control Council Law No. 10 in December 1945, which empowered each occupational regime to use mildly modified versions of the Nuremberg charges for additional trials of other major war criminals in their custody, likewise had no bearing on the course or conduct of American military trials.[47]

The U.S. military trial program and proceedings at Nuremberg were therefore distinct, taking place at different locations with different rules created to try different types of war criminals. Contrary to common assumptions, these trial programs therefore had little in common and operated largely in isolation from each other. American military prosecutors would ultimately try over 1,600 individuals in 462 separate trials in the same period of time that a total of 193 Nazi defendants were judged at Nuremberg—first by the International Military Tribunal and then during twelve subsequent trials launched unilaterally by the United States in accordance with Control Council Law No. 10.[48] So stark are the differences between the Nuremberg and American military trial programs that Nuremberg prosecutor Benjamin Ferencz argues that meaningful comparison is virtually impossible. To compare Nuremberg to the military trials, he insists, "would not be like comparing apples to oranges, but apples to trucks."[49]

The American Military Trial Program and the Law

Aside from the daunting administrative and organizational hurdles that had to be overcome before the military could begin to try the suspected war criminals who fell under its jurisdiction, the U.S. Army also had to look back through its own history for precedents on which to model future trials, and with which to justify the arrest and punishment of foreign nationals. While the Moscow Declaration, as well as the Geneva and Hague conventions, provided the military with grounds to try war criminals, they provided no specific directions for proceeding against war crimes suspects. As a result, those in charge scrambled through the legal inventory for precedents, reading back as far as the American Civil War.

As early as 1860, the United States had played an active role in the development of the modern laws of war.[50] During the American Civil War, Abraham Lincoln signed into law the Instructions for the

Government of Armies in the Field, formally defining a legal framework for the military. Based on the work of a German-American political scientist named Francis Lieber, the code became known variously as the Lieber Code and as General Order 100. It defined such fundamental issues as the application of martial law, military jurisdiction, and military necessity. It spelled out the legal status of deserters, prisoners of war, hostages, partisans, civilian scouts, and other individuals not specifically associated with belligerent armies, while also providing rules for the treatment of captured spies, messengers, and war traitors. Further, it offered regulations for the conduct of military forces in the field and provided guidelines for military occupation.[51] These rules, though drawn up in the 1860s, would nonetheless continue to be influential during the Second World War, especially in shaping the American occupation of Germany.[52]

In 1865, the first military commission court was set up to try those accused of violating the rules of war that Lieber had helped to establish. Although the first use of military commission courts can be traced back to the Mexican-American War, the trial of Henry Wirz for atrocities committed at a Confederate prison camp at Andersonville, Georgia, provided the first major trial precedent of use to prosecutors working at Dachau.[53] According to prosecutors at the Wirz trial, approximately 13,000 Union prisoners had died at Andersonville between February 14, 1864, and May 5, 1865.[54] Living in conditions not wholly incomparable to Mauthausen, many of the 30,000 interned there died of disease, starvation, and other mistreatments while the camp was under Wirz's supervision. Wirz was tried, convicted, and hanged for conspiring with Jefferson Davis and others to "impair and injure the health and destroy the lives . . . of large numbers of Federal prisoners . . . at Andersonville" and to "murder, in violation of the laws and customs of war."[55] Although some historians have argued that Wirz was ultimately a scapegoat for the abuse at the mismanaged and ill-supplied camp, his trial nonetheless produced an important legal precedent for the concentration camp cases to be heard in American military courts, given the nature of the crimes in question.

The growing consensus in the mid-nineteenth century that warfare required a standardized code of conduct was not a phenomenon limited only to the United States.[56] Rather, a movement to institutionalize an internationally recognized set of regulations for the waging of war had emerged also by the mid-1800s, culminating in global agreements still in place today. The first such convention, signed in Geneva, Switzerland, in 1864, secured humanitarian relief for wounded soldiers on the battlefield. Henri Dunant, who had founded the Red Cross the previous year, became the driving force behind the agreement, after witnessing the horrors of war in Italy in 1859. From this first Geneva Convention emerged a number of agreements that would collectively regulate the treatment of prisoners of war, civilians, and the wounded, while prescribing various prohibitions and limitations on doing battle. The agreements reached at both Geneva and The Hague, Netherlands, ultimately formed the basis of the charges employed by the military commission courts working at Dachau between 1945 and the end of 1947.

Crucial to the formulation of all war crimes cases brought before the courts in the wake of the Second World War, the Geneva and Hague conventions provided explicit rules for the treatment of the POWs interned in camps such as Mauthausen. The Fourth Hague Convention of 1907 prescribed by law that prisoners of war "must be humanely treated" and that any labor assigned to them "shall not be excessive and shall have no connection with the operation of the war."[57] Further, Article 7 of the convention required that

the Government into whose hands the prisoners of war have fallen is charged with their maintenance. In the absence of a special agreement between the belligerents, prisoners of war shall be treated as regards board, lodging, and clothing on the same footing as the troops of the Government who captured them.[58]

In July 1929, delegates from forty-four nations ratified the Third Geneva Convention, which augmented the Hague Convention of 1907 by providing further regulations for the treatment of POWs. The Convention Relative to the Treatment of Prisoners of War stated that captive soldiers must be protected against violence, intimidation, and humiliation and must be accessible to the Red Cross. Regarding the issue of interrogation, it was ruled that prisoners could not be subject to undue pressure to obtain information. Further, prisoners could not be condemned without a fair trial before a military court. Living conditions for POWs were also specifically prescribed through specific provisions for the quality and quantity of food, water, and clothing a prisoner must receive.

Germany was a signatory to both the Hague and Geneva conventions and was therefore bound by international law to uphold the regulations they contained. The flagrant violation of these rules at camps such as Mauthausen later provided American military prosecutors with an argument that those on trial broke laws that were well established when the offenses in question had occurred. Although they provided legitimacy for war crimes tribunals, however, the Geneva and Hague conventions were not without their shortcomings. Most important, neither spelled out either the conduct of proceedings or how violations of the laws of war were to be punished. Rather, enforcement was left open to signatories.[59] Some delegates at the 1907 Hague Convention had suggested that a permanent, international war crimes court be established, but concerns over issues of national sovereignty prevented the proposal from garnering the support it required for inclusion.[60] Ultimately, then, the Geneva and Hague conventions provided a set of rules for the conduct of war that constituted a part of a nation's general body of law.[61] The means of enforcement and penalties for violations of these rules remained unstated.

Because of this shortcoming, historical precursors, though few and far between, helped to provide models for the charges and trials to unfold in 1945. Unlike the Wirz trial, which was helpful in providing a precedent for the concentration camp cases, the Leipzig trials, which followed the First World War, were the first and only example of an internationally coordinated attempt to bring war criminals to justice. Though the trial envisioned by the victorious European powers in 1919 had more in common with the International Tribunal at Nuremberg than with Dachau, the invocation of the Geneva and Hague conventions nonetheless made this early attempt at war crimes prosecution a valuable example for American military prosecutors. In their pursuit of victory during the First World War, German forces committed various war crimes, including unrestricted submarine warfare, the use of poisonous projectiles, and the neglect and killing of captured soldiers in prisoner-of-war camps. Outrage at such acts prompted the Allied powers to insist that trials be a part of any peace settlement. As a result, Article 228 of the Treaty of Versailles declared that "the German Government recognizes the right of the Allied and Associated Powers to bring before military tribunals persons accused of having committed acts in violation of the laws and customs of war."[62] On February 3, 1920, the Allies presented the Germans with a list of 854 individuals wanted for trial, including General Erich Ludendorff and Field Marshal Paul von Hindenburg, Admiral Alfred von Tirpitz, and former chancellor Theobald von Bethmann Hollweg.[63] From the outset, however, the envisioned trial program faced insurmountable obstacles that soon turned the proceedings into an embarrassing illustration of the impotence of the Allied war crimes initiative.

The push to try Germans for war crimes after the First World War began with a major tactical error. Rather than determining a mechanism for the prosecution of war criminals at the time of the armistice of 1918, the issue was only raised during the Paris peace talks the following year.[64] Although the Commission of Responsibilities of the Authors of the War and the Enforcement of Penalties emerged from the talks to deal with the war crimes issue, consensus was impossible. The Americans would not back down in their opposition to the British and French proposal for international adjudication. Robert Lansing, the American representative who chaired the commission, believed observance of laws of war should be left to the discretion of the military authorities of each state.[65] American representatives rejected all suggestions offered by the other delegates.[66] As the fractures in the unity and determination of the Allies began to show, the delegates agreed to allow the Germans themselves to try those accused of war crimes, before the German Supreme Court—the Reichsgericht—in Leipzig. Of the 854 suspects initially named, the Germans were able to negotiate a far smaller list of men for trial—only 45. Hindenburg and Ludendorff were removed from the list, while the Kaiser's exile in the Netherlands also prevented him from standing before the court. The Reichsgericht dismissed out of hand the cases brought by both the French and the Belgians, citing a lack of evidence and credible witnesses.[67] Of the forty-five people the Germans agreed to try, only twelve ultimately appeared before the court. Six of them were convicted—one was released immediately, and the other five received light sentences. The British, who feared alienating moderate circles in an increasingly unstable Germany, decided not to pursue the contentious issue further, while observers sent from both France and Belgium withdrew in protest. According to the *Times* of London, the trials represented a "scandalous failure of justice."[68] The lessons learned from the Leipzig fiasco were not lost on those working to try war criminals in the wake of World War II. In his opening address to the International Tribunal at Nuremberg, Chief Justice Robert Jackson referred to the Leipzig trials to illustrate the "futility" of leaving adjudication to the vanquished.[69]

The war crimes trials organized by the international community and by the U.S. Army in the years before 1945 addressed crimes seldom comparable either in nature or scope to those committed during the Second World War. Though jurists working at Nuremberg took this as an opportunity to craft new legal concepts to cope with the unprecedented crimes of the Nazis, American military prosecutors stuck as closely as possible to army procedure and the definitions of war crimes that were spelled out in the Geneva and Hague conventions a generation earlier. Though novel twists on old legal concepts would be employed to expedite the trial process, the military commission courts working at Dachau were not designed to break with the general practices and procedures that had long governed American military justice.

Military Commission Courts at Dachau

Once the U.S. Army had cleared the way for the trials at Dachau to begin, the Judge Advocate began to forward cases to the commanding generals of the Third or Seventh armies, who in turn had the authority to appoint the courts that would preside. The courts at Dachau were essentially common-law military commissions as opposed to courts-martial.[70] These courts were to be composed of seven to nine senior officers and presided over by a high-ranking general officer, usually a brigadier general or major general. Those appointed had to be recognized as "men of stature in their professions," who had served as officers for twenty-five to thirty years.[71] Individuals appointed to the court were required to have previous experience sitting on courts-martial, though only one needed to be a lawyer. It was the duty of this lone lawyer to advise the rest of the court on legal matters, such as the admissibility of evidence. The Judge Advocate's office also assigned both the prosecution and defense teams, though defendants had the right to choose their own counsel at the court's expense, provided such costs were within reason. According to procedural guidelines, any officer of the U.S. armed forces, or any other person acceptable to the court, could act as prosecutor.[72]

The Judge Advocate's office prepared the charges used to try war criminals at Dachau, in the form prescribed for military government courts. These charges emanated from two specific areas of the law. Military jurists drew from both traditional conceptions of the laws and customs of war, as well as from the general principles of the common law. According to instructions issued by the Headquarters of United States Forces, European Theater, war crimes included

> violations by enemy nationals, or person acting with them, of the laws and usages of war of general application and acceptance, including acts in contravention of treaties and conventions dealing with the conduct of war, as well as other offenses against persons or property which outrage common justice or involve moral turpitude, committed in connection with military operations, with or without orders or the sanction of commanders.

Further,

> the term "War Criminals" may be understood to include persons who
> (i) have committed war crimes, or
> (ii) have aided, abetted or encouraged the commission of war crimes.[73]

Only war crimes committed after the formation of the United Nations on January 1, 1942, fell under the jurisdiction of the court.

The expansive definition of war crimes provided by the army is instructive. Although the above statement makes clear allusion to the Geneva and Hague conventions, it also includes more-general references to offenses not explicitly dealt with in those conventions. Because crimes against civilians remained outside the scope of international war crimes law until the Fourth Geneva Convention of 1949, alternative sources of law were required to try camp guards for crimes committed against inmates who had not been POWs. This approach, however, did not require the traditional parameters of American legal practice to be breached. The common-law tradition allowed for the prosecution of offenses that were not explicitly laid out in existing legal statutes, so long as they were universally recognized to involve violations of accepted ethical principles.[74] The above reference to offenses "which outrage common justice or involve moral turpitude" therefore helped provide a much broader conception of war crimes, allowing for the prosecution of those responsible for heinous acts that had never previously been brought before the courts. This definition of war crimes helps to illustrate the fact that, while seeking to avoid the radical legal innovations at Nuremberg, military jurists nonetheless had to adapt existing laws creatively in order to prosecute the unprecedented crimes they would be faced with.

Rules of Evidence and Procedure at Dachau

The regulations handed down to govern the trial of war criminals at Dachau combined standard rules of courtroom procedure with others that departed from legal practices in the United States. In general, the trials were to unfold in a traditional manner. According to the *Rules of Procedure in Military Government Courts,* the prosecution was instructed to begin with an opening statement outlining the facts of the case against the accused, followed by the presentation, examination, and cross-examination of its witnesses.[75] Before closing its case, the prosecution was permitted to reexamine its witnesses on new matters having arisen during cross-examination by the defense. Once the prosecution closed its case, statements by the accused or his or her representative were given, followed by the calling, examination, cross-examination, and reexamination of witnesses for the defense. Once the defense closed its case, the prosecution could recall witnesses to rebut statements or new evidence introduced by the defense and defense witnesses. After the prosecution and defense had then given their final statements to the court, the court would consider the case and then announce its findings. If the accused was convicted, the court heard statements and evidence given by both the prosecution and the defense regarding the sentences. The decisions ultimately announced by these military commissions were determined by the majority of votes cast by the court. A two-thirds majority was required for all sentences of death.[76]

Because no appellate court existed in the American military commission system, a mandatory review of each case was prepared by the Deputy Judge Advocate for War Crimes and submitted to the commanding generals of the Third or Seventh armies for approval.[77] If the death sentence had been imposed, the Judge Advocate would submit his own recommendations—based on the "Review and Recommendations" prepared by the Deputy Judge Advocate to the theater commander for final approval.[78] In place of an appeal procedure, therefore, the army (and not an independent authority) reviewed each case twice, and, for cases resulting in a sentence of death, three times.

The greatest departure from standard American judicial practice outlined in the *Rules of Procedure in Military Government Courts* involved the admissibility of evidence. The more relaxed standards dictated by the army would prove controversial at Dachau and would spur the defense to protest rigorously before the court. According to the *Rules of Procedure:*

(1) A Military Government Court shall in general admit oral, written and physical evidence having a bearing on the issues before it, and may exclude any evidence which in its opinion is of no value as proof.

(2) The court shall in general require the production of the best evidence.

To further clarify the way the court was to treat the evidence before it, an appended procedural guide stipulated that

[the above rule] does not incorporate the rules of evidence of British or American courts or of courts-martial . . . Hearsay evidence, including the statement of a witness not produced, is thus admissible, but if the matter is important and controverted every effort should be made to obtain the presence of the witness, and an adjournment may be ordered for that purpose. The guiding principle is to admit only evidence that will aid in determining the truth.[79]

This procedural stipulation would prove useful to military prosecutors. For the trial of perpetrators from camps like Mauthausen, these rules greatly aided the prosecution of crimes that sometimes had few, if any, surviving witnesses. Because Nazi camp officials made it policy to murder those who were exposed to the machinery of murder in the gas chambers, for instance, the testimony of individuals who could attest only to conversations they had heard, or to the groups of people they saw alive one moment and dead the next, was essential. From the point of view of the defense, however, such stipulations made defending their clients extremely difficult, as they allowed evidence to be heard from individuals who were at times not available for cross-examination. Defense motions to curb the right of the court to see or hear questionable evidence, including unsworn and coerced statements, would often be denied by the court if no better testimony could be found.[80]

First and foremost, these rules of evidence and procedure were designed to produce spare and expedient proceedings that could allow for the trial of thousands of war crimes suspects in a short period of time. As the army sought to use its trial program primarily to administer swift and severe punishment to war criminals, its legal authorities were less concerned with due process and legal innovation than were jurists at Nuremberg. While the latter would place great emphasis on using trial proceedings also as a way of communicating to the German public and to the world the evils of Nazism and the virtues of democracy, such pedagogical goals were of secondary importance at Dachau. According to the *Guide to Procedure in Military Courts,* the purpose of Military Government Courts and of the principal enactments reinforced by them is the protection of the Allied Forces and the advancement of their military objectives. All pertinent enactments must therefore be interpreted broadly and in accordance with their obvious intention: all courts must be conducted in view to the attainment of this purpose to the fullest possible extent . . . A technical and legalistic viewpoint must not be allowed to interfere with such a result.[81]

Further, on the effect of irregularities during proceedings, the rules stipulated permissively that

the Proceedings shall not be invalidated, nor any findings or sentence be disapproved, for any error or omission, technical or otherwise, occurring in such proceedings, unless in the opinion of the Reviewing Authority, after an examination of the entire record, it shall appear that the error or omission has resulted in injustice to the accused.[82]

Lending legitimacy to such regulations, both the U.S. Supreme Court as well as the United Nations War Crimes Commission had come to the conclusion that those to be tried for war crimes did not qualify for protection under Article 63 of the 1929 Geneva Convention.[83] This stipulated that prisoners of war had to be tried "by the same courts and according to the same procedure as in the case of persons belonging to the armed forces of the detaining power."[84] It was ruled, however, that Article 63 applied only to those whose offenses were committed when already in custody, and did not apply to war crimes or any other offenses committed prior to gaining the status of prisoner of war.[85]

The rules and regulations prescribed for war crimes trials before American military commissions help to illustrate the predicament that the army faced. Between the need for expediency on one hand, and the protection of the rights of the accused on the other, the army walked a tightrope that would at times prove perilous. Though the procedures that governed the military trials would ultimately allow for the prosecution of an astonishing 1,676 individuals in just over two years, they also fueled stinging criticism of the trial process at Dachau that would eventually cast the entire program into disrepute.

First Attempts at Prosecuting Nazi Crimes in Military Courts

Even before proceedings got under way at Dachau, the American and British military authorities conducted a number of war crimes trials that proved to be of paramount importance to Dachau prosecutors. Though military jurists at Dachau had an exceedingly small pool of historical precedents on which to draw, the British trial of perpetrators from Bergen-Belsen concentration camp, as well as the American trial at Wiesbaden of the staff of the Hadamar "euthanasia" facility, helped establish principles fundamental to the cases to be tried at Dachau.

At Lüneburg, the British army, acting under the authority of a royal warrant in June 1945, tried forty-four men and women charged with committing war crimes at Bergen-Belsen concentration camp. Bergen-Belsen, the only major camp liberated by British forces, was comparable in its record of atrocity to Dachau, Buchenwald, Flossenbürg, and Mauthausen, camps whose staff would later be tried by the American military. Bergen-Belsen had not been an extermination camp per se, yet the regimen of abuse, starvation, and slave labor that existed there, coupled with rampant disease, resulted ultimately in the deaths of more than 50,000 individuals.[86] The British prosecutors working at Lüneburg selected defendants whose diverse functions had helped the camp to operate. Ultimately, the dock contained sixteen male SS men, the highest ranking of whom were camp commandant Josef Kramer, compound commandant Franz Hössler, and camp doctor Fritz Klein. Sixteen female SS members were also tried, including the notoriously cruel compound commander Irma Grese. Aside from such high-ranking defendants, however, the majority of the accused had subordinate roles in the camp, working in administration, in the kitchen or ration store, or supervising labor battalions. The remaining twelve defendants were prisoner functionaries (kapos) of various nationalities accused of abusing fellow inmates.

Those tried in the Belsen case were charged with violating the laws and usages of war, and more specifically with being "parties to the ill-treatment . . . and deaths . . . of allied nationals."[87] Ultimately, thirty of the accused were found guilty by the court, and eleven of them sentenced to death and executed. More important, however, the court made two significant findings that would be key to the cases tried at Dachau. First, the court ruled that the defendants had helped to further an existing conspiracy to commit war crimes, even though they may not have helped plan, or had contact with, the original Nazis who created the camp system.[88] Second, Belsen was found to be a criminal enterprise, making each of the defendants vicariously liable for the crimes committed there. In reviewing the case, Brigadier H. Scott Barrett explained that "the accused were not charged with individual murders, though many such were proved against a number of them . . . [the case] was established once the court was satisfied that [the defendants] were members of the staff of the camp."[89] The principle of vicarious liability would be central to mass-atrocity cases brought before American military commission courts. When verdicts in the Dachau concentration camp case were later handed down, the court, as well as the reviewing authority, indicated that the findings of guilt and the sentences imposed reflected the American view of the Belsen case.[90]

Also important to American military prosecutors were the precedents established in the cases tried by the U.S. Army prior to the consolidation of the trial program at Dachau. On July 15, 1945, a military commission court at Freising, Germany, tried policemen

Albert Bury and Wilhelm Hafner for killing a downed American airman. The defendants denied culpability for their acts, arguing that they were only following the orders handed down by their superiors to kill "terror aviators." Following a principle established during the Leipzig trials and encoded in the U.S. Army's *Manual on the Laws of War,* however, the court rejected the "superior orders" defense and sentenced the men to death.[91] The court further refused to consider the existence of superior orders as grounds for mitigating the sentences to be handed down. The case against Bury and Hafner provided an early test of the superior-orders defense and rendered it useless for all practical purposes in future American military trials.[92]

The United States v. Hartgen et al. set an important precedent regarding the wording of the indictments leveled at the accused. At Darmstadt on July 25, 1945, eleven civilian defendants were charged with "collective participation" in the mob killing of six downed American fliers in the town of Rüsselsheim. During the trial, and in line with the newly prescribed rules of procedure for military commissions, the court accepted all testimony "having probative value to the reasonable man," including extrajudicial statements and hearsay.[93] The defense, however, was limited to arguing how much weight should be given to such evidence, and not to its general admissibility.[94] Five defendants received death sentences, and three others received stiff jail terms. During the trial, the defense had argued that technical mistakes, as well as inexact wording included in the indictment against the accused, had prevented the defendants from receiving a fair trial. In the *Review of the United States v. Hartgen et al.,* however, these objections and challenges to the particulars were ruled "technical" and ignored. The court declared that "violations of the laws and usages of war" was thus the only part of the indictments that had legal status, and that the structure and wording of the particulars, alleging conspiracy on the part of the defendants, for instance, were not essential to the charge.[95]

The extent to which military commissions were willing to over-look technical abnormalities in the course of the cases they heard was made clear most dramatically with the trial of Justus Gersten-berg, at Ludwigsburg. Gerstenberg, an uneducated member of Hit-ler's paramilitary Storm Troopers (SA), was ultimately sentenced to death for the killing of American airman Willard Holden in July 1944. The review of the trial provided a remarkable precedent re-garding the composition of military commissions. As laid out in the *Rules of Procedure in Military Government Courts,* each military commission had to include a lawyer, to advise the other commis-sion members on legal questions raised during the trials. The court that convened to try Gerstenberg, however, did not include a law-yer, nor was any attempt made to acquire one. Upon review, the objections of the defense regarding the composition of the court were rejected, and the trial ruled fair. Gerstenberg went to the gal-lows September 12, 1946. This case was not anomalous, and along with the Hartgen case, it helped to illustrate the latitude that pros-ecutors in future cases could expect from the court when dealing with technical matters big or small.[96]

Though the above cases helped to establish precedent regarding issues such as superior orders, the wording of indictments, and the impact of irregularities on trial proceedings, the "Hadamar Murder Factory" case would prove to be by far the most important in lay-ing the foundation for the mass-atrocity trials to be held at Dachau. Aside from setting an essential precedent regarding the jurisdiction of American military commissions, the Hadamar case introduced the novel concept of a *common intent* to commit war crimes. The suc-cess of this prototypical approach persuaded Dachau prosecutors to build future concentration camp cases on a similar model.

The Hadamar Asylum, overrun by American forces on March 26, 1945, had played a crucial role in the Nazis' T4 euthanasia pro-gram. Between January and August 1941 alone, for instance, the staff of the facility murdered some 10,000 Germans designated as incurably mentally ill.[97] Another 5,000 victims, including nearly 500 Polish and Russian laborers, perished there between the summer of 1942 and the spring of 1945, as the state expanded the euthanasia program to cover other undesirable groups.[98] Such victims were generally designated "tubercular" and "treated" with lethal injections of morphine or scopolamine.[99]

The trial of the staff of the Hadamar facility took place in Wiesbaden over seven days, beginning October 8, 1945. The seven accused included Alfons Klein, the administrative head of the hospital, as well as the institution's only doctor, Adolf Wahlmann. Future Watergate Special Prosecutor Leon Jaworski charged the accused with "violation of international law" and added the following specification:

> In that Alfons Klein, [et al.], acting jointly in pursuance of a common intent and acting for and on behalf of the then German Reich, did . . . willfully, deliberately and wrongfully aid, abet and participate in the killing of human beings of Polish and Russian nationality, their exact names and number being unknown but aggregating in excess of 400 . . . [100]

The charges brought before the court are instructive. First, the prosecution did not attempt to try the accused for all 15,000 murders. The War Crimes Group advised prosecutors that crimes committed by German nationals against fellow citizens did not constitute a violation of international law and therefore fell outside the jurisdiction of the court. Instead, prosecutors sought justice only for the 476 Russian and Polish victims—Allied nationals—whose names they had gleaned from captured records.[101] Second, the defendants were accused of pursuing a *common intent* to kill Allied nationals. This charge helped redefine war crimes by framing them in terms of an illegal common plan or enterprise. This reconceptualization of the offense built upon the strategies used by the British to great effect during the Bergen-Belsen case.[102]

During the course of the Hadamar trial, the court also made an important ruling regarding the admissibility of evidence, which would play out in later mass-atrocity cases. Prosecution witness and former Hadamar nurse Minna Zachow testified under oath that 10,000 Germans had been killed at the institution in 1941.[103] Although these victims were not Allied nationals and had died before the dates specified in the charges, the court overruled the ensuing objections of the defense, stating that such evidence helped to illustrate the state of mind of those working at Hadamar. In future concentration camp cases as well, the prosecution was therefore able to introduce evidence regarding crimes committed against Germans—crimes for which the defendants were not accused—to illustrate the normal operation of the facility in question. As a result, it became generally understood that the American military courts were operating within their rights when accepting such evidence for its probative value, given that so few patients or inmates left Nazi camps or euthanasia facilities alive.[104]

Prior to the mass-atrocity trials at Dachau, then, the Hadamar Murder Factory case, as it became known, proved to be a rich source of both strategy and precedent. The Hadamar trial confirmed first that international law gave the U.S. Army jurisdiction to try only those crimes committed against "non-German" nationals. While releasing the accused from prosecution for crimes committed against their own countrymen, however, the Hadamar case did establish the jurisdiction of American commission courts over crimes committed against stateless victims. Like a number of cases aimed at prosecuting German townsfolk for the mob killing of downed Allied fliers, the Hadamar case affirmed the right of American military courts to try civilians. Both of these jurisdictional precedents would prove essential for the war crimes cases to be heard at Dachau. Most important, the success of coupling the specified charges with the concept of "common intent" (termed "common design" in future trials) led Dachau prosecutors to borrow this strategy, and employ it with astonishing results in the concentration camp cases they were preparing.

The Dachau Trials Begin

By the autumn of 1945, the U.S. Army had confronted most of the significant legal questions it would face in staging war crimes trials. Military commissions had ruled on the admissibility of various forms of evidence, had dealt with and dismissed the defense of "superior orders," had sanctioned the application of "common participation" and conspiracy to international law, and had withstood challenges to the jurisdiction of the court to try foreign nationals.[105] When the first concentration camp case got under way at Dachau in November 1945, prosecutors had a solid foundation of precedent-setting cases on which to build.

The choice of Dachau as the hub of the American war crimes trial program was perhaps the most dramatic manifestation of the Allied promise, as stated in the Moscow Declaration, to return perpetrators to the location of their crimes to face justice. Situating the trial program on the grounds of the camp was also important for practical reasons. Dachau was located just over fifteen kilometers northwest of Munich and close to Landsberg Prison, where convicted war criminals could be taken for incarceration or execution. Because most of the heating and plumbing at Dachau was still in working order when the Americans arrived, three courtrooms were easily set up, the largest of which could seat between 250 and 300 individuals.[106] Camp buildings were also able to provide the substantial office space required by military personnel.[107] Such practical advantages aided the drive for expediency that propelled the military trial program. Eventually, as many as eight tribunals were able to operate simultaneously at Dachau.[108]

The location included a number of drawbacks, however. The facilities often did not permit the effective segregation of suspects and witnesses—a fact that could affect the testimony heard before the court. The choice of Dachau also raised the question of whether or not the trials were sufficiently removed from the scene of the crime. As trial stenographer Barbara Ann Murphy recalled, there was no escaping the lingering stench of death that was referred to as "the Dachau aroma."[109] The largest courtroom, where the major concentration camp cases were held, had previously been a slave labor shop that had turned out shoes and uniforms for the Wehrmacht. Remarkably, one witness who testified in the new court facility recalled having worked in the very room in which he now stood, under a kapo presently on trial in front of him.[110]

The first trial to be held at the former concentration camp was not for crimes committed in such places, however, but for the killing of downed American airmen. This trial, and dozens like it, represented the first of three broad categories of cases brought before military commission courts at Dachau. This group of cases involving the murder of downed fliers dominated the American war crimes program for the first six months of its existence. Although this partially reflects the priority given to cases involving American victims, the early concentration of such cases was also due to the fact that crimes of this sort had been under investigation since the summer of 1944, before a single camp had been liberated.[111] The second category of trials staged at Dachau grouped the concentration camp personnel from Mauthausen, Dachau, Buchenwald, Flossenbürg, Nordhausen/Mittelbau-Dora, and Mühldorf, as well as the various subcamps associated with each. Lastly, a miscellaneous category of trials, including that which dealt with the Malmédy perpetrators, encompassed disparate proceedings not associated with the other two trial groups. From the first trial at Dachau in September 1945 to the close of the program at the end of 1947, an astonishing 462 individual trials, representing cases from each of the above categories, would ultimately be conducted by the Dachau military commissions.

The Dachau Concentration Camp Case and the Concept
of a Common Design

The first trial of perpetrators from Dachau, begun on November 13, 1945, would become the archetype for all future mass-atrocity cases to be heard on the grounds of the former concentration camp. Although earlier American military trials held across Germany had helped to establish the precedents discussed above, prosecutors at the Dachau concentration camp trial drew together a comprehensive strategy for dealing with mass-atrocity cases in an expedient, effective, and fair manner. The Mauthausen trial, as well as the trials of personnel from Buchenwald, Flossenbürg, and Nordhausen, would be built on this model.

For many Americans, Dachau concentration camp, like Bergen-Belsen for the British, came to symbolize the horrors of National Socialism. Opened in March 1933, it was the first official camp set up by the Nazis, and one of the first liberated by American forces. In the long history of the camp, which spanned all of the Third Reich's twelve years, almost 32,000 people are known to have died there.[112] Aside from being subject to grueling slave labor building roads, mining gravel, or working in armaments factories, hundreds of prisoners were killed or permanently maimed in horrific medical experiments of various sorts. In Dachau and its subcamps, the Nazis consigned political opponents, "Gypsies," Jews, Jehovah's Witnesses, asocials, criminals, and other "undesirables" in the Reich to a regimen of terror, starvation, and disease. Although the small gas chamber at Dachau was never used on prisoners, those too weak to work were at times selected and gassed at Castle Hartheim, near Linz. By war's end, hundreds of thousands had passed through the Dachau camp system.[113]

The man selected by the army to prosecute the dozens of Dachau suspects now in custody in the former concentration camp would become the central figure in all the large mass-atrocity cases to be tried by American military commission courts. Lieutenant Colonel William Denson was only thirty-two years old when called to serve at Dachau. Although Denson had no experience dealing with war crimes, he had previously been involved in virtually every phase of military justice, having acted either as Trial Judge Advocate, member of the court, or defense counsel in over 130 army cases.[114] Denson was a graduate of both West Point and Harvard Law School and strove to follow in the footsteps of his father and grandfather, both of whom had held important legal positions in his home state of Alabama.[115] His family legacy, he believed, was one of humanism, typified by his grandfather, who as an Alabama Supreme Court justice had defended black Americans at a time when it was considered virtually treasonous to do so.[116] Denson's strong Christian upbringing further forged his worldview and allowed him to see his service at Dachau as part of a broader moral crusade against Nazi barbarism.[117] A slim man standing just under six feet tall, Denson spoke with a slow southern drawl and emanated a warmth that made him popular with his colleagues. Alongside his southern charm, however, Denson proved to be a brilliant and formidable prosecutor who would leave Dachau with a 100 percent rate of conviction for the 177 men he tried there. Denson had no hesitation requesting the penalty of death in the cases he argued, and ultimately succeeded in having the court impose it ninety-seven times.[118]

Denson had been at Dachau only a few short weeks when he was assigned the Dachau concentration camp case. Almost immediately, the Judge Advocate General's office placed immense pressure on him and his staff to get the trial under way. Denson was given only four weeks to prepare his case, in order that the trial start at Thanksgiving and produce headlines in time for Christmas. Owing to these demands, the pretrial work was completed by late October. Proceedings in court began November 13, 1945, in front of a standing-room only crowd. Because the opening of the trial at Nuremberg had been delayed for a week (due to problems restoring the parquet floor), the courtroom at Dachau was packed with nearly 400 members of the military elite, the press, and the local public. Among other top brass, the front row contained General Walter Bedell Smith, chief of staff to Dwight Eisenhower, and Lieutenant Colonel Lucien B. Truscott Jr., the commanding general of the Third Army. Such a scene, however, would prove to be anomalous. Within a few days of the trial's opening, the courtroom had emptied, as Goering, Hess, and other top-ranking Nazis stole the spotlight at Nuremberg.

As the forty defendants named in Denson's indictment were led into the courtroom, each received a numbered card for the purposes of identification. Their faces revealed hints of humiliation when they were instructed to place the cards around their necks.[119] The defendants were a diverse group, ranging in age from eighteen to seventy-four, and in position from kapo to commandant. The two charges and the accompanying particulars designed by the prosecution to send these men to the gallows reflected the wisdom gained from studying the precedents set and strategies employed in earlier military trials. All forty were charged with violating the "laws and usages of war,"

> in that Martin Gottfried Weiss . . . [et al.], acting in pursuance of a common design to commit the acts hereinafter alleged, . . . did at or in the vicinity of Dachau and Landsberg, Germany, between about January 1, 1942 and about April 29, 1945, willfully, deliberately and wrongfully encourage, aid abet and participate in the subjugation of civilian nationals of nations then at war with the German Reich to cruelties and mistreatment, including killings, beating, [and] tortures.[120]

The second charge read much the same, save that "subjugation of civilian nationals of nations then at war with the German Reich" was replaced with "subjugation of members of the armed forces of nations then at war with the German Reich."[121]

For the Dachau case, as well as all future mass-atrocity cases to be tried before American military commissions, the concept of a "common design" to commit war crimes became the essential element of the charges brought by the prosecution.[122] Though conceptually similar to the charge of conspiracy used at Nuremberg, common design did not oblige the prosecution to illustrate the existence of a previously conceived plan or agreement to commit the crime in question. For conspiracy to be proved at Nuremberg, prosecutors had to provide evidence that the defendants had planned, prepared, or initiated the crime of waging an aggressive war.[123] At Dachau, on the other hand, the common-design charge required prosecutors merely to illustrate that the accused had participated in the maintenance of a criminal enterprise that resulted in the deaths of inmates. As with the Hadamar case, the underlying principle was that of vicarious liability. There was no need to prove that the actions of each defendant resulted in the death of a specific individual, but only that the defendants were aware of the ultimate purpose or product of the institution they helped to maintain. At least in theory, the camp cook was therefore as criminally culpable as the hangman, and could be caught within the same judicial net.

For Denson and his team, three main steps were required to establish the guilt of the accused. First, the prosecution had to show that there was in force at Dachau a system to ill-treat prisoners and commit the war crimes described in the charges. Second, the prosecution had to illustrate that each of the defendants was aware of this system. Last, it was essential to prove that each of the individuals now on trial aided and abetted, or participated in enforcing this system.[124] It was argued, for instance, that even the guards who remained in watchtowers outside the confines of the camp had aided and abetted this "common design" by making sure prisoners could not escape. Further, kapos—the prisoner functionaries—were also deemed part of this common design, as they helped administer the camp and took orders from the SS.[125] The prosecution contended that it was impossible for those working at Dachau to remain ignorant of the daily regimen of torture and death that defined prisoner life there. Overflowing crematoria and emaciated inmates were an everyday part of the landscape of the camp.

The defense neither seriously disputed the familiarity that any-one stationed at Dachau for any length of time would have with these crimes, nor the existence of the system that produced them. Rather, the defense focused on the nature of the *relationship* be-tween each of the accused and the common design alleged by the prosecution.[126] The defense rigorously challenged evidence and tes-timony that linked any one of the accused to a specific act of cruelty or killing. In his summation before the court, however, Denson re-minded the judges that

> this case could have been established without showing that a single man over in the dock at any time killed a man. It would be suffi-cient to show that there was in fact a common design, and that these individuals participated in it, and the purpose of that com-mon design was the killings, beating and tortures, and the subjec-tion to starvation.[127]

The prosecution succeeded in convincing the court that although many of the defendants had never known each other, and had served during different periods of the camp's existence, the accused had all knowingly participated in the upkeep of an inherently criminal in-stitution. After reviewing 2,000 trial exhibits and hearing 170 wit-nesses, all 40 defendants were judged guilty, and 36 sentenced to death.[128] The trial had lasted a mere four weeks.

The Dachau Case and the Establishment of the Parent Trial System

Aside from introducing a prosecutorial strategy founded on the con-cept of a common design to commit war crimes, the Dachau trial was also the first of a number of so-called parent concentration camp cases. The parent trial system used at Dachau, like the catchall common-design charge, was implemented in the interests of expediency. The basic concept was to hold an initial trial for each major concentration camp whose personnel were in American custody, and then use the findings of the court in each case to rapidly try other members of these institutions in subsequent hearings without having to reestablish the evidence. According to instructions given by the American army,

in such trial of additional participants in the mass atrocity, the prosecuting officer will furnish the court certified copies of the charge and particulars, the findings and the sentences pronounced in the parent case. Thereupon, such Military Government Courts will take judicial notice of the decision rendered in the parent case, including the findings of the court (in the parent case) that the mass atrocity operation was criminal in nature and that the participants therein, acting in pursuance of a common design, did subject persons to killings, beatings, tortures, etc., and no examination of the record in such parent cases need be made for this purpose. In such trials of additional participants in the mass atrocity, the court will presume, subject to being rebutted by appropriate evidence, that those shown by competent evidence to have participated in the mass atrocity knew of the criminal nature thereof.[129]

In this way, the burden of proof was shifted onto the accused in these subsequent proceedings. The accused was left with few options but to argue that he was not present at the camp; that it was a case of mistaken identity; that he did not act in the capacity alleged; or that there were extenuating circumstances.[130] These subsequent trials consisted of groups usually of seven to ten men and were often completed within a day. The Dachau main case alone would ultimately spawn 118 subsequent proceedings, involving 492 defendants.[131]

With the close of the Dachau "parent" trial in December 1945, Denson and his team of prosecutors had established a comprehensive strategy for dealing with the mass-atrocity cases to be brought before American military commissions. Prior to the centralization of the army's war crimes program at Dachau, earlier trials had helped to establish the necessary precedents regarding the jurisdiction of military courts, the rules of procedure and evidence, and the impact of irregularities on trial proceedings. Although the Belsen and Hadamar trials had introduced novel modifications of the concept of criminal conspiracy, the Dachau trial had firmly established the most crucial concept that would underpin future prosecutions—the concept of a "common design" to commit war crimes. The common-design charge at once allowed prosecutors to net large and diverse groups of defendants, while removing the burden of connecting each of the accused to a specific act of abuse or killing. The "parent trial" system added further efficiency to this process, allowing for subsequent trials of war crimes suspects before courts that had already taken judicial notice of the criminality of the concentration camp in question. By the time Denson and his team began preparing a case against the personnel of Mauthausen, they possessed a streamlined strategy for dealing with perpetrators of mass atrocity in the expedient manner that the army demanded.

CHAPTER 2

American Investigators at Mauthausen

When the first war crimes investigators entered Mauthausen on May 6, 1945, concentration camps Auschwitz, Majdanek, Bergen-Belsen, and Buchenwald had already fallen into Allied hands. Yet despite the horrific scenes that their Russian, British, and American counterparts had reported from these camps, investigators were scarcely prepared for what they discovered. Aside from the masses of dead that littered the camp, the gas chamber and crematoria provided evidence of mass murder on a near-industrial scale. In the weeks that followed, investigators set to work piecing together the crimes committed within the camp's walls, deeply affected by their visceral confrontation with atrocity. Understaffed and ill-equipped, war crimes investigators came to rely wholly on an organized body of survivors intent both on telling their stories and seeing their former captors face justice. Camp survivors played a crucial role in every aspect of the investigation process—from the gathering of evidence to the interrogation of suspects. This remarkable working relationship forged between liberator and liberated fundamentally shaped the investigation and lived on to influence the proceedings at Dachau.

Only six weeks after entering Mauthausen, investigators submitted the report that would form the basis of the indictment ultimately brought against dozens of camp personnel. This report, compiled by a team of men who arrived at Mauthausen with little more than an anecdotal knowledge of the concentration camp system, helps to shed light on early perceptions of Nazi criminality. Though the report presented compelling evidence that revealed the criminal nature of the camp itself, investigators reached conclusions wholly at odds with current understandings of Mauthausen and the role it played in the Nazi state. In stark contrast to current scholarship, investigators contended that Mauthausen was an extermination camp best compared to Auschwitz-Birkenau. Because Mauthausen was not built expressly for mass murder and did not play a central role in the genocide of European Jewry, historians instead group it with concentration camps such as Dachau, Sachsenhausen, and Buchenwald, which served as severe penal institutions for the social and political enemies of the Reich.[1] Ultimately, however, it was the flawed vision of Mauthausen put forth by war crimes investigators that would inform proceedings at Dachau. To understand both the findings and the dynamics of the American investigation, one must first understand Mauthausen and its place within the Nazi system of incarceration and terror.

Mauthausen Concentration Camp: A Brief History

Immediately following the Anschluss in March 1938, SS leader Heinrich Himmler made a number of visits to stone quarries in the region of Upper Austria in order to find a practical and profitable location for the establishment of a new concentration camp. Himmler was intent on exploiting slave labor in order to corner the market on the production of stone—the material that Hitler's grandiose architectural plans helped make a crucial commodity in the Third Reich. To coordinate this enterprise, Himmler established the German Earth and Stone Works Corporation (Deutsche Erd- und Steinwerke GmbH, or DEST) on April 29, 1938, and began the process of acquiring the quarries and brick works that would supply the raw materials for the planned remodeling of cities such as Berlin and Linz. Mauthausen concentration camp, like camps Flossenbürg and Gusen, was founded in order to assist this goal, while at the same time acting as a penal institution and execution ground for the enemies of the Reich.

"An Honor for Upper Austria"

Within weeks of Himmler's first visit to the quarry at Mauthausen, August Eigruber, the gauleiter (Nazi district leader) of Upper Austria, announced that his province would have the "special honor and distinction" of having within its bounds a concentration camp for the "traitors of Austria."[2] The first transport of inmates, made up of German and Austrian common criminals, arrived at Mauthausen on August 8, 1938. These prisoners, along with many others who soon followed, constructed the first buildings in the camp and toiled in the Wiener Graben—the massive stone quarry that provided Mauthausen with its raison d'être.[3] Through slave labor, the camp grew into a massive, fortresslike compound strikingly different from German camps such as Sachsenhausen, Dachau, or Buchenwald. Mauthausen took on castlelike dimensions, complete with high stone walls and granite guard towers to match. Surrounded by picturesque countryside on a hilltop high above the town on the Danube that shared its name, Mauthausen was an imposing site from both inside and out. Excluding the quarry, the camp grew to cover 150,000 square meters, contained ninety-five buildings, and spawned forty-nine subcamps.[4] It lay only twenty kilometers from Linz, the town where both Hitler and Adolf Eichmann had once attended school.

Prior to the outbreak of the Second World War, the inmate population of Mauthausen was small, the living conditions survivable, and the mortality rate relatively low.[5] After September 1939, however, the population of Mauthausen began to expand and diversify rapidly. Alongside the growing number of political prisoners from within the Reich came a huge influx of inmates from the newly conquered territories of Poland, Czechoslovakia, Belgium, Luxembourg, the Netherlands, and France. To help accommodate the growing prisoner population, work began on Gusen, the first and largest subcamp of Mauthausen, located at another quarry site five kilometers to the west. As the population of Mauthausen grew, conditions deteriorated. Overcrowding and insufficient sanitation brought epidemic disease. A brutal regimen of slave labor weakened prisoners further. Despite the torturous twelve-hour workdays prisoners spent in the quarry, they received less than half the calories required to sustain physical health.[6] As a dubious symbol of the climbing death rate this brought, Heinrich Kori Ltd. installed the first of three crematoria at Mauthausen in May 1940.[7]

Mass Killing and "Extermination through Work"

By the beginning of 1941, the SS considered Mauthausen the harshest penal institution in the Greater Reich. In January, Reinhard Heydrich, chief of the Reich Security Main Office (RSHA), issued a decree that underscored the unique place of Mauthausen in the Nazi system of incarceration and terror. Heydrich's decree separated all concentration camps into three classes of ascending severity and prescribed the sort of prisoner suitable for each. Class I camps included Dachau, Sachsenhausen, and the main camp of Auschwitz, and were to be used for "protective custody prisoners who are least encumbered and have the definite possibility of improvement." Class II camps, which included Buchenwald, Flossenbürg, Neuengamme, Groß-Rosen, and Auschwitz II–Birkenau (under construction), were for those "who were heavily encumbered protective custody prisoners [who] still held the possibility of reeducation and improvement." Class III was reserved for the worst type of prisoners and consisted of Mauthausen alone. This camp was to receive "heavily encumbered protective custody prisoners who are incorrigible as well as criminals who have had previous sentences and asocials, which means those . . . who are barely educable."[8] Heydrich's categorization of Mauthausen as the harshest of all concentration camps was soon borne out in death-rate statistics. In 1941, the year that Heydrich's decree was signed, 8,200 prisoners out of a total population of 15,900 died at Mauthausen—a full 52 percent of those interned there.[9] In comparison, 2,700 of Dachau's 7,500 inmates perished (36 percent); 1,522 out of a total of 7,730 at Buchenwald (19 percent); and 1,816 out of 11,111 at Sachsenhausen (16 percent).[10]

In line with Heydrich's decree, Nazi officials in Berlin increasingly used Mauthausen as the execution ground for a wide array of perceived "enemies of the Reich." The camp received hundreds arrested under the Night and Fog Decree of December 1941. Issued by Field Marshal Wilhelm Keitel, it provided for the arrest and secret execution of anyone thought to imperil the German occupation forces in Western Europe. By 1942, resisters from France, Belgium, and Holland had been killed there, as had hundreds of Spanish Republicans, Soviet POWs, Dutch Jews, Poles, and Czechs.[11] Most died in the two-story building in the camp that housed the prison, the execution chamber, the gallows, and the crematoria. The camp SS killed some in the so-called photo gallery, where prisoners posed for mug shots in front of a mock camera that dispensed bullets. Camp executioners also used the gallows in the adjacent room, where a collapsible stool allowed for thirty hangings per hour.[12] By the spring of 1942, however, experiments with poison gas led to the construction of both a gas van and gas chamber at Mauthausen. The gas chamber, measuring 3.5 by 3.7 meters, was located in the same building as the crematoria and could kill thirty to eighty prisoners at a time.[13] It claimed its first twenty-six victims—Soviet prisoners of war—on March 23, 1942, and would eventually be used to murder between 3,500 and 5,000 people.[14] When the gas chamber at

Mauthausen ceased functioning on April 29, 1945, it earned the dubious distinction of being the last such facility to function during the Second World War.

Despite the existence of a functioning gas chamber, Mauthausen should not be confused with the so-called Operation Reinhard camps of Treblinka, Sobibor, and Belzec, designed expressly for the murder of Europe's Jews. Still, Mauthausen was a key site in the Nazi program of "Extermination through Work" *(Vernichtung durch Arbeit)*. This program was not conceived to facilitate the destruction of European Jewry—though it certainly contributed to this end—but was rather intended to eradicate a broad spectrum of undesirables who fell into the hands of the Nazis. Oswald Pohl, head of the SS Economic and Administrative Main Office (WVHA), implemented Extermination through Work in a bid to harmonize the drive for SS profit with the ideological war against the Reich's enemies. In a letter to Himmler dated April 30, 1942, Pohl explained that "the war has quite clearly changed the purpose of the concentration camp. Our task is now to direct its functions towards the economic side."[15] In line with Pohl's plan, and in direct consultation with Hitler, Minister of Justice Otto Thierack agreed to deliver "anti-social elements for the execution of their sentence to the Reichsführer-SS to be worked to death. [This includes] persons under protective arrest, Jews, Gypsies, Russians and Ukrainians, Poles with more than 3-year sentences, Czechs and Germans with more than 8-year sentences."[16] The impact of this program on the mortality rate at Mauthausen was devastating. On average, 9.7 percent of the prisoner population at the camp died *each month* between July 1941 and April 1943.[17] Of the roughly 10,000 prisoners sent to Mauthausen and Gusen between November 1942 and early 1944 in accordance with Thierack's decree, some 6,700 died in the same period.[18] As a letter sent from Mauthausen staff to the firm Topf and Sons suggests, even the camp SS was overwhelmed by the massive increase in deaths. Nazi officials requested that the company clarify as soon as possible the maximum number of corpses per day that could be burned safely in a single one of its crematoria ovens without endangering its continued operation.[19]

Industry and Expansion

In March 1943, Albert Speer, the German minister of armaments, inspected Mauthausen, keen on exploring the possibility of diverting slave laborers away from the DEST quarries and into the production of war materials. Mauthausen remained out of the range of Allied bombers into 1944, making it a crucial strategic location for the resource-strapped Reich. As a result of Speer's recommendations, a major expansion of Mauthausen began, as did the redirection of many prisoners into the production of various materials essential for the war effort. Construction started on a massive network of subcamps that stretched through eastern Austria and even into Germany (at Passau). Camps under the jurisdiction of headquarters at Mauthausen sprang up to supply slaves for the V-2 rocket factory at Ebensee; the Heinkel aircraft factories at Hiterbrühl and Schwechat-Floridsdorf; the Daimler factory at Steyr; the missile experimental center at Schlier; the Messerschmitt factory at Gusen; Steyr-Daimler-Puch armaments production at Melk; the Nibelungenwerke tank factories at St. Valentin; the Hermann Goering Werke in Linz; the mines at Eisenerz; the agricultural factory at St. Lambrecht, and an array of other disparate industrial interests. Eventually, more than forty subcamps were built that along with Mauthausen held as many as 85,000 prisoners.[20]

The diversification of labor in the Mauthausen concentration camp system considerably changed the dynamics of prisoner life. Outright extermination of the prisoners was no longer the central purpose of the Mauthausen camps, as the needs of the Reich temporarily overshadowed the ideological war against opponents of Nazism. For the first time, mortality rates at Mauthausen began to fall, due in part to the introduction of "Class I" and "Class II" prisoners into the camp population. Between May 1943 and March 1944, the monthly death rate fell to 1.9 percent.[21] Life for all prisoners in the Mauthausen system of camps did not necessarily improve during this period, however. Those who remained in the main camps of Mauthausen and Gusen continued to toil in the quarries for DEST or in other industrial concerns, and to die at horrific rates. Conditions in the subcamps also varied to a considerable degree and were sometimes as bad as those in the parent camp. A full 8,200 of the 27,000 who labored in tunnels at Ebensee, for instance, died there.[22]

Disintegration and Destruction

By the autumn of 1944, conditions at Mauthausen had again begun to deteriorate, this time to levels that would drive the death rate to the highest point in the camp's history. As the Germans retreated westward, masses of inmates from camps such as Auschwitz poured into Mauthausen and its subcamps, causing massive overcrowding. The population expanded also with the creation of a women's camp at Mauthausen in September 1944. To make matters worse, a decree signed by Himmler the previous May forbade the release of prisoners from Mauthausen for the duration of the war.[23] To deal with the swollen camp population, the Mauthausen SS accelerated extermination operations to cope with those who had not already fallen victim to disease or starvation. Camp administrators reduced food rations in the overflowing sick camp by 50 percent to facilitate the death of the weak, who could no longer provide profit for DEST or help produce war materials.[24] Routine in the camp began to break down, supplies dwindled, and death rates skyrocketed. The SS ordered the digging of mass graves for the burial of an eventual total of more than 10,000 bodies that workers in the crematoria could not burn fast enough.[25]

To reduce the prisoner population further, the gassing facility at Castle Hartheim near Linz was put at the disposal of Gauleiter Eigruber and the camp SS. Initially built as an asylum for the mentally ill, Hartheim had already been the site of mass murder during the T4 "euthanasia" program. Toward war's end, however, Hartheim became an auxiliary killing facility for prisoners from Mauthausen. The camp SS, intent on keeping the fate of those transported to Hartheim secret, euphemistically referred to the facility as both "Dachau Sanatorium" and "Bad Ischl Sanatorium," and more generally as a "convalescent home" and "recuperation camp." Though smaller but significant numbers of prisoners from Mauthausen and Gusen had been gassed at Hartheim in 1941 and 1942, the most frequent usage of the "euthanasia" facility began in mid-1944, leading to a total death toll of some 5,850 prisoners by December of that year.[26]

This last phase of the camp's history also saw a major influx of Jews into Mauthausen. Prior to 1944, most Jews who were sent to the camp arrived as Gestapo arrestees for political offenses. However, in mid-1944, Jews began to arrive from Auschwitz, in order to build the underground armaments production facilities at Ebensee. By early 1945, the stream of Jews from Auschwitz increased greatly, as tens of thousands were evacuated to Mauthausen and away from the Soviet advance. By all accounts, the camp SS subjected the Jews at Mauthausen to the worst conditions and assigned them the dirtiest and most laborious jobs. The life expectancy of a Jew in Mauthausen was only a few weeks.[27] The subcamps that housed the largest number of Jews tended to have the highest mortality rates, suggesting that Mauthausen did play an important role in the Final Solution in the last year of the war. Subcamp Melk, for instance, had a prisoner population made up almost exclusively of Jews. In the single year that it existed, roughly one-third of the 15,000 prisoners interned there died.[28] Of the 8,078 Jews interned at Ebensee, 3,110 died—nearly 40 percent.[29] The worst mortality rates, however, occurred just outside the fences of Mauthausen main camp, in a series of large tents set up to house the 8,500 Hungarian Jews who arrived during the first week of April 1945. Between 150 and 200 died there per day, due largely to disease and starvation in an overcrowded enclosure that contained no beds or sanitary facilities.[30] Overall, approximately 25 percent of those who perished in the Mauthausen camp system were Jews, despite the fact that Jews had only arrived in significant numbers in the final year of the war.[31]

For all prisoners at Mauthausen, the last months were the most terrible. Beginning at the end of March 1945, most satellite camps were dissolved, and their inmates either concentrated at Mauthausen parent camp, marched farther into the Reich, or simply murdered by the SS. Already-desperate conditions caused by meager rations and horrific sanitary conditions became exponentially worse. Between January and April, an average of 12.5 percent of the prisoner population died per month.[32] In Mauthausen and Gusen, this represented 205 deaths per day.[33] The Mauthausen SS also stepped up the pace of industrial killing, gassing 1,200–1,400 people in April alone.[34] When liberation came on May 5, 1945, at least 100,000 of the 197,464 people known to have passed through Mauthausen and Gusen had died there.[35]

The American Army at Mauthausen

The Liberation and Its Wake

The American platoon that first reached Mauthausen on May 5, 1945, started out at dawn from its base at Katsdorf with orders to "investigate a German stronghold" nineteen kilometers to the south and to check whether a bridge over the Gusen River at St. Georgen could support heavy tanks.[36] Led by a staff sergeant of the Eleventh Armored Division named Albert J. Kosiek, the twenty-two soldiers drove southward from their base along the Gusen valley road, where subcamps of Mauthausen dotted their route. First Gusen III, then Gusen II and Gusen I were discovered, but not investigated. The guards who remained in these camps were so willing to surrender that Kosiek simply delegated a small number of men to supervise their arrest and then moved on. The prize was to be Mauthausen main camp, which, Kosiek was told along the way, held "four hundred SS men ready to give up."[37]

At 9:30 A.M., Kosiek's platoon climbed the hill toward Mauthausen and entered the main gate to the jubilation of the prisoners who still had life enough to greet them. The survivors, one soldier wrote home, looked like "ghosts in a nightmare."[38] Heaps of dead and scores of dying lay sprawled around the camp. Kosiek's men were both shocked and overwhelmed—their platoon of fewer than two dozen had no supplies to aid those in need and totally insufficient manpower to administer the thousands they had liberated. Perhaps fortunately for Kosiek, the SS men he expected to discover there had fled in the preceding days, leaving in their place the police formation of the Vienna fire brigade. They surrendered without incident and were disarmed with the help of former prisoners. With the arrival of a second platoon led by Staff Sergeant Leander Hens, the Americans inspected all corners of the camp, including the gas chamber and crematoria. Then, after promising to return the next day, they left as quickly as they had come.

Finding themselves in the absence of both their former captors and their American liberators, the surviving inmates at Mauthausen set up an improvised system of governance that helped bring security and order to a chaotic and desperate situation. Even prior to liberation, a number of prisoners within Mauthausen had met secretly and created an International Committee designed to represent inmates according to national origin. During a clandestine meeting on April 29, 1945, these inmates elected Dr. Heinrich Dürmayer, an Austrian Communist, to govern the new body, and chose others to lead smaller committees that represented the various nationalities of the thousands who passed through the camp.[39] The International Committee held its first official meeting on liberation day in order to establish both its authority and the basic rules by which it would operate. Delegates agreed that each committee would be autonomous and should organize its own office to assist inmates of common origin. Committees took on the responsibility of insuring such essentials as equitable food distribution and sanitation, while enforcing order.[40] Most important in this regard was the prohibition of summary justice and mob violence directed at kapos—the prisoner-functionaries who had acted under the camp's SS authority in return for special privileges. Despised by regular inmates for the harsh discipline they imposed, the kapos at Mauthausen were confined to the prison block along with the other German and Austrian criminals from whose ranks they had been drawn. In the further interest of security, the head of the Russian Committee received the task of defending the camp against the possible reappearance of the SS.[41] While some prisoners fled the camp altogether, most waited anxiously for the American return.

The Americans Return: War Crimes Investigators at Mauthausen

Little more than twenty-four hours after Kosiek and his men walked back out of Mauthausen's main gate, a new American patrol arrived under Lieutenant Colonel Richard R. Seibel. Like Kosiek's platoon, Seibel's men were totally overwhelmed. As a result, American authorities at Mauthausen were wholly dependent on the International Committee that had crystallized in their absence. An improvised system of administration emerged, in which prisoner committees carried out the wishes of the American authorities in the camp while representing the needs of former inmates. Together, American servicemen and the prisoners they freed began the momentous task of organizing food and proper sanitary facilities, caring for the sick, and burying the dead. This collaboration between liberator and liberated was forged out of necessity but proved to be essential not only in establishing order in the wake of liberation, but in investigating the crimes that had occurred there. More than any other factor, the cooperation of an organized and willing body of survivors allowed for the successful investigation, apprehension, and ultimate trial of a huge number of Mauthausen perpetrators.

War crimes investigators at Mauthausen, the first of whom reached the camp the same day as Seibel's platoon, operated according to a directive issued by Theater Judge Advocate Telford Taylor in April 1945. These men, led by Major Eugene S. Cohen, often had no prior experience dealing with war crimes and therefore required instruction both on practical techniques and tactics as well as on basic legal principles. Taylor's directive therefore laid out effective methods for the interrogation of witnesses and coached investigators on the sort of evidence necessary to establish the corpus delicti—the essence of the crime. Taylor sought to ensure that investigation teams provided reports that would allow prosecutors to establish prima facie cases against those accused of war crimes.[42] As investigators working at Mauthausen soon discovered, however, chronic understaffing and a lack of resources made the completion of their task exceedingly challenging.

One of the first war crimes investigators to enter Mauthausen was future Nuremberg prosecutor Benjamin Ferencz. A young Jewish lawyer from New Jersey, Ferencz was drawn to war crimes work and to the "action" to be found in the liberated camps.[43] Unlike many of the other military personnel aiding Cohen at Mauthausen, Ferencz had gained considerable prior experience investigating atrocities at Flossenbürg, and the killing of downed American fliers in small towns throughout Germany. Ferencz recalled with frustration the lack of both quality and quantity of staff that he had to work with at Mauthausen. Though the office of the Deputy Judge Advocate for War Crimes had stipulated that investigation teams include two legal officers, a medical officer, a forensic evidence expert, a warrant officer, a court reporter, a stenographer, a photographer, an interpreter, and two drivers, Ferencz remembered working with much less.[44] "In my particular outfit," Ferencz recalled, "the officers assigned there were mostly shell-shocked tank officers who were sent to this new unit as a form of recreation and rehabilitation. They sat around with no idea what to do."[45] For Ferencz and those he worked alongside, creativity and improvisation were key.

For war crimes investigators at Mauthausen, the most important form of improvisation involved recruiting former prisoners to perform the tasks that American servicemen were not available to do. War Crimes Investigation Team 6836, one of the groups commissioned to investigate and report on atrocities committed at the camp, complained that chronic understaffing had left them few options:

> Our military staff . . . is entirely inadequate. For example, we have one military stenographer and one interpreter. Improvisation became necessary. We had the CIC [Counter Intelligence Corps] screen and clear British, American, Austrian, German, Stateless victims and employed them . . . Further improvisation compelled us to use our drivers as clerks, clerks as guards, interpreter as prescreener, stenographer as testimony coordinator, etc, etc.[46]

To facilitate the participation of the International Committee, the Americans issued military government passes to its representatives. Accordingly, war crimes investigators empowered the committee's chairman, Heinrich Dürmayer, to "go anywhere at any time to carry out the business and administration of Mauthausen in the interest of the American Army."[47] Similar privileges were extended to committee leaders such as Premysl Dobias, an Austrian appointed as official interpreter to the American authorities.[48] Investigators put other former inmates to work tabulating data, writing out histories of the camp, making lists of the names of the SS staff, assisting in interrogations, and gathering statements from witnesses.

The International Committee played a key role in securing the participation of hundreds of survivors in the investigation process. Committee leaders impressed upon former inmates the duty they had to assist the Americans in reconstructing the crimes that occurred at the camp as well as in identifying the guilty parties. On May 8, 1945, Dr. Ludwig Soswinski, head of the Austrian Committee, posted a decree instructing all former prisoners of their obligation:

> The international court for the investigation of war criminals has sent its representatives here. It is our duty and our right to support the work being done to reveal these crimes. Everyone of us who knows something about incidents of the following sort should make their names known to their block secretary, so that he can be called as a witness.
> Incidents include:
>
> 1. The murder of comrades that you yourself witnessed.
> 2. Shootings of fleeing prisoners, which you yourself saw.
> 3. Experiments of any sort on prisoners.
> 4. Sadistic tortures that you yourself experienced or witnessed.
>
> Report yourselves immediately, because this work must proceed.[49]

As a result, investigators and representatives of the committee took hundreds of prisoner statements, which together ultimately formed the basis of the cases built against the Mauthausen perpetrators.

Though both the International Committee and American authorities at Mauthausen made overtures to secure the participation of former prisoners, many survivors illustrated their own determination to be part of the investigation process. Simon Wiesenthal, then a thirty-six-year-old Jew from Buczacz, Poland, had been liberated from Mauthausen after surviving a number of death marches from other camps abandoned by the Nazis. In a letter to Lieutenant Colonel Seibel dated May 25, 1945, Wiesenthal implored the American camp commander to accept his services:

Having spent a number of years in thirteen Nazi concentration camps, including Mauthausen from which I was liberated by the American forces on May 5th and where I still am staying at the present . . . [I am] desirous to be of help to US authorities to bring the Nazi criminals to account . . . With all the members of my family and of my nearest relatives killed by the Nazis, I am asking of your kindness to place me at the disposal of US authorities . . . I feel that the crimes of these men are of such magnitude that no effort can be spared to apprehend them.[50]

Wiesenthal was but one of a large number of former Mauthausen inmates determined to play a role in bringing Nazi perpetrators to justice. The dozens of survivor-volunteers who assisted American authorities helped to compensate for the lack of properly trained military personnel bemoaned by Benjamin Ferencz and other war crimes investigators working at Mauthausen.

Evidence

For war crimes investigators, it was immediately clear that while understaffing made their task difficult, evidence for the crimes committed at Mauthausen would not be lacking. First, there were the hundreds of former prisoners who remained in the liberated camp, eager to provide eyewitness testimony and often willing to write and submit their own reports. Second, prisoners turned over crucial documentary evidence they had hidden in the days and weeks before liberation, which provided details of the deaths of tens of thousands. Despite the efforts of the camp SS to destroy the paper trail that chronicled their crimes, courageous prisoners risked death to preserve damning material for future use.

More than any other piece of evidence gathered by war crimes investigators, the death books of both Mauthausen and Gusen proved to be vital in the investigation and ultimate trial of the SS staff. These books, which record the deaths of nearly 72,000 prisoners, survived through the efforts of a prisoner clerk named Ernst Martin. Sent to Mauthausen for his anti-Nazi activities in Innsbruck, Martin worked as a secretary in the office of the camp's chief physician.[51] By posing as a "dumb and disinterested clerk," Martin gained the trust of his Nazi overlords and was put in charge of updating the death books on a daily basis.[52] In the final weeks of Mauthausen's existence, the camp SS ordered Martin to collect and then burn all the documents kept in the office where he worked. During the eight days Martin spent in the crematoria carrying out his task, he risked his life removing and stowing away the seven books listing the dead of Mauthausen, five that listed the dead of Gusen, and a separate book used to record the deaths of Soviet prisoners of war. Aside from the names of the deceased, the books list the time and date of death, reported cause of death, and the nationality of the victim.[53] Although Martin was ordered not to record the true causes of death, the books clearly reflect mass murder. On March 19, 1945, for instance, 275 Jewish prisoners are listed to have died of heart trouble at Mauthausen between 1:15 A.M. and 4:30 P.M. They died alphabetically, one after the other, from Ackerman to Zyskind.[54] Investigators and prosecutors could scarcely hope for better evidentiary material.

The most remarkable documentary evidence given over to war crimes investigators was a unique collection of photographs taken by camp personnel.[55] In 1940, the SS set up an official photographic service within the Political Department at Mauthausen—the dreaded office where Gestapo agents carried out the interrogation of prisoners. Run by two SS officers and various prisoner assistants, the office (known as the Erkennungsdienst) kept photos of new arrivals in the camp, as well as ethnographic photos intended to bolster Nazi racial theories. Apparently for administrative purposes, camp staff also photographed prisoners "shot while trying to escape," as well as those publicly executed.[56] As with the death books, hundreds of these photographs were secretly preserved by the inmates who worked with them. For more than three years, Spaniards Antonio Garcia and Francisco Boix Campo made duplicate copies of the negatives they handled, and distributed them to other prisoners, who hid them in various locations around the camp. In a similar fashion, Casimiro Clament Sarríon smuggled out and then buried a collection of photographic portraits of the camp SS also kept by the Political Department. Benjamin Ferencz, the investigator who received these photographs, remembered being "moved by the blind faith which inspired the unknown prisoner [later revealed as Clament Sarrion] to risk his life in the conviction that there would one day come a day of reckoning."[57] Like the death books hidden by Ernst Martin, the remarkable photographic record preserved by inmates of Mauthausen depicted atrocity in unambiguous terms and revealed the identity of the perpetrators.

The Commandant

For many survivors, the desire to participate in the investigation of war crimes at Mauthausen stemmed from a determination to see the camp SS captured and brought to justice. More than any other figure, survivors and investigators alike were fixated on the whereabouts of Commandant Franz Ziereis, who had fled with the rest of the Mauthausen personnel shortly before the arrival of American forces. In a striking illustration of the close cooperation between former prisoners and their liberators, American soldiers organized small units of willing Mauthausen survivors to carry out manhunts in the surrounding region. Members of the Eleventh Armored Division requisitioned horses from the local population, armed the volunteers, and scoured the countryside for perpetrators that former prisoners could identify. Though these improvised units ultimately caught few of the camp SS, all were relieved and elated that Ziereis was one of them.[58]

The liberated prisoners despised Commandant Ziereis not only because of his position, but also because of the active role he played in meting out punishment and executing death sentences in the camp. Aside from the first few months of Mauthausen's existence, Ziereis served as the highest SS authority at the camp for the seven years it operated.[59] Born in 1903, Ziereis was a dedicated National Socialist who had served in the Reichswehr during the Weimar era before joining the SS. Though largely uneducated, Ziereis compensated for his shortcomings with good looks, energy, and determination. His rise within the ranks was quick: after serving at camps Buchenwald and Oranienburg, Ziereis was appointed to lead Mauthausen at age thirty-four. Though not arrogant to his SS underlings, he walked with a swagger, often with his hands on his hips. His stance was such that Spanish inmates in the camp nicknamed him "el Pavo"— the peacock.[60]

On May 23, 1945, the same day that Heinrich Himmler took his life in Allied custody, a small detachment of American soldiers and former Mauthausen prisoners spotted Ziereis in civilian clothing trying to hide by an Alpine hut in Spital am Pyhrn. Following an attempt to flee, Ziereis was shot through the back and upper arm.[61] His pursuers carried him back to the field hospital at Gusen for interrogation, suffering from massive blood loss. When he finally succumbed to his wounds, former prisoners seized his body and hung it on display from the barbed wire that surrounded the camp.

A series of photographs of Franz Ziereis on his deathbed show a disheveled man perhaps resigned to his fate, surrounded by the former prisoners he once ruled over.[62] While receiving numerous blood transfusions and smoking heavily, Ziereis spent his final hours detailing his service at Mauthausen and laying blame wherever he could. Though a number of former inmates and war crimes investigators asked questions of Ziereis, the most intensive interrogation, lasting between five and six hours, was conducted by a former Austrian political prisoner named Hans Marsalek.[63] According to

Marsalek, the questioning of Ziereis was seldom more than superficial and was undertaken without proper preparation, owing to the time constraints imposed by the former commandant's rapidly ebbing strength. Though reportedly lucid during questioning, Ziereis at times drifted in and out of consciousness. To make matters worse, Marsalek complained of constant distractions, the interruptions of visitors, as well as the general chaos of the conditions at Gusen. Nonetheless, Ziereis would prove to be an important font of information for war crimes investigators, who had yet to have access to other senior members of the Mauthausen staff.[64]

Likely aware that his death was imminent, Ziereis doled out incriminating information concerning the activities of himself and his subordinates. The interrogation, as recorded by Marsalek, suggests a man whose attitudes were rife with contradiction.[65] Ziereis at once admitted taking pleasure in whipping prisoners, while claiming he was driven to nervous breakdown by the sight of starving inmates. He boastfully exaggerated the number of dead at Mauthausen, and yet tried to take credit for shielding the camp population from destruction in the days before liberation. Ziereis also made bizarre claims about his superiors in Berlin. He wished to personally shoot "scoundrels" *(dieser Schuft)* such as Himmler and Pohl, and maintained that Hitler was an insane syphilitic.[66] However, while Ziereis's awareness of his own impending death may have made him a more truthful subject than his underlings who were to face trial, investigators were well aware that his claims could not be taken at face value. Throughout the course of the investigation, Ziereis's contentions would have to be weighed against the testimony of survivors as well as other camp personnel.

The most important information provided by Ziereis concerned the responsibilities of various members of the Mauthausen staff, the relationship between the administration of Mauthausen and Nazi authorities, and the activities of the SS in the final days of the camp's existence. Ziereis contended that SS chief post physician Dr. Eduard

Krebsbach had ordered the building of the gas chamber at Mauthausen, whereas camp pharmacist Erich Wasicky had invented the gas van used there.[67] As numerous eyewitnesses would confirm, Ziereis admitted to driving the gas van back and forth between Mauthausen and Gusen and explained that it was Krebsbach who had selected those killed in this fashion. Ziereis identified Gauleiter August Eigruber as chiefly responsible for the starvation conditions at Mauthausen, because provisioning the camp fell under his jurisdiction. Though Ziereis admitted to taking part in numerous executions of those prisoners sent to Mauthausen expressly for death, he claimed that such killings were undertaken only upon the orders of the RSHA in Berlin. He further explained that Berlin had ordered the routine killing of those working the crematoria, as well as prisoner orderlies employed in the camp hospital. Ziereis contended that Himmler, Pohl, and Ernst Kaltenbrunner (successor to Heydrich) had variously ordered him to murder all remaining prisoners in anticipation of the Allied approach. Ziereis claimed to have thwarted these orders, considering them to be odious and "nonsensical."[68]

The information obtained during the interrogation of Franz Ziereis proved to be both important and misleading. War crimes investigators were alerted to the role of men such as Krebsbach, Wasicky, and Eigruber, all of whom would be tried at Dachau for their crimes. Ziereis's claims provided a basis for the interrogations of these and other suspects, many of whom would admit to the activities alleged by the former commandant. In his attempt to pass the buck upward, Ziereis also implicated various officials in Berlin, many of whom other prisoners could place at Mauthausen during its seven years of operation. The contentions of Ziereis also had a negative impact on the investigation, however. His boastful claims regarding the numbers of dead at Mauthausen led investigators to draw inaccurate conclusions that were later cited in the reports they filed, and perpetuated by prosecutors at Dachau. Though Marsalek remembered reproaching Ziereis for his gross exaggerations, the former commandant claimed that almost 400,000 had died in the confines of Mauthausen, while a staggering 1.5 million had been taken to Hartheim and gassed.[69] Ziereis's claims help to explain why American war crimes investigators and prosecutors alike referred erroneously to the "million" dead at "Mauthausen extermination camp."[70]

Eugene S. Cohen and the Findings of War Crimes Investigators at Mauthausen

The Cohen Report

Between May 6 and June 15, 1945, Major Eugene S. Cohen compiled the official report that chronicled war crimes at Mauthausen and later formed the basis of the indictment brought against the accused at Dachau.[71] Nearly 300 pages in length, the Cohen Report drew together 143 witness statements, as well as a wealth of documentary evidence including maps, official Nazi records, and photographs. To a truly extraordinary extent, the report reflected the tremendous input of former prisoners who had not only laid down their accounts for war crimes investigators, but who had also preserved the most important documents the report contained. Though the wealth of evidence collected and presented by Cohen helped reveal the extent of the crimes committed at Mauthausen, however, the conclusions that he drew from this material were often highly inaccurate and sometimes at odds with the records at his disposal. When faced with a lack of concrete evidence, Cohen made inferences. The erroneous conclusions he reached were taken seriously by prosecutors at Dachau and perpetuated in the courtroom.

The introduction to the Cohen Report outlines the conclusions drawn by war crimes investigators working at Mauthausen and salutes the International Committee for "securing the best witnesses and covering all phases in the preparation of this case for trial."[72] The considerable degree to which Cohen depended on former prisoners is immediately evident when examining the body of his report. Aside from dozens of survivor statements concerning specific crimes at Mauthausen, a number of former prisoner-functionaries submitted lengthy reports, outlining the history and function of the camp, that Cohen included unabridged. These well-placed prisoners had observed Mauthausen as near "insiders," in daily contact with the camp SS and privy to information revealed to few others. The weight and authority that Cohen gave to their reports would be mirrored in the trial at Dachau, where a number of former prisoner-functionaries testified virtually as expert witnesses.

The central feature of the Cohen Report was a twenty-three-page exhibit prepared by former inmates Ernst Martin and Josef Ulbrecht. The two prisoner clerks, both of whom had worked at different stages keeping the death books in the office of the camp's chief physician, provided Cohen with an in-depth analysis of mortality at Mauthausen. Privy to the way information was recorded and often falsified on the orders of camp authorities, Martin and Ulbrecht clarified how the death books were to be interpreted. They emphasized that although the death books record 71,856 deaths, thousands more went unregistered. Among those absent from the death books were the thousands gassed at Hartheim, thousands of the Hungarian Jews who perished in the tent camp and at Gunskirchen, and Soviet prisoners of war targeted by the so-called Bullet Decree (Kugel Erlass, or "Aktion K").[73] Aside from numbers alone, however, Martin and Ulbrecht offered authoritative testimony concerning the actual causes of death of prisoners. They explained, for instance, that "shot while trying to escape" was a euphemism for murder. The "escapees" in this case were usually weak prisoners the SS chased into no-man's-land and deliberately shot. To further clarify the manner in which the death books needed to be interpreted, Martin and Ulbrecht reported that most of the suicides they registered in the books were also deliberate killings, either by hanging, electrocution on the camp fence, or through drowning in the latrines. Those gassed, they explained, they generally recorded as having died of disease.[74]

In addition, as well as presenting an analysis of mortality at Mauthausen, Martin and Ulbrecht gathered together reports made by other prisoner-functionaries providing firsthand accounts of various aspects of the camp's operation. Dr. Vratislav Busek, a Czech professor incarcerated in Mauthausen since 1942, provided a particularly detailed report on medical atrocities he witnessed firsthand while working in the hospital and sick camp.[75] Busek emphasized the murderous role played by doctors in the camp, both in carrying out horrific medical experiments and in the selection of inmates for mass killing. In the sick camp itself, starvation conditions facilitated the deaths of many who entered, and drove others to cannibalism. Those who remained, Busek explained, were often weeded out by doctors through lethal injections and gassing. With a remarkable sense of objectivity, Busek detailed atrocities of the most heinous sort. Certainly owing in part to Busek's report, eight of the sixty-one defendants chosen for the first Mauthausen trial would be medical personnel. Like Martin and Ulbrecht, Busek was well educated and well placed during his internment in Mauthausen. As such, he represented the model witness and, like Martin and Ulbrecht, would be among the first called to testify at Dachau.

Though Cohen prominently featured the testimony of Martin, Ulbrecht, and Busek, the bulk of his report consists of statements made by "ordinary" prisoners concerning specific incidents they had witnessed. Many exhibits are little more than a paragraph, in which individuals identify a single camp guard who had abused them, or a specific atrocity they had witnessed. Yet despite the fragmentary nature of these statements, a remarkably detailed picture of war crimes at Mauthausen emerges when all these exhibits are pieced together. What is most striking about the evidence presented by many individual prisoners is the exceptional care and attention to detail with which they recorded information while still incarcerated. In testament to their determination to bear witness, many prisoners secretly recorded the date a crime was committed, the nationalities and numbers of victims, and the perpetrators involved, believing that there would come a day when such information would be used to punish their captors. Dr. Michael Major was able to specify, for instance, that on February 16, 1945, between 2 and 3 P.M., some 500 to 600 new arrivals were murdered; Wolfgang Sanner could detail how all of the 47 Allied soldiers brought to Mauthausen on September 6, 1944, were killed, and by whom.[76] These statements, and many like them, record disparate crimes, and yet helped to reveal patterns for investigators and prosecutors to work with. Former prisoners repeatedly singled out SS personnel Hans Spatzenegger, Andreas Trum, and Josef Niedermayer for their excessive cruelty. Survivors who witnessed mass killings often reported the presence at Mauthausen of medical personnel such as doctors Eduard Krebsbach and Friedrich Entress, as well as camp pharmacist Erich Wasicky. The statements included by Cohen further revealed that torture was carried out in the Political Department, that labor in the Wiener Graben was often tantamount to a death sentence, and that treatment in the sick camp generally meant death and not recovery.

Cohen's Conclusions

Cohen's conclusions, which appear at the beginning of his report, prescribe the way in which the reader is to interpret the collected materials. Though the exhibits gathered by Cohen provide unambiguous evidence of mass atrocity, the conclusions he drew from this material regarding the nature and extent of crimes at Mauthausen are flawed and at times difficult to explain. When examining these conclusions, it is important to bear in mind the time in which Cohen was writing. Although the liberation of Buchenwald and Bergen-Belsen brought news of Nazi concentration camps to the wider world, their role in the National Socialist state was not fully understood. Further, the particular nature of the crimes committed against the Jews had yet to be grasped, and the term "Holocaust" yet to be given to describe this. For Cohen, the camp system as a whole was the most extreme manifestation of the Nazi drive for unbridled political control in a totalitarian state.

According to Cohen, his report illustrated that Mauthausen "ranked with Auschwitz as by far the largest and worst of all Concentration Camps."[77]

> The evidence collected in this case shows very clearly that the whole purpose of the MAUTHAUSEN Chain of concentration camps was extermination of human beings for no other reason than their opposition to the Nazi way of thinking . . . The other [sub-] camps were not exclusively used for extermination but prisoners were used as tools in construction and production until they were beaten or starved into uselessness, whereupon they were customarily sent to MAUTHAUSEN for final disposal.[78]

Further, Cohen estimated that

> between 1,500,000 and 2,000,000 political prisoners are known to have been incarcerated and labeled for extermination at the Mauthausen system of concentration camps from available records . . . [79] The total number of victims is impossible to estimate, but with HARTHEIM Castle (a building used for the mysterious disposal of people) . . . almost 2,000,000 are counted from among the German Records themselves.[80]

The first issue raised by Cohen's conclusion concerns the designation of Mauthausen as an extermination camp. The reasons Cohen categorized the camp in this way are relatively clear. The existence of the gas chamber, which was last used only a week before Cohen and his men arrived at Mauthausen, suggested that murder on a near-industrial scale was a part of the camp's regular function. Testimony concerning mass killing at Hartheim, in the gas van, and through other means certainly strengthened this contention. Further, Ernst Martin's report went into great detail concerning the methodical nature of killing at Mauthausen, starting with the selection of prisoners for death, the removal and storage of dental gold, and the ultimate cremation of corpses. As explained in the first section of this chapter, however, historians generally reserve the term "extermination camp" for the gassing facilities in Poland set up by the Nazis for the express purpose of murdering European Jewry. Mauthausen, in contrast, is grouped alongside the German concentration camps. Cohen's description of Mauthausen helps to reveal the difficulty of assigning the camp to either one of these categories. In this regard, the comparison he drew to Auschwitz is skewed and yet instructive. On the one hand, Auschwitz stands in stark contrast to Mauthausen: its primary function became the destruction of European Jewry, and its victims numbered over a million.[81] On the other hand, Cohen's report clearly illustrates that production-line killing formed part of Mauthausen's raison d'être, distinguishing it from its German counterparts.

The most problematic of Cohen's conclusions concerns the estimates he provides for the number of Mauthausen's victims. Cohen approximated that between 1.5 million and 2 million died in the camp—a number fifteen to twenty times too high.[82] The reasons for this gross overestimation are difficult to identify. With the reports of Martin, Ulbrecht, and Busek on hand, Cohen did not lack reliable information concerning the number of dead. Although the death books deal only with registered deaths, Busek puts the total number of all Mauthausen's victims at 138,000—a figure deemed reasonable by two American military physicians who inspected the camp and reported to Cohen.[83] Curiously, Cohen states that the numbers cited can be found in the "available camp records" and directs the reader to exhibits 4, 81, and 213.[84] However, the specific records he cites—Martin and Ulbrecht's report; a German document concerning deaths at Mauthausen on April 29, 1945; and the death books—do not support his contention.

Where then did Cohen come up with his estimate of the camp's total number of victims? One likely source is the interrogation record of Franz Ziereis, in which the former commandant of Mauthausen boasts of over a million dead. Strangely enough, however, Cohen neither includes nor discusses Ziereis's interrogation in his report, suggesting that he did not base his findings on this document. Another possibility is that Cohen made his own calculations, based on the overall size of the prisoner population and the efficiency of murder at the camp. War Crimes Investigation Team 6836—the same team that worked under Cohen—made the following inferences in a secondary report on Mauthausen prepared in January 1946. Borrowing from the Ziereis interrogation, the report stated that 76,540 people were incarcerated in Mauthausen and its subcamps, where mass murder was carried out with "assembly line efficiency." "If the turnover occurred weekly," the report continued, "the yearly murder production approximated over 3,000,000, if monthly, 840,000."[85] Considering the real numbers that Cohen himself had to work with, it is likely that his conclusions can be attributed at least in part to such imprecise reasoning.[86]

Both the reports of Cohen and the men of War Crimes Investigation Team 6836 reveal a sense of deep moral outrage gained from confronting evidence of almost unimaginable atrocity. The huge number that Cohen presented may also reflect the expression of this outrage, borne out in a general tendency to emphasize and accept as fact the most extreme account of Nazi crimes the evidence would allow. In their struggle to accurately describe the horror of the crimes they reported on, investigators used the most severe language at their disposal. Therefore, the application of terms such as "extermination" and "death camp," as well as comparisons to Auschwitz, can also be explained in part by the need

Cohen felt to communicate the truly heinous nature of the atrocities at Mauthausen to those who would never see the evidence firsthand.

After laying out his conclusions concerning the crimes committed at Mauthausen, Cohen reserved his final words for the future prosecutors charged with indicting the accused:

> Although direct evidence is not established against all the members of the SS guards in this disreputable chain, the presumption should be that all of them are equally guilty of these mass murders and that the burden of proof is upon them to prove their innocence.
>
> The SS organization was a purely voluntary one and since its purposes were obviously criminal, in violation of the Geneva and Hague Conventions, and the loss [sic] and rights of humanity, any member recorded or accused in the MAUTHAUSEN chain should be considered a perpetrator until he himself proves otherwise.
>
> It is the belief of the Investigator-Examiner that the theory of "Association des Malfaiteurs" should be employed most stringently in a case as virulent and as atrocious as the MAUTHAUSEN setup.[87]

Cohen's suggestions are interesting, especially when matched against the charges that would ultimately be leveled against the accused at Dachau. Writing at a time before the Nuremberg Charter, and before the first judicial attempts to try concentration camp personnel, Cohen recognized the utility of combining the concept of a criminal conspiracy with violations of the Geneva and Hague conventions. His statement concerning an assumption of guilt mirrors the way many defendants were ultimately dealt with under the Dachau "parent trial" system. In the subsequent proceedings spawned by the main concentration camp cases, the burden of proof was shifted onto the accused, as discussed in Chapter 1. Though it is impossible to say whether or not Cohen's particular suggestions influenced those assigned to try the Mauthausen case, his conclusions help to illustrate the fact that strategies employing variations of criminal conspiracy to deal with Nazi crime arose independently of those that were to operate at Nuremberg.

Arrests and Interrogations

While the Cohen Report was instrumental in laying the groundwork for the prosecution of Mauthausen perpetrators at Dachau, its most immediate contribution to the judicial process was in identifying hundreds of suspects to be arrested and interrogated by military authorities. By the time Cohen filed his report, the two men at the top of the Nazi hierarchy at Mauthausen were already dead. Commandant Ziereis had died in American custody at Gusen, following his interrogation. Georg Bachmayer, Ziereis's second-in-command, made certain to avoid such a fate by killing himself, along with his wife and children.[88] As the Cohen Report made clear, however, key perpetrators remained at large. Exhibit 2, prepared by the International Committee, listed the names of some one hundred camp personnel, as well as information that helped facilitate their arrest.[89] Making use of camp records preserved by former prisoners, the International Committee furnished Cohen with details of each man's period of service in the Mauthausen camp system, as well as his rank, hometown, address, and next of kin. The dozens of eyewitness accounts also included as exhibits in Cohen's report helped to provide details of the crimes committed by many of those listed.

Though the circumstances surrounding the arrest and interrogation of the majority of Mauthausen perpetrators are not known, some generalizations can be made. Those suspected by American military authorities of committing war crimes did not receive the protection offered to prisoners of war by the Geneva Convention. A bona fide prisoner of war could not be coerced into giving information and could not be threatened, insulted, or exposed to disadvantageous treatment if he refused to speak.[90] Both the United States

Supreme Court and the United Nations War Crimes Commission ruled, however, that involvement in war crimes nullified an individual's right to receive the benefits associated with prisoner-of-war status.[91] Robert H. Jackson, chief prosecutor at the International Military Tribunal at Nuremberg, therefore advised military authorities to treat all war crimes suspects as common criminals. In a letter to President Truman on June 6, 1945, Jackson explained that he instructed the War Department to deny war crimes suspects

the privileges which would appertain to their rank if they were merely prisoners of war; to assemble them at convenient and secure locations for interrogation by our staff; to deny them access to the press; and to hold them in close confinement ordinarily given suspected criminals.[92]

In line with this policy, those suspected of committing war crimes at Mauthausen were confined to various enclosures throughout Germany and Austria and treated as common criminals. Resented by their captors and lacking the protection of prisoner-of-war status, these men were at times subject to interrogation methods that would cause scandal both at Dachau and eventually in Washington.

It appears that interrogation strategies were left largely to the discretion of the interrogator. Generally speaking, the questioning of each individual war crimes suspect revolved around information gathered on each arrestee in the days, weeks, or months leading up to his apprehension. Reflecting the priorities of the U.S. Army, virtually all suspects as well as witnesses were also interrogated on what they knew about the killing of American and Allied prisoners of war in German hands. During the course of the trials at Dachau, however, many defendants (including a number in the Mauthausen parent case) claimed that their statements on these matters had been obtained through coercion. Though some investigators were called to the stand to defend their actions, they denied any wrongdoing. For instance, Paul Guth, who interrogated a number of

Mauthausen defendants, denied using undue pressure on his subjects and insisted that it was always "easier to get them with honey than with poison."[93] Benjamin Ferencz, however, recalled having no qualms both humiliating and threatening the lives of those he interrogated in order to get the information he sought. Ferencz explained, for example, that when investigating cases involving the killing of downed fliers, he would have the local *Bürgermeister* round up the people in the area where the crime occurred and tell them to write out what happened or they would be shot. "That seems to make a big impression," Ferencz noted. "You tell me the truth or I'll kill you!"[94]

Ferencz further related a story concerning the interrogation of an SS colonel, in order to illustrate the method he used to get information for a concentration camp case. While Ferencz could no longer remember the name of the detainee in question or the camp at which he served, his account sheds some light on the way in which information may have been obtained from some of the Mauthausen accused. Once the suspect had refused to speak, Ferencz explained that he took out his pistol in order to intimidate him:

What do you do when he thinks he's still in charge? I've got to show him that I'm in charge. All I've got to do is squeeze the trigger and mark it as *auf der Flucht erschossen* [shot while trying to escape] . . . I said "you are in a filthy uniform sir, take it off!" I stripped him naked and threw his clothes out the window. He stood there naked for half an hour, covering his balls with his hands, not looking nearly like the SS officer he was reported to be. Then I said "now listen, you and I are gonna have an understanding right now. I am a Jew—I would love to kill you and mark you down as *auf der Flucht erschossen,* but I'm gonna do what you would never do. You are gonna sit down and write out exactly what happened—when you entered the camp, who was there, how many died, why they died, everything else about it. Or, you don't have to do that—you are under no obligation—you can write a note of five lines to your wife, and I will try to deliver it . . ." [Ferencz gets the desired statement and continues:] I then went to someone outside and said "Major, I got this affidavit, but I'm not gonna use it—it is a coerced confession. I want you to go in, be nice to him, and have him re-write it." The second one seemed to be okay—I told him to keep the second one and destroy the first one. That was it.[95]

The fact that Ferencz threatened and humiliated his subject and then reported as much to his superior officer is instructive. While one cannot assume that other war crimes investigators used similar interrogation methods as Ferencz, it does point to the existence of a culture in which such methods were deemed acceptable.

Though the details of the arrest and initial interrogation of those suspected of committing war crimes at Mauthausen remain for the most part obscure, the case concerning August Eigruber provides an important exception to this rule. As gauleiter of Upper Austria, Eigruber had held ultimate authority over the Mauthausen camp system. Initially wanted by Nuremberg prosecutors for his role in the Anschluss, he had been a friend to Hitler and was a fanatical National Socialist who joined the illegal Austrian wing of the party as a teenager and controlled Upper Austria at thirty. Numerous statements included in the Cohen Report identified Eigruber as the instigator of some of the most brutal mass atrocities committed at Mauthausen.

Owing to his rank, Eigruber became the object of a coordinated manhunt and, unlike any other suspect wanted for war crimes at Mauthausen, caught the attention of the news media. An article from the *New York Herald Tribune* captures the sense of intrigue that surrounded Eigruber's arrest. An October 15, 1945, headline read, "Eigruber Trap Used U.S. Agent as Nazi's Driver."[96] According to the story, Eigruber's arrest had been kept secret since his apprehension on a mountain road near St. Parkraz, Austria, on August 11. Counterintelligence had managed to install one of its agents as Eigruber's chauffeur; the man gained the former gauleiter's confidence and persuaded him to leave hiding to seek refuge in Vienna. The chauffeur then drove Eigruber to a hairpin curve, where a faked accident forced them to halt. When those at the accident scene requested help, both the chauffeur and the bodyguard got out of their car, allowing American agents to move in. According to the report, the bodyguard offered fierce resistance, but Eigruber surrendered calmly. Though Eigruber's name has largely been forgotten, the newspaper report illustrates the interest with which he was once viewed. According to the story,

> He has been one of the most eagerly sought of the Nazi hierarchy not only for the role he played but also for the testimony on incriminating orders given him by his superiors. He is believed to know something about German preparations for the entry into Czechoslovakia, the murder of American flyers and the finances of Austria. His place of confinement is being kept secret but he will go on trial at Nuremberg with other ranking Nazis.

Though this interest in Eigruber seems to stem from his initial inclusion among those to be tried at Nuremberg for his part in a perceived Nazi conspiracy, his subsequent interrogation reveals that war crimes investigators were most interested in what had occurred at Mauthausen.

Once Eigruber was in American custody, war crimes investigators found him uncooperative and pompous. While imprisoned, he indicated to his cell mates that he had no intention of answering the questions of his American captors. "The best thing is to commit suicide," he told them. "If I had a pistol I would make an end right now."[97] When under interrogation, Eigruber stated that he understood he was considered a war criminal, and therefore he had no intention of giving away information that would incriminate him or any of his comrades.[98] Throughout the course of his questioning, however, Eigruber boasted about his achievements and flaunted his National Socialist credentials. Though he would not admit to taking part in specific crimes, he spoke of the virtues of the concentration camp system and the role he played within it. According to Eigruber, Mauthausen was built so that "political prisoners could be reeducated, the asocial elements could be taught to work and to think socially, and the Jewish enemies of the state could be eliminated!"[99] Proud of being the highest authority at Mauthausen, Eigruber freely admitted that he confirmed numerous death sentences to be carried out at the camp "without hesitation," totally convinced of the justice of such measures. "All upstanding National Socialists like myself," Eigruber exclaimed, "take responsibility for what we have done and ordered."[100] However, when questioned about his participation in specific incidents, Eigruber revealed nothing. Even in the weeks leading up to his trial, war crimes investigators would obsess over how to break his will and extract a meaningful confession.

Aside from the unfruitful interrogation of Eigruber and a few other suspects questioned by American authorities in the second half of 1945, the investigation of war crimes at Mauthausen wound down with the submission of Cohen's report that summer. The intensive interrogations of most of those who would eventually be tried for crimes committed at Mauthausen were left for those working at Dachau to carry out in the month leading up to their trial. These latter interrogations, discussed in Chapter 3, yielded an astonishing collection of signed confessions that would play a key role in the case made by American prosecutors.

When preparation for a trial of camp personnel began in January 1946, prosecutors had a rich body of evidence on which to draw. Owing in no small part to the efforts of a remarkable group of camp survivors, war crimes investigators pieced together an extraordinarily detailed chronicle of atrocity at Mauthausen. Though the Cohen Report failed to set into proper perspective the crimes committed at Mauthausen, it nonetheless provided prosecutors with extensive eyewitness testimony and hard documentary evidence sufficient to indict dozens of suspects. To a large extent, the case that American prosecutors presented to the court at Dachau would mirror the findings of the Cohen Report, and reflect the misperceptions of its author.

CHAPTER 3

The Prosecution Crafts Its Case

Toward the end of 1945, the Judge Advocate's Office referred the Mauthausen case to trial, following an assessment of masses of evidentiary materials submitted by Major Eugene S. Cohen and other war crimes investigators who had worked at Mauthausen and its subcamps. Although officials in the Judge Advocate's Office had reviewed thousands of cases concerning atrocities committed in the American zone of occupation, against American personnel or in concentration camps overrun by American forces, the Mauthausen case was one of a much smaller number ultimately chosen for trial at Dachau.[1] Lieutenant Colonel William Denson, assigned by the Judge Advocate to lead the prosecution team, worked with a small group of lawyers, military personnel, and former concentration camp inmates to indict dozens of perpetrators from Mauthausen and its subcamps detained by American forces. Though the paper trail is scant, the recollections of Denson and other members of his team allow us to retrace the prosecution's steps in crafting their case against the Mauthausen accused, the pressures under which they worked, and the strategies Denson employed in the course of his preparations. One cannot understand the Mauthausen trial itself without first understanding this process.

William Denson and His Team

In the first weeks of 1946, the Judge Advocate granted Lieutenant Colonel Denson only ninety days to prepare a single case against more than sixty defendants accused of committing war crimes at Mauthausen. Though the thirty-two-year-old Harvard Law School graduate had arrived in Germany in early 1945 with no experience prosecuting war criminals and with little knowledge of the atrocities committed by the Nazis, he was the obvious choice for such an assignment.[2] While working at Dachau in the preceding months, Denson had built a reputation as an honest, efficient, and formidable military prosecutor. In December 1945, Denson had persuaded a military commission court to convict all forty defendants in the first Dachau concentration camp trial and to send thirty-six of them to the gallows.[3] Denson's use of the innovative charge of participating in a common design to commit war crimes had allowed him to prosecute large numbers of concentration camp personnel in a single trial and to set the stage for a series of rapid subsequent proceedings for others accused of committing similar crimes at the same institution. The army, under pressure from Washington to deal with the war criminals in its custody as quickly as possible, saw Denson's expedient prosecutorial strategy as the best way forward.

With little time to spare, Denson turned to the reports of war crimes investigators in order to familiarize himself as quickly as possible with Mauthausen, its subcamps, and all that had occurred there. According to his own admissions, Denson struggled to believe what he read. "To look at [these reports] and to read them was not to comprehend them," he later recalled.[4] Though Denson had already prosecuted the Dachau case, Major Cohen's immense report on war crimes at the Mauthausen main camp suggested atrocity on a scale he had yet to encounter. "The events were so horrible, so sadistic, so monstrous," Denson remembered, "that they were incredible."[5] For Denson, Mauthausen could not be presented to the court simply as another Dachau, or as resembling any other concentration camp liberated by American forces. Drawing on the flawed conclusions of the Cohen Report, Denson deemed Mauthausen to have been "an extermination camp serving the Nazis in the west the same as Auschwitz and Treblinka operated in the east."[6] For Denson, the Mauthausen case was to be different.

Aside from familiarizing himself with the Cohen Report and the evidence submitted by war crimes investigators, Denson used the first days of his assignment to gather together a small staff to aid him in constructing his case. The most important member of Denson's staff was Paul Guth, a twenty-two-year-old intelligence officer who had already worked with Denson on the Dachau concentration camp case. Originally from Vienna and of Jewish descent, Guth was particularly passionate about the prosecution and punishment of those who had worked in the camps. When Denson first met Guth in the summer of 1945 while working on cases involving the killing of Allied airmen, he was immediately impressed by Guth's fervor as well as his skill as an interrogator. Denson invited Guth to join his staff and promised him a promotion to lieutenant—a commission that would earn Guth the extra points necessary to leave the military and return to the United States to finish his law degree at Columbia.[7] Though Guth dreamed of returning home to finish school, he nonetheless relished his work at Dachau and his role in the creation of what he saw as a new era of international justice.[8] By the time preparation for the Mauthausen trial began, Guth was already Denson's most trusted assistant and confidant, and was primed to take on much of the responsibility for both gathering witnesses and interrogating defendants.

Working alongside Denson and Guth were a number of others who came to Dachau with varying degrees of experience with war crimes and with the law in general. The lawyers on Denson's team included Captain Charles Matthews of Texas, Captain Myron N. Lane of New York, and Lieutenant Colonel Albert Barkin of

Massachusetts. Barkin, who had previously managed the office of General Lucien B. Truscott at the headquarters of the Judge Advocate General in Munich, had no prior experience prosecuting war crimes cases. The Judge Advocate's decision to assign Barkin to the case initially concerned both Denson and Guth, who feared that the newcomer might use his superior age and rank to take control of the case.[9] Despite such concerns, however, Barkin proved to be a cooperative and capable addition to Denson's team. Denson had little choice but to make the best of any qualified staff put at his disposal, given the general lack of trained personnel assigned to the military war crimes investigation and trial program. In total, Denson, Guth, and Barkin were part of a prosecution team that never exceeded 22 members. To put this in perspective, Chief Prosecutor Robert Jackson had a staff of over 650 working under him at Nuremberg to try 22 defendants—roughly one-third the number of accused that Denson's modest team would eventually indict.[10]

The Search for Witnesses

The most pressing task that Denson and his staff faced was the gathering of witnesses to corroborate the statements made in war crimes reports, to identify perpetrators, and eventually to testify at trial. In the months that followed the end of the war in Europe, however, this was no simple matter. First, American military witnesses, who had either been incarcerated in Mauthausen or were members of the liberating force, had returned home or been redeployed to other theaters of the war. Second, civilian witnesses either returned to the thousands of towns and cities that the war had torn them from, or sought shelter in the dozens of displaced-persons camps that dotted Germany and Austria. Finally, hostile witnesses, fearing prosecution themselves, made every effort to conceal their identities and disappear into the postwar landscape.[11] Owing to these difficulties and to the limited number of staff at Denson's disposal, Denson's team focused on the displaced-persons camps, where the largest concentrations of camp survivors were found. Paul Guth, who took charge of the search for witnesses, created his own efficient system to sort through the DP camp populations. Flanked by a translator and reporter, Guth entered each camp, set up a portable table and typewriter, and instructed the superintendent to bring forth residents one by one for questioning. In this way, Guth processed large numbers of potential witnesses and determined whether or not they had information that could tie the suspects named in war crimes investigation reports to specific crimes. So successful was this system that years later, Guth likened the DP camps to the "icing on the cake" in the process of locating witnesses for trial.[12]

Like the war crimes investigators who worked at Mauthausen in the wake of liberation, Guth enlisted former concentration camp inmates to help him complete the work for which American staff were unavailable. One of the most important in this capacity was Baron Hans Karl von Posern. A German lawyer originally from Dresden, von Posern had been a member of the Nazi Party in the 1930s but was incarcerated in Mauthausen for his criticism of certain National Socialist policies. Von Posern had in fact arrived at the American enclosure at Dachau as a prisoner, considered worthy of trial for his activities as a prisoner-clerk. Stranger still was the fact that Guth himself had interrogated him some months before and declared him a "borderline case."[13] Owing to a lack of evidence, American authorities dropped the charges against von Posern, allowing him to then join the defense team at the first Dachau concentration camp case as co-counsel. On one hand, Guth's use of von Posern appears bizarre: the former Nazi had faced serious charges about his own behavior as a prisoner—charges that would later be revived and would result in his own conviction before a Dachau court.[14] On the other hand, Guth's choice underscores the improvisation that was required of American investigators in order to get their job done. Desperately lacking in trained personnel, Guth had secured the assistance of a professional lawyer not only intimately familiar with the American war crimes trial process, but also with Mauthausen itself. Von Posern proved to be an important and controversial figure in the Mauthausen trial, both by aiding in the organization of the case and in providing witness testimony on the stand.

Denson also came to rely heavily on the help of a former concentration camp prisoner as he began the process of interviewing the witnesses that Guth located. Ruppert Kohl was a committed Communist from Vienna who had spent the entire war incarcerated in Mauthausen. Kohl had been interviewed by Guth at a DP camp as a potential witness and volunteered his services to the American staff as a translator. Denson immediately took to Kohl and took him on as a trusted member of his staff.[15] Kohl acted not only as translator, but as a much-needed liaison between Denson and American occupation authorities in Austria. Kohl played a particularly important role negotiating the release of witnesses from Vienna, a development that Seventh Army Staff Judge Advocate General Mark Clark had initially attempted to prevent. In Clark's mind, the Russians, who controlled the lion's share of the city, would consider the removal of witnesses "kidnapping."[16] Through the talents of Kohl and the direction of Denson, a settlement was reached in which witnesses could be taken out five at a time. Like von Posern, Kohl proved to be a competent substitute for trained American staff and played a significant role in readying the Mauthausen case for trial.

With the assistance of Kohl, Denson screened the witnesses that Guth gathered, assessing the credibility of the information each provided and evaluating the impression each would make on the stand. Though Denson had read the accounts of dozens of survivors in the reports of war crimes investigators, he still struggled with the stories that witnesses presented him with. As Denson later recalled, the atrocities recounted were at times so horrible and so cruel that he initially feared that the witnesses he interviewed were "drawing on fantasy rather than reality."[17] "The biggest problem I had after I was designated to prosecute these cases," Denson remembered, "was believing, or getting testimony that could be believed because of its nature." However, as witness after witness corroborated the reports of previous interviewees, Denson's doubts dissipated. "Finally I got to the point," Denson recalled, "where I could believe almost anything."[18]

Though Denson's ongoing encounter with atrocity had eroded his own doubts, a central problem remained: how would a court, hearing these witnesses for the first time, be made to believe testimony that had taken Denson weeks to come to terms with? For Denson, the answer lay in redoubling efforts to find the most credible witnesses available, while conceiving of a strategy to "condition the court" to believe the testimony it would hear.[19] Denson and his team took great pains to conduct thorough interviews with dozens of potential witnesses, assessing not only their testimony, but the way witnesses sat, the sort of facial expressions they made, and how eloquently they could express themselves.[20] Good witnesses were noted to have made "a good and honest impression" or to have appeared to be "calm and objective."[21] Other witnesses, such as brothers Mozes and Joel Trompetter, had recounted stories for war crimes investigators that were "so gruesome, that confirmation or repudiation by wholly disinterested witnesses" was deemed necessary.[22] Denson sought witnesses who could speak not only to the worst excesses that occurred at Mauthausen, but also to the more "normal" abuses that occurred at the camp on a daily basis. Denson feared that even the best witness would be unable to convince a court of the extent of atrocity at Mauthausen if it had not first heard testimony concerning incidents that could have taken place in any severe penal institution. In this way, Denson's strategy was to select witnesses who could be used to gradually "condition the court" to hear testimony of an increasingly disturbing nature.

Though Denson and his team interviewed dozens of potential witnesses in the months before the trial, it was clear from the outset that a few key figures would be central to the prosecution's case. First, well-placed former prisoner-functionaries Ernst Martin, Dr. Josef Podlaha, and Dr. Wolfgang Sanner were obvious choices, given their extensive knowledge of the inner working of Mauthausen as illustrated in the accounts they submitted for inclusion in the Cohen Report (see Chapter 2). Second, and perhaps most important, was Lieutenant Jack Taylor, a member of the U.S. Navy Reserve from Hollywood, California, who had spent the last month of the war interned in Mauthausen. Arriving at the camp March 29, 1945, Taylor had survived torture at the hands of the Gestapo and was rescued from the gas-chamber line minutes before his scheduled execution. For Denson, Taylor was the ideal witness. While Ernst Martin had been a Communist and Sanner once a member of the Nazi Party, Taylor was a homegrown American military man who could take the stand in uniform and testify in the plain English that was common to the court. In the immediate wake of the liberation of Mauthausen, Taylor had even put together his own report detailing the entry ritual at the camp, the tortures that occurred there, food, sanitation, and the fate of the other Americans with whom he had arrived.[23] Denson went to great lengths to bring Taylor back to Germany from his home in California, despite his protests and frail health. Though Taylor insisted that his report had provided all the necessary information the army could possibly need, and that "re-association with these experiences" would do him "irreparable mental and physical damage," Denson insisted on his return.[24]

Selecting Defendants

The process of selecting defendants for trial involved a number of important steps. The first and most basic involved the identification of perpetrators through the use of standardized questionnaires. This innovation, introduced by Paul Guth in the months prior to the Dachau concentration camp trial, required each and every one of the 15,000 detainees in American custody to complete a form that detailed his or her name, date and place of birth, nationality, and education level, as well as his or her rank, place of service, position, and membership status in Nazi organizations.[25] Remarkably, Guth discovered that a number of suspects confessed in their questionnaires to crimes for which there had been no prior evidence.[26] Aside from studying these questionnaires, Denson and his team also combed through the reports and evidentiary materials gathered by war crimes investigators in the wake of the liberation of Mauthausen to glean the names of those allegedly involved in specific atrocities. Once these efforts had narrowed the pool of suspects to those who had served at Mauthausen in a capacity that likely implicated them in the atrocities that occurred there, the witnesses that Denson and his team had screened were asked to identify in lineups individual suspects whom they could connect to specific atrocities. As well as simply identifying perpetrators, survivors involved in this process were allowed the opportunity to provide a statement concerning the activities of each chosen suspect and to say whether or not they considered the suspect to have been "good" or "bad."[27] As with the earlier investigation phase, therefore, the use of lineups allowed survivors to play a key role in the process of selecting the defendants who would stand trial for atrocities committed at Mauthausen.

Although the study of war crimes reports and the use of questionnaires and lineups allowed Denson to identify a large group of potential defendants, the Judge Advocate General's Office instructed him to select from this pool the sixty he felt were most suited for trial.[28] In line with the parent trial system, those suspects not initially chosen would be dealt with later, in subsequent proceedings.[29] Accordingly, Denson did not seek out a comprehensive group of defendants so much as a representative one. First, he sought defendants who held key positions in the various areas of operation at

Mauthausen, in order to illustrate to the court the "common design" that gave the camp its raison d'être.[30] To round out this picture, Denson also decided that approximately 20 percent of the defendants should be rank-and-file camp personnel.[31] Paul Guth later expressed a deep discomfort with this part of the selection process. Choosing these defendants from the masses of other "low-ranking murderers and local thugs" in custody was, in Guth's words, akin to "a throw of the dice or a spin of the roulette wheel."[32] Despite the promises of the parent trial system, Guth feared that the majority of other lower-level functionaries from Mauthausen were unlikely to be tried unless they could be linked to specific killings.[33]

Guth was more comfortable with the secondary aspect of the selection process, which simply consisted of "picking the easy cases" according to the evidence on hand.[34] In contrast to Guth, Denson was totally convinced of the justice of the selection process. "I never put a man on trial whose guilt was questionable in my belief," Denson later declared. "In fact, I was so convinced of this guilt that I would have been satisfied to put the noose around their necks with my own hands, and spring the trap."[35]

Sixty-One Men from Mauthausen

Although the general process that Denson and his team used to choose defendants is known, the specific reasons that governed the selection of each of the sixty-one individuals eventually brought before the court in the Mauthausen parent trial must remain a matter of speculation, for there is little evidence on this matter. Nonetheless, the logic behind Denson's choices can be deduced from the defendants he selected. First and foremost, Denson sought out representatives of each of the main camp offices, as well as defendants who had served at various Mauthausen subcamps. Because subsequent proceedings against Mauthausen personnel would be based on the findings of the court at the parent trial, Denson sought to introduce evidence concerning the farthest reaches of the Mauthausen system. In this way, eligible defendants for future trial could be drawn not only from the main camp, but also from subcamps such as Gusen, Ebensee, and Melk, as well as from the euthanasia facility at Hartheim. The defendants Denson ultimately chose therefore reflected not only a short-term strategy geared toward securing the maximum number of convictions in the parent case, but also a long-term strategy aimed at insuring that the maximum number of perpetrators from the camp system would eventually face justice.

By far the highest-ranking defendant ever brought before the courts at Dachau was August Eigruber, chosen by Denson to stand trial for his role in atrocities committed at Mauthausen. As gauleiter of Upper Austria, Eigruber had ultimate authority over the region, as well as over the Mauthausen camp system within it. Unlike the other defendants Denson would select, Eigruber had been a candidate for trial by the International Military Tribunal at Nuremberg, for the role he was assumed to have played in the Anschluss.[36] Denson's interest in Eigruber, however, had little to do with the gauleiter's contributions to Nazi expansionism, but was rooted instead in ruthless acts of violence and murder attributed to him. Though investigators could not establish direct command channels linking Eigruber with Commandant Ziereis, the gauleiter's "intense personal interest" in Mauthausen was illustrated by his frequent visits to the camp and by witnesses who placed Eigruber at the scene of numerous mass executions there.[37]

Denson, who repeatedly stressed his ignorance of the goings-on at Nuremberg, became aware of Eigruber in the course of his own examination of the witnesses and evidence at his disposal. "His name kept on coming up in preparation for the Mauthausen trial," Denson later recalled, "yet nobody seemed to know where he was . . . Finally I figured he might be in custody at Nuremberg."

After reaching Nuremberg chief prosecutor Robert Jackson on the telephone, Denson located Eigruber and secured his release for trial at Dachau. Referring to the biblical story on which the Jewish holiday of Purim is based, Denson assured Jackson that he would hang the former gauleiter "as high as Haman."[38]

Though much less is known about the specific reasons that the other defendants—those who represented the inner workings of Mauthausen—were selected, Denson's choices from among the camp leadership follow his overarching strategy. Because Commandant Franz Ziereis had succumbed to his wounds in American custody in May 1945, Denson had to settle for lower-ranking officials in order to present to the court evidence concerning the chain of command within the camp. Denson located, already in custody, Adolf Zutter and Viktor Zoller, both of whom had served at different times as adjutants to Ziereis. The adjutants at Mauthausen held authority over the prison compound within the camp ("the bunker"), as well as over the crematorium and armory. They also coordinated the guard units and were responsible for the enforcement of camp regulations and the internal penal system. From the reports of war crimes investigators, Denson learned that Zoller and Zutter were also both implicated in the so-called Dawes case, which involved the killing of fifteen captured American servicemen at Mauthausen in January 1945.[39] Alongside the two adjutants, Denson also selected Karl Struller, a sergeant major who worked in camp headquarters, as well as Julius Ludolf, who had served as commandant at subcamps Loiblpass, Gros Raming, and Melk.

As with the office of the Commandant, Denson had to make do with lesser officials from the "protective custody camp leadership," or *Schutzhaftlagerführung*. Camp leader Georg Bachmayer, second-in-command to Ziereis, had made certain to avoid his boss's fate by killing himself, along with his wife and children, in anticipation of the Allied advance. Bachmayer's office was responsible for the entire camp compound, for the inspection of subcamps, for the deploy-

ment of labor, for capital punishment and discipline, and for security. To answer for the crimes of Bachmayer's office, Denson selected
Hans Altfuldisch, who, as Bachmayer's immediate subordinate, had
acted as second prison compound commander. Also selected for trial
were three so-called rapport leaders—Josef Niedermayer, Andreas
Trum, and Josef Riegler—who were under the authority of the prison
compound commanders and who were responsible for the general
prisoner population and for meting out punishment and carrying
out executions. Under their authority were the block leaders, of
whom Denson selected Emil Müller, Franz Huber, and Erich Miessner. These men were each in charge of an individual block and were
responsible for the discipline and order of their prisoners, as well as
for the counting of their prisoners during roll call. While Denson had
evidence that linked each to specific atrocities, he likely also chose
these defendants for the diverse locations in which they worked.
Müller had not only served at Mauthausen, but at subcamp Steyr;
Huber had worked at subcamp Hinterbrühl; Niedermeyer had been
responsible for Mauthausen's prison and for the infamous Block 20,
where condemned prisoners awaited execution; Miessner held authority over the so-called tent camp, which housed Hungarian Jews
marched from Auschwitz in the final months of the war. In selecting
these defendants, Denson sought to present to the court the full
function and expanse of the Mauthausen system and to show that
the "common design to commit war crimes" extended far beyond
the confines of the main camp.

As Mauthausen was a key site of the Nazi program of "Extermination through Work," Denson sought out those responsible for
the backbreaking slave labor that defined camp life.[40] The highest-
ranking defendants were Johannes Grimm, in charge of the murderous labor in the Wiener Graben, and his immediate subordinate Otto
Drabek. Further, Denson chose Andreas Trum and Herman Pribyll,
responsible for the general deployment of prisoner labor at Mauthausen and Ebensee respectively. Falling under the authority of the

work service leaders were the detail leaders, who led individual slave-labor gangs. Drawn from this rank were Heinrich Häger, Wilhelm Mack, Rudolf Mynzak, Willy Eckert, Paul Kaiser, and the notoriously cruel Hans Spatzenegger.[41] Like the block leaders selected by Denson, these men worked at diverse locations, including in the main camp, in the Wiener Graben, as well as at subcamps Gunskirchen, Gusen, and Linz.

Despite the horror meted out on prisoners by the various camp authorities described above, no office at Mauthausen inspired more fear than the Political Department, through which the camp's Gestapo operated. Led by Karl Schulz, the Political Department was responsible for the interrogation and torture of inmates, for processing execution orders from Berlin, and for keeping files on all prisoners within the Mauthausen camp system. Because Schulz remained at large, Denson had no choice but to do what he had done with regard to the offices of Ziereis and Bachmayer—select lower-level operatives.[42] Denson's most prominent defendant from the department would be sixty-two-year-old Werner Grahn, the former chief criminal secretary of the Gestapo at Mauthausen and head of the translation office. Besides Grahn, Denson selected Hans Diehl, Joseph Leeb, and Wilhelm Müller, all of whom were clerks in the Political Department and all of whom were identified by witnesses as having participated in the torture and killing of prisoners.

Likely as a result of the great emphasis placed on the murderous role of doctors in the Cohen Report, as well as in the report on Ebensee submitted by Charles S. Deibel, eight of those that Denson selected for the Mauthausen parent trial were medical personnel.[43] Most notorious was chief physician Dr. Eduard Krebsbach, referred to as "Spritzbach" by various survivors because of his preferred method of killing through lethal injection.[44] Ernst Martin, who had provided extensive testimony in the Cohen Report and who would be one of Denson's star witnesses, described Krebsbach as "a sadist of the worst sort." Like Commandant Ziereis on his deathbed, Martin also implicated Krebsbach as instrumental in the construction of Mauthausen's gas chamber. Denson also chose the chief physicians who succeeded Krebsbach after his dismissal in August 1943.[45] Like Krebsbach, Dr. Friedrich Entress and Dr. Waldemar Wolter were implicated in the mass killings at Mauthausen, both in the hospital and in selecting prisoners for the gas chamber. From the subcamps, Denson chose Dr. Willy Jobst, the notoriously cruel chief physician at Ebensee, and his assistant Gustav Kreindl. According to the report of war crimes investigator Lieutenant Charles B. Deibel, Jobst and Kreindl had turned the hospital at Ebensee into a site of mass killing through lethal injections, as well as deliberate starvation and exposure.[46] To further build the picture of medical atrocities in the Mauthausen camp system, Denson also added chief dental officer Dr. Walter Höhler, as well as his predecessor Dr. Wilhelm Henkel, both of whom allegedly dealt with the collection of dental gold from corpses in the gas chamber and crematoria complex. Lastly, Denson selected camp pharmacist Erich Wasicky, who reportedly controlled the lethal substances used both in the gas chamber and in the injections prepared by the camp physicians.

The selection of a number of defendants from the camp's administrative office reveals how far Denson was willing to go in order to map out every aspect of the Mauthausen camp system and paint the most complete picture possible of its functions. The office of administrative leader Xavier Strauss was responsible for the camp's warehouses, the personal effects of prisoners, the laundries, workshops, and kitchens, and the general economics of the camp.[47] To answer for the starvation that defined daily life in the Mauthausen camp system, Denson selected from this office Hans Hegenscheidt, responsible for food distribution at the camp, as well mess sergeant Otto Streigel. Further, Denson selected Hans Eisenhöfer, the chief of personal effects at Mauthausen and the custodian of dental gold.

Denson hoped to use Eisenhöfer to illustrate to the court the organized plunder that accompanied the program of mass killing at the camp. In Denson's mind, administrators bore responsibility for the atrocities that occurred at Mauthausen, even if their individual duties did not involve violence. At least in theory, the concept of a common design to commit war crimes allowed Denson to charge the cook at Mauthausen alongside the executioner, so long as each chosen defendant recognized that violence was a chief product of the camp system they helped to sustain.

By far the largest group selected for trial were the rank-and-file guards who occupied the towers surrounding the camp and who prevented the escape of prisoners at work sites and during transports. As Paul Guth explained, there was a random element to the selection of these defendants. However, there were nonetheless distinguishing features of the guards Denson chose. First, witnesses had either connected each of these men to specific atrocities in the statements they gave, or had identified them directly in lineups. Second, the nineteen guards chosen represented eleven subcamps, including Gusen I and II, Eisenerz, Redl-Zepf, Ebensee, Wiener-Neudorf, St. Georgen, Steyr, and Loiblpass. Only August Blei, as guard compound commander, held a position of significant importance. The rest—Stefan Barczay, Karl Billmann, Willy Brünning, Michael Cserny, Ludwig Dörr, Heinrich Fitschok, Heinrich Giese, Herbert Grzybowski, Paul Gützlaff, Viktor Korger, Kaspar Klimowitsch, Franz Kautny, Kurt Keilwitz, Ferdinand Lappert, Josef Mayer, Theophil Priebel, Adolf Rutka, and Thomas Sigmund—were low-ranking guards who, according to German policy, had not been permitted to enter the camp compound.[48] The guards whom Denson chose also reflect the demographic shift that occurred at Mauthausen after the winter of 1941–1942, when the almost exclusively German and Austrian staff was diversified to include other nationals, in order to fill the ranks.[49] Of the nineteen guards chosen by Denson, ten were from Germany, three from Czechoslovakia, two from the Sudeten-land, two from Yugoslavia, one from Romania, and one from Hungary.

For Denson, responsibility for the crimes committed at Mauthau-sen extended even beyond the camp's rank-and-file personnel to encompass civilians as well as prisoner-functionaries. In reviewing the Dachau parent trial, the Deputy Judge Advocate for War Crimes had confirmed that "the law of war is addressed not only to com-batants and public authorities of state, but to anybody, including civilians, regardless of status or nationality, who assists or partici-pates in violations thereof."[50] With this established, Denson chose a number of defendants who had never held an official rank in the Mauthausen camp system. First, he selected kapos Willy Frey, Ru-dolf Fiegl, and Georg Gössl, all of whom were implicated in atroci-ties described either in the reports of war crimes investigators or by survivor-witnesses. Second, Denson chose Vinzenz Nohel, the sole defendant to represent Castle Hartheim. Though a civilian, Nohel had acted as "fireman" at the euthanasia facility, reportedly stok-ing the crematory ovens and assisted in gassings.[51] Finally, Denson chose a number of those who represented the business interests of DEST, the German mining corporation set up by Heinrich Him-mler. Denson selected Leopold Trauner, the supervisor at the quarry at Gusen, as well as Anton Kaufmann, who ran the Gusen supply warehouse. Also from DEST was Johannes Grimm, who managed the Wiener Graben. While the latter two figures were required to take on Waffen-SS ranks in the spring of 1942, their prior service as civilian employees of DEST would nonetheless be subject to the scrutiny of the court.

The sixty-one defendants whom Denson ultimately chose present a diverse picture of the system of authority within the camp. Defen-dants ranged in age from twenty-one to sixty-two and included forty-two Germans, twelve Austrians, three Czechs, two Yugoslavians, one

Romanian, and one Hungarian.[52] Alongside Mauthausen main camp, the defendants had served at more than fifteen subcamps, as well as the Hartheim euthanasia facility. However, in a pattern common to nearly all of the hundreds of cases tried at Dachau, Denson selected no female defendants and would use no female witnesses.[53] The fact that Denson chose no one to represent the women's camp at Mauthausen, set up in September 1944, is remarkable, given his determination to paint the most complete picture possible of the Mauthausen camp system. Denson's reasons for not choosing female defendants are not clear, but the ultimate consequence was regrettable. As a result of Denson's decision, there would be no one in the courtroom to represent either the 4,000 female prisoners registered in the camp or the dozens of female SS guards who had terrorized them.[54]

Extracting Confessions

Once Denson and his team had reviewed the available evidence and selected witnesses and defendants for trial, Paul Guth assumed responsibility for the crucial task of extracting confessions from the accused. Though many of the defendants chosen by Denson had already supplied incriminating information during the questioning they faced upon arrest or while in custody, Guth sought signed statements from each of the sixty-one that would be unimpeachable in the courtroom. In the six weeks that remained before trial, Guth employed to stunning effect the techniques he had learned while training both at Camp Ritchie in Pennsylvania and at the Twenty-first Army Group Intelligence Center in Divizes, England. The confessions that Guth ultimately extracted from the defendants would prove to be among the most important pillars of the case presented to the court by Denson and his team.

Although the Theatre Judge Advocate's Office advised war crimes investigators on various methods of interrogation that had proved successful in the past, the army refrained from dictating specific procedures to its personnel. "[We do not want] to commit investigating teams or individual investigators to an unalterable method of interrogation," the Theatre Judge Advocate stipulated. "On the contrary, it is believed to be important that there be left to all investigators a latitude of judgment and an elasticity of procedure, so that the courses of action most appropriate to each factual situation may be followed."[55] Accordingly, Paul Guth, like Benjamin Ferencz and other investigators before him, was relatively free to extract statements from the accused through means he saw fit. The Theatre Judge Advocate's Office emphasized that the most important thing was simply that written confessions—deemed to be of "inestimable value"—be extracted from defendants facing trial. Given that each statement was recorded in the words of the accused and signed upon completion, the defendant could not easily argue that his words had been misunderstood, misrepresented, or taken out of context. In fact, Guth and others working on extracting confessions were advised to tell the accused that each should use the definitive nature of such statements to their advantage. The Judge Advocate suggested that investigators "tell the prisoner that in order to avoid any misunderstanding of what he has said, it might be best for him to put the facts in his own handwriting; that the record will then be clear and unmistakable."[56] The Judge Advocate further explained that one should not be surprised if such simple methods are highly effective. "The average German prisoner," wrote the Judge Advocate, "has been found to possess an extreme weakness for wanting to write."[57] Guth found the sixty-one defendants from Mauthausen to be no exception.

The strategies that Guth developed to extract confessions from the sixty-one men stand in stark contrast to the gruff techniques employed at times by Benjamin Ferencz, as described in Chapter 2. In Guth's opinion, it was always "easier to get them with honey than with poison."[58] Guth, who at twenty-two still had a boyish face, compensated for his lack of physical stature with a number of cunning techniques aimed at gaining the confidence of the accused. Guth later recounted having taken to heart what one of his instructors at Army Intelligence had taught him. "If you want to get confessions from Germans," he was told, "imitate a Prussian Officer. Behave like Herr Doktor Guth and watch what happens. There will be no need to shout." Rather than intimidate, Guth opted for flattery, or for the promise of better treatment in exchange for information. As Guth explained later, one has to "give the prisoner the impression you are trying to help him, that he has your sympathy . . . The prospect of clemency is a powerful inducement." In general, Guth explained,

> the process of interrogation starts by looking for a lead. If a prisoner writes in a questionnaire that he was a *Blockältester,* or block leader in the camp, you might casually mention that some other prisoner has already admitted seeing him kill a prisoner or turn someone over for "processing." Most block leaders killed somebody, so your intimation about eyewitnesses should provoke a degree of cooperation. "Actually," he will say, "I was like a father to the prisoners. It was Sergeant so-and-so who was the beast." Then, of course, you summon Sergeant so-and-so who will predictably deny everything. "Not me," he will say. "It was the *other* so-and-so. Ask that one over there. He'll tell you it wasn't me. He saw it happen." Now you have another lead.[59]

Many of the sixty-one men Guth sought confessions from had already admitted to participating in atrocities, though none acknowledged the criminal nature of their actions. In such cases, Guth needed only to persuade the accused that they should clarify in writing the statements they had made to American authorities when first detained. Some of the rank-and-file defendants justified their actions according to the instructions they received from their superiors. When questioned upon arrest, Willy Brünning, for instance, admitted to shooting seven sick prisoners who were no longer able to march, simply because "there was an order to kill such people."[60] Some of those higher up the chain of command made boastful statements about their activities that appear to reveal a resignation to their fate. Second camp commander Hans Altfuldisch freely described to his captors how he had "led the gassing of 250 Slavic men and women, who had to strip down in the presence of the SS leaders."[61]

Most shocking to investigators had been the statements of those who continued to justify mass killing as beneficial to society as a whole. Vinzenz Nohel, the so-called fireman who had stoked the crematory ovens at Hartheim Castle, argued that "people who are not able either to live properly or to die should be killed according to the most humane means possible. This is definitely more humane and sensible than to let them live, and endanger the general population."[62] Dr. Eduard Krebsbach, who admitted to selecting and then killing scores of sick prisoners in the camp, recoiled at the suggestion that what he had done was criminal or even morally wrong. "I was instructed to kill people through injections, when I was of the opinion that the state would only be hindered by them . . . It's the same with humans as with animals. Animals which are born crippled or unfit for life are killed shortly after birth. On humanitarian grounds, the same thing should be done to humans, in order to prevent disaster and misfortune!"[63] With such statements in hand, Guth appears to have had little trouble persuading those chosen for trial to write out more-detailed statements, in part on the pretext that they could elaborate on the justifications they felt permitted their actions.

Though Guth ultimately succeeded in getting confessions from nearly all the defendants chosen by Denson to stand trial, the stiff resistance offered up by Gauleiter August Eigruber presented Guth with his greatest challenge. When previously interrogated by American authorities, Eigruber had boasted of his National Socialist credentials but signaled that he had no intention of giving away information that would incriminate him or his comrades. He reportedly advised others in custody to commit suicide rather than talk.[64] Though he had not admitted to taking part in specific atrocities, he extolled Nazi anti-Semitism and the virtues of the concentration camp system.[65] Despite the failure of both British and American authorities to extract a confession from Eigruber, Guth was determined to succeed, especially given that the former gauleiter was the highest-ranking of the defendants selected for trial. Rather than intimidate Eigruber, Guth chose to set up a scenario designed to trick him into confessing. In the waiting room and in the washroom outside his office, Guth placed businessmen from Linz who knew Eigruber. These men, likely fearing prosecution themselves, went along with the ruse, telling Eigruber as he awaited questioning that one "is well treated here" and that "if you give them a little something, they will let you be."[66] Once inside Guth's office, Eigruber was offered fine Cognac to further bring his defenses down. To the surprise of all, especially Denson, Guth emerged with a signed confession.[67] Although Eigruber had only admitted to being present during an execution at Mauthausen, such a confession, Denson hoped, would be sufficient to illustrate the former gauleiter's participation in the common design to commit war crimes at the camp.

The signed confessions that Guth extracted from the Mauthausen defendants in the six weeks that preceded their trial would prove central to the case presented to the court by Denson and his team. Virtually bereft of any expressions of contrition or remorse, these statements reflect instead a misplaced belief among the accused that the best way to defend their actions was to claim that atrocities had occurred as a result of orders handed down by superiors. Though the methods used to extract confessions from all of those brought before military commission courts at Dachau would later cause considerable scandal in Washington, the statements of the Mauthausen defendants would be thrust to the fore by Denson and his team. As will be discussed in Chapter 4, these signed confessions had a major impact on the proceedings at Dachau and would contribute significantly to the conviction of the accused. At the same time, however, the validity of these statements would be rigorously contested by the defense and would bring Guth's methods under the scrutiny of the court.

The Charges and Particulars

By the spring of 1945, when Denson turned his attention to drafting the charge to be brought against the Mauthausen accused, American military jurists had already confronted the major legal questions surrounding the trial of war criminals on German soil. Military commission courts had withstood various challenges to their jurisdiction and had made important rulings concerning the admissibility of various forms of testimony and documentary evidence. Further, American military courts had dealt with and dismissed the defense of "superior orders" and had sanctioned the application of "common participation" and conspiracy to international law.[68] Building on these precedents, Denson himself had introduced the novel charge of "participating in a common design to commit war crimes" at the first Dachau concentration camp trial, laying down an efficient strategy for dealing with large groups of defendants in a single proceeding. To a large degree, the Mauthausen charges and particulars would mirror those brought against the forty defendants at the Dachau trial, while at the same time reflecting lessons Denson had learned through the course of this earlier effort.

As with the Dachau concentration camp case, Denson rooted the charges to be brought against the Mauthausen accused in preexisting international law.[69] Denson claimed that he could never have prosecuted war criminals according to the charges created for the Nuremberg tribunal and still have kept a clean conscience. For Denson, charges in use at Nuremberg such as crimes against humanity were "ephemeral in nature" and "as broad as the world is big."[70] Such charges were invalid, according to Denson, because they were ex post facto in nature, created after the atrocities in question had occurred. Instead, the Mauthausen defendants, like the Dachau defendants before them, would be tried according to what Denson contended were "their own standards of conduct."[71] Denson insisted that what had occurred in the concentration camps during the Second World War had been illegal even under German law and that there was no need to look beyond the laws and treaties to which Germany remained a party.[72] Article Three of the Weimar Constitution, which the Nazis never abrogated, was key in this regard, as it stated that "the rules of International Law are considered an integral part of the German Constitution."[73] For Denson, the Geneva and Hague conventions provided ample ammunition to try and to hang those responsible for atrocities at Mauthausen, while maintaining what he saw as the legitimacy of the postwar trial program.

The charges and particulars that Denson designed to prosecute the sixty-one Mauthausen defendants were brief and to the point. Those chosen for trial would be tried for "violations of the laws and usages of war." Aside from the charge, Denson added the following:

Particulars: In that Hans Altfuldisch [et al.] . . . , German nationals or persons acting with German nationals, acting in pursuance of a common design to subject the persons hereinafter described to killings, beatings, tortures, starvation, abuses, and indignities, did, at or in the vicinity of the Mauthausen Concentration Camp, at Castle Hartheim, and at or in the vicinity of the Mauthausen sub-camps—Ebensee, Gross-Raming, Gunskirchen, Gusen, Hinterbrühl, Lambach, Linz, Loiblpass, Melk, Schwechat, St. Georgen, St. Lambrecht, St. Valentin, Steyr, Vienna, Wiener-Neudorf, all in Austria—at various and sundry times between January 1, 1942 and May 5, 1945, willfully, deliberately and wrongfully encourage, aid, abet, and participate in the subjugation of Poles, Frenchmen, Greeks, Yugoslavs, Citizens of the Soviet Union, Norwegians, Danes, Belgians, Citizens of the Netherlands, Citizens of the Grand Duchy of Luxembourg, Turks, British Subjects, stateless persons, Czechs, Chinese, Citizens of the United States of America, and other non-German nationals who were then and there in the custody of the German Reich, and members of the Armed Forces then at war with the German Reich who were then and there surrendered and unarmed prisoners of war in the custody of the German Reich, to killings, beatings, tortures, starvation, abuses and indignities, the exact names and numbers of such persons being unknown, but aggregating many thousands.[74]

The charges and particulars crafted by Denson are instructive, both in their similarities to, and differences with, previous mass-atrocity cases. Like all the cases already tried by American military prosecutors in Germany, Denson's charge implicitly invoked the Geneva and Hague conventions by citing the accused for violations of the "laws and usages of war." As with the Dachau trial, combining this charge with the concept of a common design to commit such acts freed Denson from the need to connect any of the accused to a specific act of atrocity. Unlike the conspiracy charge used at Nuremberg to try the major figures of the Third Reich, "common design" also freed Denson from the burden of having to show the existence of a previously conceived plan or agreement to commit the crimes in question.[75] To prove the guilt of the Mauthausen defendants, Denson would only have to follow the steps taken to successfully convict all forty defendants at the Dachau trial. First, Denson would have to illustrate that there existed at Mauthausen a system to commit war crimes that led to the deaths of thousands; then that each defendant was aware of this system; and that in some way, each defendant had participated in the maintenance of this system.[76] In this regard, Denson's strategy for prosecuting the

Mauthausen accused was virtually identical with the one employed to send those responsible for atrocities at Dachau to the gallows.

Despite the similarities of the charges and particulars crafted for both the Dachau and Mauthausen trials, Denson incorporated a number of important changes into the latter that would help make the Mauthausen case more airtight. First, Denson amalgamated the two charges used at the Dachau trial into a single, inclusive charge. The Dachau defendants had been charged first with committing war crimes against "civilian nationals then at war with the German Reich," and second with war crimes committed against "members of the Armed Forces of nations then at war with the German Reich." At the Dachau trial, therefore, Denson had had to prove two distinct charges against the accused, despite the fact that both charges involved the killing and torture of concentration camp inmates. For the Mauthausen trial, Denson sought to avoid the unnecessary complications that dual charges brought by crafting a single charge that encompassed war crimes committed against all non-German nationals in the custody of the Reich. In this way, Denson's new streamlined charge no longer differentiated between victim groups at Mauthausen and therefore allowed for the presentation of a single body of evidence to support the prosecution case.

Aside from collapsing into a single category those named as victims of the atrocities in question, Denson sought to make the charges and particulars more expansive by explicitly naming the subcamps at which war crimes had allegedly occurred. Denson had charged the defendants at the Dachau trial simply with war crimes committed "at or in the vicinity of Dachau and Landsberg, Germany." As preparations for subsequent proceedings against Dachau personnel got under way, however, it became evident that such wording provided a loophole for some to escape conviction by claiming that their crimes had been committed at locations not named in the original charges. Therefore, by naming Mauthausen, Hartheim, sixteen subcamps, and the vicinity of each, Denson created a more durable parent case that could be used as the basis for subsequent proceedings brought against defendants who had committed crimes in the farthest reaches of the expansive Mauthausen camp system.

Though the charges and particulars crafted for the Mauthausen trial permitted the efficient prosecution of a large and diverse group of offenders for diverse crimes committed at diverse locations, they also raised a number of problems. First, American military courts only claimed jurisdiction over war crimes that had occurred after the formation of the United Nations on January 1, 1942. As a result, Denson could not prosecute the accused for crimes committed at Mauthausen during the first three and a half years of its existence. Second, while Denson expanded the charges to include crimes committed against all non-German nationals, the accused did not have to answer for atrocities visited upon the thousands of Germans whom the Nazis had incarcerated in Mauthausen as political prisoners, as so-called asocials, or because they were Jews or "Gypsies." The charges and particulars in fact make no mention of Jews whatsoever, despite the fact that roughly one-quarter of all Mauthausen's victims were Jewish. The aforementioned jurisdictional limitations also precluded the prosecution of personnel from Hartheim Castle for the murder of thousands of handicapped Germans under the T4 euthanasia program during the first two years of the war. Unlike the gassing of Mauthausen inmates there, the majority of murders at Hartheim remained outside the purview of the court because they were not war crimes, because they were committed before 1942, and because the victims were German nationals. Each of these issues foreshadowed, if not predetermined, the way the Mauthausen camp system would be presented in the courtroom and how military judges would define the role of Mauthausen and the crimes committed there in their judgment.

By March 1946, Chief Prosecutor Denson's case was ready to present to the military commission court at Dachau. Although Denson had hundreds of potential witnesses and defendants to draw from, those ultimately selected were chosen not only to secure convictions, but to prove to the court that a common design to commit war crimes underpinned the activities of all those that worked at Mauthausen and its subcamps. In this way, Denson strove to present a case so extensive that it could serve as the foundation for a series of future trials of Mauthausen perpetrators not named in the parent case. How Denson's strategy would play out in the courtroom had yet to be seen.

Lead war crimes investigator Major Eugene S. Cohen at Mauthausen subcamp Ebensee, May 17, 1945. (Courtesy United States Holocaust Memorial Museum)

Survivors show the crematoria to American personnel inspecting Mauthausen, May 1945. (Courtesy United States Holocaust Memorial Museum)

Camp survivors assisting war crimes investigators at Mauthausen by counting the dead, May 1945. (Courtesy United States Holocaust Memorial Museum)

Camp survivors in the central roll-call yard at Mauthausen, May 1945. The last chimneys on the right stem from crematoria 1, 2, and 3. The farthest building is the camp "infirmary," followed by the camp prison, or "bunker." The gas chamber is located in a basement that connects the two buildings belowground. (Courtesy United States Holocaust Memorial Museum)

The Death Books of Mauthausen, rescued from destruction by camp inmates just prior to liberation, record the deaths of 72,000 prisoners. War crimes investigators could scarcely hope for better evidentiary material. (Photo courtesy of the author)

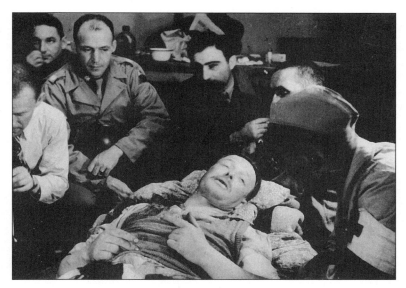

Mortally wounded Mauthausen commandant Franz Ziereis at the Gusen field hospital hours before his death, May 24, 1946. American personnel interrogate him with the assistance of camp survivors. (Courtesy United States Holocaust Memorial Museum)

Chief Prosecutor Lieutenant Colonel William D. Denson in the Dachau courtroom.

(National Archives and Records Administration, U.S. Army Signal Corps)

The nine Mauthausen trial judges in the Dachau courtroom. In the middle is the court's president, Major General Fay B. Prickett; to his left sits the court's only lawyer, A. H. Rosenfeld. (Courtesy United States Holocaust Memorial Museum)

The sixty-one Mauthausen trial defendants stand in the dock behind the defense team. (National Archives and Records Administration, U.S. Army Signal Corps)

Lieutenant Commander Jack Taylor testifies for the prosecution on the first day of trial, March 29, 1946. (Courtesy United States Holocaust Memorial Museum)

The sixty-one Mauthausen trial defendants wait to enter Courtroom A at Dachau. (Courtesy United States Holocaust Memorial Museum)

A Mauthausen survivor identifies a defendant in the dock for the court.
(Courtesy United States Holocaust Memorial Museum)

Opposite, top: August Eigruber, former gauleiter of Upper Austria, undergoes cross-examination in the Dachau courtroom. Chief Prosecutor William Denson stands in the center. (Courtesy United States Holocaust Memorial Museum)

Opposite, bottom: The typically empty spectators' gallery in the Dachau courtroom during Mauthausen trial proceedings. (Courtesy United States Holocaust Memorial Museum)

Defense counsel Lieutenant McMahon asks Vinzenz Nohel, the civilian "fireman" who had stoked the crematory ovens at Hartheim Castle, to identify his signed confession for the court. (National Archives and Records Administration, U.S. Army Signal Corps)

Defendant Viktor Zoller, former adjutant to Commandant Ziereis, is asked to read to the court entries from the death records kept by the Political Department at Mauthausen, which implicate him in the killing of prisoners. Standing to Zoller's right is assistant defense counsel Major Ernst Oeding. Above Zoller stands Paul Guth, Denson's twenty-two-year-old assistant, who extracted signed confessions from the majority of the defendants. Denson stands to his left. (National Archives and Records Administration, U.S. Army Signal Corps)

Defendant Hans Altfuldisch, second prison compound commander at Mauthausen, receives his death sentence, May 13, 1946. (National Archives and Records Administration, U.S. Army Signal Corps)

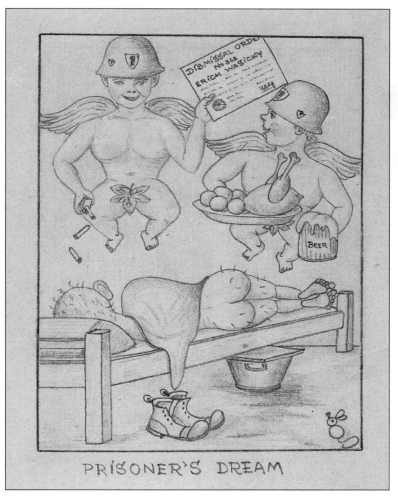

PRISONER'S DREAM

A wishful illustration drawn by camp pharmacist Erich Wasicky while awaiting execution at Landsberg Prison. Wasicky was responsible for dispensing the lethal substances used both in the gas chamber and in the deadly injections used to kill Mauthausen inmates. (Courtesy United States Holocaust Memorial Museum)

Mauthausen trial convicts awaiting execution on the gallows at Landsberg Prison, May 27, 1947. *Top left:* Chief Mauthausen physician Dr. Eduard Krebsbach. *Top right:* Rapport leader Josef Riegler. *Bottom left:* Hans Spatzenegger, the notoriously cruel work-detail leader from the Wiener Graben quarry. (National Archives and Records Administration, U.S. Army Signal Corps)

CHAPTER 4

The Defendants in the Dock

As Chief Prosecutor William Denson put the final touches on the statement he would present to the court on the first morning of the Mauthausen trial, he had every reason to feel confident. Less than four months earlier, he had achieved a 100 percent rate of conviction in the first Dachau concentration camp trial, before a similar military government court. Denson's use of the innovative charge of "participating in a common design to commit war crimes" had therefore already proved to be highly effective in prosecuting the large groups of defendants chosen for the mass-atrocity parent cases. Further, American military judges at Dachau had shown themselves more than willing to make use of the relaxed rules of evidence spelled out in the procedural guide for such trials—a fact that greatly eased the evidentiary burden on Denson and his team.

Nonetheless, the prosecution faced new challenges with the Mauthausen case. First, the indictment named sixty-one men, a potentially unwieldy number of defendants, 50 percent larger than the group chosen for the Dachau camp case. Second, the Dachau trial had allowed defense counsel for the Mauthausen case to fully grasp and prepare to meet Denson's chosen prosecutorial strategy and, in particular, the intricacies of the "common design" charge. For Denson, the wisdom of his choices of both defendants and witnesses would be put to the test, as would the strength of the preparatory

115

work done by war crimes investigators and interrogators in the months leading up to the trial. Although the prosecution, the defense, the accused, and the assembled witnesses would view the trial from the differing perspectives their roles entailed, the opening of proceedings at Dachau nonetheless represented a long-awaited moment of truth. Despite the fact that some two hundred witnesses would take the stand, verdicts would be announced within six weeks.

The Mauthausen Trial Begins

At the southern end of the former concentration camp of Dachau, just inside the main gate, lay the large one-story building that contained the courtrooms where American military personnel would try thousands of lower-level Nazi perpetrators. The Mauthausen case, like the other mass-atrocity cases, would be argued in Courtroom A, which occupied the 200-meter-long main expanse of the U-shaped structure. The eastern and western wings of the building, each of which jutted seventy meters toward the center of the camp, housed Courtrooms B and C respectively and were reserved for smaller proceedings brought against those suspected of killing downed American fliers, or for concentration camp personnel not included in any of the "parent cases." Above the main entrance to the courthouse hung a sign nailed up some months earlier by war crimes investigator Benjamin Ferencz. It read "Dachau Detachment War Crimes Group," and in smaller letters, "Judge Advocate Division, United States Forces European Theatre."[1] Those who entered the courtroom through its main doors faced a massive American flag that decorated the far wall and hung above the heavy five-meter table where all eight members of the court sat. On the left side of the room stood two rows of tables for the members of the prosecution; on the opposite side of the room stood the tables for the defense, as well as six rows of stadium-style risers to seat the accused. In the middle of the floor, facing the members of the court, sat a single chair on a carpeted block, reserved for those giving testimony. Though the spectators' gallery could seat nearly 300, the court would seldom play to a full house.

On March 29, 1946, only twelve weeks after the Deputy Judge Advocate for War Crimes had assigned William Denson the enormous task of building a case against dozens of perpetrators from the Mauthausen camp system, proceedings at Dachau began. Shortly after 10 A.M., armed guards wearing white helmets and gloves escorted the sixty-one accused into the courtroom. According to a brief press report, the men appeared "self-confident, lively, even arrogant" as they shuffled to find their place in the stands.[2] Once all were present, save for the members of the court, an American MP ordered all to rise for the entry of the judges. The eight men who composed the military commission did not wear judges' robes, but uniforms that revealed their military ranks. Major General Fay B. Prickett, president of the court, entered alongside Colonels J. C. Ruddell, Garnett H. Wilson, John B. Smith, Lyman D. Judson, Raymond C. Condor, Carl J. Martin, and the court's only lawyer, A. H. Rosenfeld. President Prickett's neatly pressed and well-decorated green uniform, coupled with his wavy graying hair and silver-rimmed glasses, commanded respect as he opened proceedings with a formal statement detailing the time, place, and circumstances of the trial.

No sooner had Prickett opened proceedings than the defense, led by Lieutenant Colonel Robert W. Wilson, launched a spirited attempt to have the Mauthausen case dismissed on the grounds that the court was without jurisdiction over the accused. Article 63 of the Geneva Convention, argued defense counsel, protected prisoners of war from facing trial except before the same courts and according to the same procedures as for persons belonging to the armed forces of the detaining power. Well prepared for such a motion, Denson quoted Article 63 directly, showing that this stipulation applied only to crimes committed while the accused were already prisoners of war. Instead, Denson argued that because the sixty-one men were suspected war criminals, they were to be considered unlawful belligerents, making the provisions of the Geneva Convention concerning POWs inapplicable. In line with Denson, Prickett dismissed the motion, ruling that it was well-established international law that members of an armed force or civilian nationals of an enemy country could be prosecuted for war crimes by properly constituted courts of the occupying forces. The Dachau concentration camp trial itself provided the most immediate precedent for such proceedings.

With the first challenge from the defense easily deflected, Prickett called on each defendant to state his full name, age, place of residence, nationality, and military status. Further, Prickett assigned each a numbered white card on a string to be worn around the neck for easy identification. According to a brief report in *Heute* magazine, ex-gauleiter Eigruber grimaced as he received number thirteen, perhaps because of its unlucky connotation, or simply because of the humiliation of being reduced to a number. Once each defendant had adjusted the twine around his neck, Prickett read the charges and particulars to the accused, then turned to ask each if he understood the crime he was charged with. "Nein!" retorted Hans Altfuldisch, the former prison compound commander who was first to be called upon. Interjecting on his behalf, assistant defense counsel Major Ernst Oeding insisted that he had tried to explain the charges but did not fully understand them himself.[3] Oeding, an impressive-looking character once described as "John Wayne with a receding hairline," contended that it was simply not possible to explain to the accused how participating in a common design constituted a crime.[4]

Following Oeding's lead, civilian defense counsel Alexander Wolf raised the same objection. "I couldn't make my people understand, . . ." he protested. "I don't understand myself, and I have practiced law for many years."[5] To clarify matters, Denson read a definition of the term "common design" from *Black's Law Dictionary*, which described it as "a community of intention between two or more persons to do an unlawful act." With that, the court declared the charges sufficiently explained and moved to ask each of the accused to enter a plea.

Before the court could continue, however, the defense presented a series of motions designed to discredit the charges brought against the accused. First, Wilson asked the court to quash the charges and particulars on the grounds that common design did not constitute a crime. As Denson was quick to remind the court, however, the accused were charged with participating in a common design *to commit war crimes*. The particulars, he explained, laid out a number of specific offenses, including killings, beatings, and torture. Siding with Denson, the court again rejected the argument of the defense, spurring Wilson to introduce a new motion asking that the court order the prosecution to make the charges against the accused more specific. The defense contended that it was not possible to adequately defend the accused against crimes that had purportedly occurred over a three-and-a-half-year period, in eighteen separate locations. Again, however, Denson quickly convinced the court that such a motion was not warranted. Aside from referring to the Dachau concentration camp trial that he had already argued, Denson drew upon the precedent established in the Yamashita trial.[6] In that case, the court had ruled that "violations of the law of war triable before a military tribunal need not be stated with the precision of a common law indictment."[7] Denson further stated that any defendant would know perfectly well what "killings at Ebensee between 1942 and 1945" meant, if they had been there.[8]

The final motion put forth by the defense asked the court to dissolve the current proceedings in favor of trying each of the defendants separately. Defense counsel argued that the sixty-one accused were of "wildly different level of responsibilities and authority," a fact that was sure to lead to confusion. Further, Wilson and his team argued that some of the best witnesses for the defense were other defendants, a fact prejudicial to any testimony they might give. If the defendants were to remain lumped together, were they therefore being charged with conspiracy, or with individual acts? If the latter was the case, who committed them, and when? Where? The accused, Denson responded, remained accused of a single offense, participating in a common design to commit war crimes—there was little to muddle or confuse. Defense counsel Patrick McMahon railed against this strategy, insisting that Denson was "trying to allege and prove a conspiracy, but does not wish to be bound by the rules that make a conspiracy what it is."[9] As before, however, the court's consideration was brief. Having already ruled on the legitimacy of the charges, the court declared that no injustice would be done to the accused if tried as a group.

With the motions of the defense out of the way, Prickett turned to the sixty-one defendants and asked each to state his plea. One after the other, the accused snapped their heels together and answered "Nicht schuldig!"[10] August Eigruber, who had already shown himself to be defiant in the face of interrogation, refused to enter a plea, stating instead that he did not understand the charge. Wasting no time, Prickett instructed court reporters to register a not guilty plea, and moved on. Defense counsel interjected on behalf of a defendant only once, as Vinzenz Nohel, the civilian "fireman" who had stoked the crematory ovens at Hartheim, also entered a not guilty plea. Lieutenant McMahon asked that the court consider a plea of insanity from Nohel, and the appointment of an insanity commission. McMahon insisted that Nohel, as the result of an accident that had occurred in 1919, could neither state the difference between a mistake and a lie, nor between a tree and a bush.[11] To keep the proceedings rolling, Prickett deferred examination of the issue to a later date, asked the rest of the accused for their pleas, and requested that Denson proceed with his opening statement to the court.

The opening statement that Denson presented, representing fewer than three full pages of text, drew upon the conclusions reached in the reports of war crimes investigators, while summarizing the major points that the prosecution intended to prove. Denson turned toward the bench and began:

> We expect the evidence to show that the victims of [Mauthausen and its subcamps] were gathered throughout the continent of Europe from those countries who were at one time at war with Germany or who had been overrun by the German Army . . . [as well as] prisoners of war of countries then at war with the German Reich.
>
> We expect the evidence to further show that these victims constituted in the main the intelligentsia of Continental Europe, those persons who had the intestinal fortitude . . . to stand up to the Nazi yoke of oppression.
>
> We expect the evidence to show that this Mauthausen Camp was operated by the SS [who] employed in minor capacity prisoners to do their dirty work. In other words, these SS men put in charge of the political prisoners who were brought to Mauthausen, German criminals who were many times much more dangerous . . . and that they permitted these German criminals to exercise authority over the prisoners . . . and to commit atrocities that are alleged in the particulars.
>
> We further expect the evidence to show . . . that somewhere between 165,000 and a million and a half persons were killed in Mauthausen and in the by-camps of Mauthausen. We expect to show . . . that there was a planned scheme of extermination that was carried on in Mauthausen and its by camps . . . Prisoners, although there for their political beliefs or their religious beliefs or as prisoners of war, were used in such a manner so as to derive the greatest economic value from their services. They were . . . fed a diet which was calculated ultimately to end in their death.

Mauthausen and its by camps, we expect the evidence to show, was nothing more than a many-headed hydra of extermination and that these 61 men that are on trial before this court either encouraged, aided, abetted, or participated in a "common design" to subject the Poles, Russians, the Czechs, the Americans, to killings, beatings and tortures.[12]

Denson's opening statement is instructive not only for what it includes, but also for what it does not. Its brevity is in itself remarkable—to open a case against sixty-one men, for crimes allegedly committed against hundreds of thousands of victims at more than a dozen locations, Denson spoke for less than five minutes. In doing so, he signaled that this was not to be a trial designed to serve pedagogical ends and reveal the crimes of the Nazis to the wider world. Denson had concluded from the Dachau concentration camp case that the public had little interest in following such proceedings. Instead, expediency would define the approach of Denson and his team, as they set out to convict sixty-one men in a trial that all knew could not last more than a number of weeks.[13] Denson signaled to the court that he sought simply to prove, as quickly as possible, that there was at Mauthausen a general system that produced atrocity, that the existence of this system was known to the accused, and that each of the accused had, in some way, participated in the maintenance of this system.

Denson's vision of Mauthausen was both expansive and flexible, and served to justify the prosecution of such a disparate group of defendants under a single charge. His description of the ever-evolving Mauthausen camp system as a "many-headed hydra of extermination" further ascribed a common purpose to the farthest reaches of this system based on mass murder. To give credence to this contention, Denson used a remarkable set of mortality statistics that allow for a margin of error of over one million victims. This was almost certainly Denson's attempt to balance the massive overestimations produced in the Cohen Report with the more sober calculations of prisoner-functionaries Ernst Martin and Josef Ulbrecht in the report they wrote to accompany their submission of the camp's death books. Whereas Denson may have attempted to temper Cohen's conclusions with more reliable statistics, the few members of the press who covered the opening of the trial drew dramatic conclusions about Mauthausen and its place within the Nazi camp system that threatened to skew the historical record. Brief articles in both *News of Germany* as well as the *Washington Times-Herald* trumpeted the possibility of 1.5 million victims, the latter paper referring also to the "planned scheme of extermination" that gave Mauthausen its purpose.[14]

Certainly the most problematic aspect of Denson's opening statement concerns his description of the victims of the Mauthausen camp system. Despite the fact that more than 10,000 of those who lost their lives at Mauthausen were German or Austrian, these victims went unacknowledged.[15] In fact, German prisoners were introduced only as ruthless criminal kapos more brutal than the Nazis themselves. Owing to the limits of American military jurisdiction, however, Denson could only prosecute the accused for war crimes committed against non-German nationals. Claiming that Mauthausen's victims were either POWs, or those "gathered throughout the continent of Europe from those countries who were at one time at war with Germany or who had been overrun by the German Army," was therefore a half-truth that subverted the historical record in order to meet the needs of the law. The claim that Mauthausen's victims were "in the main the intelligentsia of Continental Europe" was equally skewed. While well-educated survivors had provided significant assistance to American war crimes investigators and would be prominent witnesses at trial, they represented a small portion of the tens of thousands incarcerated in the Mauthausen camp system. Further, Denson made no mention of Jewish victims, nor of any prisoners persecuted by reason of race. Though his reference to those incarcerated for their religious beliefs

may be an allusion to the 25,000 Jews who lost their lives at Mauthausen, Denson still failed to acknowledge the centrality of Nazi
racial ideology and its genocidal character. For Denson, Mauthausen
was to be seen as the ultimate tool of political control in a ruthless
totalitarian state. Its victims, Denson proposed, were martyrs who
had willingly resisted an odious ideology.

The Prosecution Case

Witnesses on the Stand: Presenting Mauthausen to the Court

Only five hours after officially opening proceedings in the Dachau
courtroom, Major General Prickett instructed Chief Prosecutor
Denson to call his first witness. Building on the strategy developed
during the Dachau concentration camp trial, Denson planned to
introduce witnesses in such a way as to "condition" the court to accept evidence of an increasingly disturbing nature. To do so, Denson would first call to the stand those who could collectively lay a
foundation of knowledge for the court, allowing those behind the
bench to become familiar with the Mauthausen camp system, its
functions, and its staff, as well as its victims. Once the court had a
full appreciation of the murderous nature of Mauthausen and its
subcamps, Denson reasoned, it could then be presented with witnesses whose individual accounts of atrocity might otherwise have
proven too much to process. Aside from simply illustrating the nature of the inherently criminal nature of the camp system, Denson
further hoped his witnesses would directly connect each defendant
to the crimes described. In the coming weeks, therefore, Denson
aimed gradually and cautiously to build a complete picture of atrocity at Mauthausen and to frame it within the concept of the common design to commit war crimes that the charges alleged.

Lieutenant Commander Jack Taylor, the American Mauthausen
survivor who had compiled his own report on atrocities at the

camp and who had returned to Germany against his will at Denson's insistence, was the first to take the stand. Though Taylor had spent only five weeks in Mauthausen, Denson knew that a military witness, speaking the plain American English common to the members of the court, would most quickly "condition" the presiding judges to hear testimony concerning the heinous crimes that had occurred at the camp. As the first to present evidence to the court, Taylor was asked to recount from his experiences the camp's most basic functions. To this end, Denson began by having Taylor recall for the court his arrival at Mauthausen, including the questioning, beating, and removal of clothes and hair that were standard components of the entry ritual that almost all prisoners were subjected to. Denson then asked Taylor to describe the layout of Mauthausen, name its subcamps, and describe for the court the various categories of prisoners incarcerated in the camp system as a whole. Taylor went on to detail the backbreaking slave labor in the camp, as well as the overcrowding, starvation, and horrific sanitary conditions that contributed to the deaths of thousands and nearly led to his own.[16]

Although Denson intended to use Taylor's testimony to give basic information about the Mauthausen camp system, Taylor also provided the court with its first taste of the horrific descriptions of atrocity that would become a standard feature of the testimony of almost all the prosecution witnesses to appear before the court. Taylor told the court how, upon arrival at Mauthausen at the beginning of April 1945, he had witnessed aspects of the mass-killing process while laying tile in the newly built crematorium that adjoined the gas chamber. "The regular procedure for the gas chamber," Taylor testified, "was twice a day gassing, 120 at a time normally . . . With the new crematorium it increased the facilities to about 200–250 a day, I believe."[17] He further explained that while he had not personally witnessed all forms of killing in the camp, he had collected eyewitness accounts from other former prisoners that described clubbing to death with wooden shovels or picks, axes, hammers, and so forth; hacking to pieces by dogs specially trained for that purpose; injections into the heart and veins of magnesium chloride and benzene; exposure—naked into zero weather after a hot shower, scalding water shower followed by cow-tail whipping to break the blisters and tear the flesh away; mashing in a concrete mixer; drowning; beating men over a 150 meter cliff to the rocks below; beating and driving men into the electric fence . . . Forcing men to drink a great quantity of water, and then jumping onto their stomachs . . . ; buried alive . . . red-hot poker down the throat, etc.[18]

This shocking list of atrocities drew the first day's proceedings to a close and helped shape the emerging landscape of the trial. On the following morning, the *Washington Times-Herald*—one of the few papers to report on the proceedings—drew on Taylor's testimony, concluding that even a camp as notorious as Dachau was "a country club" in comparison to Mauthausen.[19]

Whereas the court learned much about the nature of Mauthausen and its subcamps from Taylor's testimony, defense counsel learned how relaxed would be the rules of evidence at the Mauthausen trial. In describing atrocities at the camp, Taylor at times had reported only what others told him, explaining that with regard to certain crimes, he knew "nothing from an eyewitness account."[20] He often paired portions of his testimony with phrases such as, "as I heard the story."[21] Defense counsel insisted that such testimony went "beyond single hearsay" and amounted to little more than rumor. "In other words," Major Oeding explained, "it wasn't told to me by somebody who saw it, but it was told to me by somebody who heard it from somebody else, and on down the line."[22] In a pattern that would come to define the reactions of the court to the protestations of the defense, however, Oeding's ensuing objection was quickly overruled. In a similar fashion, the court rejected defense counsel's request that photographs of the gas chamber identified by Taylor not be taken into evidence because "no connection [was] shown with any particular defendant in this case."[23] The court made it known that it intended to take full advantage of the Rules of Procedure in Military Courts, which allowed for the consideration of any form of testimony that the judges decided was of probative value.[24]

Though Taylor admitted during cross-examination that he had not seen a single one of the defendants commit an act of violence, his testimony, Denson argued, all went to illustrate the existence of the common design to commit war crimes that each of the accused participated in.[25] Although attributing particular acts of violence to specific defendants would help to reveal the nature of the common design in place at Mauthausen, Denson reminded the court on various occasions that such evidence was not required to establish the guilt of the accused. Taylor had painted a vivid picture of atrocity for the court and confirmed Mauthausen's place as an "extermination camp" designed explicitly for "killing and disposal."[26] In this regard, therefore, Taylor's testimony had served Denson's aims effectively. The fact that the judges were being won over by Denson's argumentation is hinted at in the only question Taylor faced from a member of the court. "I would like your opinion," Colonel Martin asked before dismissing Taylor, "on whether or not you think it would be possible for anybody who was in the camp at that time not to have known [what] was going on?" Taylor's answer directly addressed a crucial aspect of Denson's case: that the accused were aware of the nature of the common design they had participated in. "I don't see how it would be possible not to know," Taylor replied.[27]

Following Taylor's testimony, Denson called to the stand a series of former prisoner-functionaries whose in-depth knowledge of the various departments in which they had worked allowed them to present detailed testimony concerning both Mauthausen's staff and function. Unlike those who testified before the International Military Tribunal at Nuremberg, these German-speaking witnesses did not have the benefit of instant translation. Instead, the Dachau court used a series of interpreters whose frequent mistakes provided the only source of amusement during the trial.[28] All witnesses were asked questions in English, which were then translated into their own language by court staff. Most problematic in this regard was the fact that witnesses or defendants who had a grasp on English had early exposure to the question, before it was put to them by the interpreter. This was made all the worse with the use of other languages such as Yiddish or Polish, which required translation between English, German, and the third language, in order that all present understood the testimony given. Aside from creating confusion, the problem of court translation underscored the lack of resources provided to military jurists at Dachau.

Former camp clerk Ernst Martin was the first prisoner-functionary to take the stand. In order to help establish his credibility, Denson first had Martin confirm his professional qualifications as an engineer and describe the antifascist activities that had led to his incarceration. Though Denson would question Martin extensively about various aspects of the Mauthausen camp system and would ultimately keep him on the stand longer than any other witness, it was Martin's familiarity with the death books—the prosecution's most important piece of documentary evidence—that made his testimony vital. As he had done for war crimes investigator Eugene S. Cohen, Martin told the court both how he had kept the death books, as well as what they revealed and obscured.[29] In testimony that illustrated the remarkable foresight with which Martin acted while still a prisoner, he explained that he had used a subtle code when registering each death that allowed him to secretly denote if prisoners had been murdered.[30] To illustrate to the court both how this code functioned and to drive home the overall evidentiary value of the death books, Denson asked Martin to identify the volume currently in front of him and to turn to entry 2,768. "The prisoner did not die a natural death, is that correct?" "He did not die a natural death,"

Martin responded. "How do you know that?" Denson asked. Martin continued:

I notice it because it was a Polish Jew who was in Block 5. That was a quarantine block, and in quarantine it was impossible to get "shot while trying to escape" because he couldn't get out of the camp. The time of death was [also] noted in intervals of exactly five minutes apiece, which in practice is not possible when someone is trying to escape.

"Did you make any notation after the place of birth," Denson asked, "to tell you whether or not that man died an unnatural death?" "After the birth place," Martin explained, "a period."[31]

Aside from explaining the information entered in Mauthausen's death books, Martin described the backbreaking slave labor in the Wiener Graben quarry, and how both work detail leader Hans Spatzenegger and work service leader Andreas Trum were among the most cruel and feared personnel stationed at the camp.[32] Martin testified that Dr. Krebsbach had conducted medical experiments on prisoners, that Dr. Henkel had administered lethal injections, that Dr. Entress had selected prisoners for gassing, and that camp pharmacist Erich Wasicky had dispensed the necessary Zyklon B.[33]

Though the defense had for the most part allowed Martin to testify uninterrupted, his implication of defendants Niedermayer and Struller in the shooting of prisoners following the mass outbreak of February 1945 brought a vigorous objection from Major Oeding. "It was rumored," Martin had explained, "that there were Russian officers amongst [the victims]." In one of the first successful objections brought by the defense, the court ruled that any testimony based on rumor be stricken from the record. To the ire of the defense, however, Denson satisfied the court merely by having Martin substitute the word "rumor" with the phrase "the common knowledge of the prisoners."[34] During cross-examination, however, Oeding continued his attack, forcing Martin, like Taylor before him, to reveal how little firsthand knowledge he had of incidents that specifically involved the defendants in the dock. "Did you ever see any one of those sixty-one men shoot anybody?" "No," Martin replied. "Did you ever see any of those sixty-one people gas anybody?" "No." "Did you ever see any of those sixty-one people inject anybody?" Oeding asked. "I did not see them inject them, but I saw them accompany them." "Did you ever see any of these sixty-one accused beat anybody to death?" "No." "Did you ever see personnel mishandled in the stone quarry?" "No," Martin replied. "Thank you. No further questions, sir."[35]

Unfazed by the challenges offered by the defense to Martin's testimony, Denson called his next witness, Dr. Joseph Podlaha, in order to present evidence to the court concerning medical atrocities at Mauthausen. Podlaha, a professor of surgery from Brno, arrived at Mauthausen with a transport of Czech intellectuals and was put to work assisting Nazi doctors in the camp's hospital. Podlaha recounted for the court how defendant Krebsbach had sent him to SS Dr. Hans Richter at Gusen, where he was forced to operate on hundreds of healthy prisoners. Podlaha went on to describe the general disdain of the SS doctors for the sick, and told the court how ailing prisoners admitted to hospital had their calorie intake reduced to between 300 and 500 calories to facilitate their deaths.[36] Asked by Denson to tell the court what nutrition a regular prisoner received, Podlaha testified that they received only 1,000 calories a day—roughly one-third the amount required to sustain life when performing the obligatory hard labor.[37] For the sick who did not fall victim to either starvation or the horrific sanitary conditions in the camp hospitals, there were selections for gassing, carried out, Podlaha testified, by defendants Krebsbach and Trum, among others. "The weak prisoners had to undress," Podlaha explained, "and [Dr. Krebsbach] picked them out, saying 'You, and you, and you,' and they were put aside . . . The next day these prisoners were reported as dead."[38]

Though Denson focused primarily on Podlaha's knowledge of medical conditions and atrocities at Mauthausen, he also elicited testimony concerning the treatment of Jews in the camp system. First, Podlaha told how all the Jews on his transport from Czechoslovakia in February 1942 were singled out upon arrival at Mauthausen and killed within days. Further, Podlaha explained that while medical facilities in the camp system were woefully inadequate, Jews were permitted no medical attention whatsoever until mid-1944. In one of the few occasions during the trial where the prosecution explicitly sought to draw out evidence concerning the fate of Jews at the camp, Denson asked Podlaha if he could tell the court from his own observations what the average life span of any Jew in Mauthausen was. "One could say 14 days at maximum," Podlaha explained, "but one could later say that after two or three days they were killed or murdered." "Was there ever a time in Mauthausen when all the Jews, regardless of nationality, were killed off?" "Yes . . . That was toward the end of 1943 'til April 1944; there were no Jews in Mauthausen then."[39] Though the defense made Podlaha clarify that his testimony concerning life spans, as well as earlier testimony concerning the nutrition prisoners received, was only educated guesswork, his firsthand accounts of the activities of the doctors in the dock no doubt made a significant impression on the court.

Following Podlaha's testimony, Denson called Austrian minister of education Dr. Felix Hurdes to give evidence concerning the camp's prison block. Though Hurdes would describe brutal beatings he witnessed while in solitary confinement there and would give extensive testimony concerning the role of defendants Neidermayer and Eigruber in such abuse, the objections of the defense soon overshadowed the evidence he gave. As Hurdes was an Austrian citizen, Major Oeding argued, the abuses he suffered were "outside the Charge sheet," as the particulars drafted for the Mauthausen case provided only for crimes committed against non-German nationals and made no mention of those perpetrated against citizens of Austria.[40] To counter this contention, the prosecution sought to portray Austria as an innocent victim of Nazi aggression, rather than as a once-dedicated component of Hitler's empire. "May it please the court," Lieutenant Colonel Barkin began, "we are trying cases of individuals who were confined because their beliefs were then opposed to the Third Reich, and Austria was not a part of the German Reich until Germany invaded the country."[41] "Whatever happened before the Anschluss," Oeding countered, "is not before this court . . . In 1942, this man was a citizen of the German Reich . . . [as] recognized by the American Government."[42] In striking terms, this exchange revealed how the historical record of the war period could at times be bent or manipulated in order to suit the needs of the law and the charges before the court. For the defense, it was necessary to portray Austria as Hitler's willing partner, in order to render crimes committed against Austrians outside the jurisdiction of the court. For the prosecution, on the other hand, it was necessary to depict Austria as an innocent victim of Nazi aggression, so as to present the German citizenship of Austrians during the war period as null and void. Though Dr. Hurdes may not have seen himself as a willing member of Hitler's Reich, the widespread Austrian support for the Anschluss makes the depictions of the prosecution questionable at best. Despite the problematic portrayal of Austrian victimhood, however, the court again ruled against Oeding. "This court," Prickett declared, "does not recognize the barring of any witness in this court. The motion is overruled."[43]

After Hurdes, Denson called Wolfgang Sanner to testify, in order to present evidence concerning the slave-labor program at Mauthausen. Prior to Sanner's appearance on the stand, the first four days of the trial went relatively smoothly for Denson and his team, objections of the defense notwithstanding. Denson's decision to introduce Sanner—a former member of both the Nazi Party and the SS—was risky. Though Sanner had been incarcerated at Mauthau-

sen reportedly for aiding victims of Nazi persecution, he had acquired the knowledge Denson sought to elicit by working as a kapo
in the camp's labor distribution office. As such, Sanner revealed one
of the central dilemmas the prosecution faced in selecting its witnesses: was it worth presenting witnesses to the court whose background was questionable, and yet whose positions as privileged prisoners allowed them unique vantage points to report on aspects of the
camp system and the activities of the accused? It was a gamble.

Denson had barely introduced Sanner when the defense lodged
its first objection, claiming that Sanner's testimony was outside the
scope of the trial, given the witness's German citizenship.[44] Having
ruled on this issue with witness Hurdes, however, the court overruled the defense and allowed the prosecution to proceed. For the
moment, Denson drew from Sanner the detailed information and
eyewitness testimony that had made his inclusion as a prosecution
witness worth the risk his background posed. Adding to the foundation built by previous witnesses, Sanner detailed the hierarchy of
offices at the camp, who headed each, and what each had been responsible for. Sanner described the backbreaking labor in the Wiener Graben, and how defendant Spatzenegger had driven one prisoner off the quarry cliff and another toward no-man's-land to be
shot by guards.[45] Denson prompted Sanner to recall the activities of
others in the dock by listing the names of two dozen of the accused.
In this way, Sanner, often in little more than a sentence, identified
Altfuldisch, Eckert, Diehl, Entress, Eigruber, Trum, Grahn, Höhler,
Hegenscheidt, Henkel, Krebsbach, Leeb, Ludolph, Blei, Niedermayer, Wilhelm and Emil Müller, Struller, Striegel, Trum, Wasicky,
Wolter, Zoller, and Zutter and summarized their responsibilities, as
well as any violent incidents each had participated in.

Given the opportunity to cross-examine Sanner, defense counsel
David Hervey seized upon the prosecution's concept of a common
design in an attempt to discount its validity while calling Sanner's
credibility into question. After having Sanner confirm that he had

held authority over other prisoners while working as kapo of labor distribution, Hervey asked him if he had worked under the authority of the camp SS. "Yes," Sanner replied. "You were in a position of authority the same as these capos [*sic*] who have been charged here, is that correct?" Hervey asked. "Yes." "Do you consider that you were participating in a common design to carry out the purposes of the—alleged purposes of the camp?"[46] Though the court sustained the objection of the prosecution to such questioning and prevented Sanner from responding, the defense had illustrated a weakness in the common-design concept. If kapos like Frey and Gössl sat in the dock, accused not of individual atrocities but of participating in the upkeep of a criminal enterprise, how was kapo Sanner any less culpable?

Determined to continue in this line of questioning, the defense changed tack in order to take aim at a different aspect of the common-design charge—the contention that the participation of all the accused, including the kapos among them, had been willing. "What would have happened to you had you refused to obey a superior's orders in Mauthausen camp?" Hervey asked. "I would have been beaten, possibly killed, possibly hanged, I don't know," Sanner replied.[47] After having Sanner confirm for the court his membership in both the SS and Nazi Party, Hervey concluded his cross-examination. While the defense had not undermined the factual quality of Sanner's testimony, Hervey had brought out pressing questions that Denson would have to answer when asking the court to rule on the role and responsibility of the three kapos in the dock.

The prosecution's next witness, Czech law professor Vratislav Busek, had worked as a clerk in the sick camp and took the stand to provide evidence chiefly concerning mass-killing operations at Mauthausen and at Castle Hartheim. Busek's appearance illustrated Denson's confidence that his previous witnesses had sufficiently conditioned the court to hear what would amount to the most disturbing testimony brought out at the trial. In a well-spoken manner that betrayed his education, Busek first described for the court how he and his fellow inmates had deduced the fate of the prisoners they had watched both defendants Krebsbach and Wolter select in the sick camp:

> One or two large Reich mail cars . . . whose windows were painted blue came in. Forty people were put into these cars at a time, chiefly people who were suffering from a severe case of tuberculosis . . . At first, we didn't know where those people were being driven to. We were told they were going to a recuperation camp. Gradually we learned what was behind this, and this happened in the following manner: Our comrades in the garage learned that the distance of the trip back and forth was usually about thirty kilometers. This they judged from the amount of benzene used. Then once, on the same day, the clothing and the artificial limbs and artificial teeth of prisoners who had left the same morning came back and were found on the same day. In that manner we became convinced that this was a matter of killing.[48]

Continuing, Busek went on to describe how the SS had forced him to take part in selections for the gas chamber in the final weeks of the camp's existence. After trying in vain to sabotage this action, Busek testified, the most he and his comrades could do was select the weakest among the sick, in the hopes of saving those who may have had the strength to survive.[49] In simple yet evocative language, Busek described the awful scene as he led the sick to their deaths.

> That was a terrible procession of corpses which I led at the time. First of all, the people were starved. They ate grass along the way. A dog ran by on the roll call place. He defecated there and two prisoners wanted to eat that. Only with effort could I get them away from it. By the time I had gotten out of the sick camp so many people were lying on the ground that I had to call for a car and had to load

fifty-five or fifty-six people on it. When the march continued, twenty-six or thirty other people fell down, whom we brought up there with all the available means of transportation. At the main gate to the main camp, work service leader Trum met me—[50]

Without letting Busek finish his sentence, Major Oeding interrupted, labeling his testimony "the most inflammatory evidence I have heard in my entire life" and asked the court to disallow it unless such incidents could be directly tied to any one of the accused.[51] Seizing on Oeding's depiction of the testimony, the prosecution fired back, arguing that testimony dealing with the depth of atrocity at Mauthausen was necessarily highly inflammatory and would "shock the conscience of all." Siding with the prosecution, the court allowed Busek to continue, and to identify defendants Wolter, Jobst, Krebsbach, and Entress as chiefly responsible for the gassing action. In a move likely aimed at preventing Busek from elaborating on the scenes of atrocity that had clearly shocked the court, the defense made little use of its opportunity to cross-examine the witness and allowed him to be excused after a few quick questions. Denson's strategy had succeeded.

To complement Busek's testimony concerning mass killing at the camp, Denson next called Hans Marsalek, the former prisoner clerk who had led the interrogation of Commandant Ziereis on behalf of American war crimes investigators. Though the prosecution had Marsalek identify twenty-four defendants and list atrocities each had participated in, Denson and his team were most interested in showing how, in his interrogation, Ziereis had implicated a number of the accused in mass murder and had also emphasized the role Mauthausen had played in exterminating the perceived enemies of the Reich. First, Marsalek told the court how Ziereis portrayed defendant Krebsbach as chiefly responsible for the killing of the sick:

Dr. Krebsbach introduced the injections in the camp, while on the other hand the gassings were introduced by Dr. Wasicky. At the same time he [Ziereis] pointed to the fact that the murder of the thirty-eight people from Linz and Steyr on the 28th of April, 1945 was done upon the orders of Eigruber.

Reinforcing Denson's contention that Mauthausen was an extermination camp, Marsalek told the court how Ziereis had spoken of a new killing facility to follow the decommissioning of Hartheim:

> After the crematories in Castle Hartheim were taken away, a new such institution about twelve kilometers away from there was planned, and that this institution was to have the size of Auschwitz. The planning stages of the work had been concluded; however, the construction was never done. Railroad tracks were supposed to lead to the gas chamber.[52]

During cross-examination, the defense cast Marsalek's testimony as "99 percent hearsay" and insisted, as it had with previous witnesses, that he differentiate the crimes he had actually seen the defendants commit from those he had only deduced to have occurred. For instance, Lieutenant McMahon asked Marsalek to tell the court again about an incident concerning the murder of twenty-eight Dutch Jews, but to do so only by recalling what he had seen with his own eyes. "I want to know about the killing," McMahon instructed Marsalek, "only the killing."

Marsalek: Trum removed a Kapo from the punishment company and ordered him to take these men to the stone quarry. It was common talk among the SS that the killing of those Dutchmen would now start—

McMahon (interrupting): If the court please, we want to know what he saw.

President: Tell the witness he is to tell only what he saw.

Marsalek: At about four in the afternoon, the dead bodies were dragged up, and [those who survived the day's labor] were sent into confinement. I was in the arrest [bunker] with Spaniard

Juan Diego the same evening in order to check out how many of the 28 were remaining . . . The [remaining] Dutchmen were marched out the next morning . . . I saw the kitchen commander Striegel go out with a stick, and coming back I saw the SS men after they had already shot everybody. Among them was Struller. We then received the death reports about those 28 Dutchmen.

McMahon: You don't know who did the shooting, do you?

Marsalek: I do not know who shot . . .

The cross-examination of Marsalek revealed a common weakness in the testimony of many of those who knew of atrocities at the camp. Although Marsalek could logically deduce what had occurred through his familiarity with SS protocol, through conversations he overheard, and through the death reports he received immediately after the killings, he had not witnessed the actual crime. Nonetheless, the court consistently rejected the attempts of defense counsel to have such testimony stricken from the record. Mass atrocities, the prosecution showed, were seldom committed in clear view of other prisoners, but were perpetrated rather in secluded areas of the camp and especially in the basement of the bunker. Testimony of the sort Marsalek gave, though not in conformity with commonly applied rules of evidence, was therefore the best the court could hope for. As guidelines set out for the courts at Dachau made clear, accepting such evidence was well within the purview of military judges.

Witnesses on the Stand: "Everyday" Atrocity at Mauthausen

Though Denson would still call more than forty witnesses to the stand in the following week of the trial, Marsalek was the last witness called to testify at length about a core element of the Mauthausen camp system. With the court now conditioned to hear diverse testimony concerning the various manifestations of atrocity at Mauthausen and its subcamps, the remaining witnesses would often be called upon to describe a single event sometimes involving only one defendant, and would be dismissed from the stand minutes later.

Over the course of the following week, French survivor Maurice Lampe, for instance, described for the court the mass killing of captured Soviet officers at Mauthausen and the role played by Hans Spatzenegger. Polish physician Anthony Goscinski identified Fiegl as having participated in experimental gassings in barracks at Gusen, whereas Krebsbach, he testified, had ordered the removal of tattooed skin from prisoners in the autopsy room there.[53] Frederick Ricol described the abuse he had received at the hands of Wilhelm Müller in the Political Department, and Czech resister Richard Dietel identified Trum, Striegel, and Altfuldisch for beatings, and Hegenscheidt for the killing of escaped Russian POWs. Hans Schmehling of Strasbourg described his tenure as kapo of the "mass grave detail," and how he and his men had buried more than 10,000 corpses. Schmehling further described beatings at subcamps Schlier and Gunskirchen involving Barczay, Miessner, and Frey, and an incident in which Trum had killed 500 new arrivals from Sachsenhausen one winter's night by forcing them to strip naked in the roll-call yard and then spraying them with cold water. Survivor Johann Scheuch testified that Grimm and Drabek were present at the killing of 500 Dutch Jews in the quarry, while Melk survivor Hermann Hofstadt testified how he had seen Ludolph kill inmates in the camp hospital. Polish survivor Wilhelm Ornstein described the process used to shoot and hang prisoners in the crematoria complex where he worked and how he had seen defendants Altfuldisch, Niedermayer, Riegler, and Eigruber present during the execution of American and British POWs there. By the end of the second week of the trial, the prosecution had introduced witnesses who had given damning testimony concerning each of the defendants and all of Mauthausen's major subcamps.

Though most of these witnesses delivered their testimony largely unhindered by the protestations of the defense, there were a number of notable exceptions. Certainly the most problematic witness called to the stand by Denson and his team was former kapo Hans Karl von Posern, the onetime Nazi Party member who had acted as defense counsel at the Dachau concentration camp trial and who had aided Guth in the preparation of the Mauthausen case.[54] Problems with von Posern began when the defense brought out inconsistencies in his alleged eyewitness account of a brutal incident involving defendant Grahn. From a vantage point gained by climbing atop the roof of the camp's kitchen, von Posern first testified, he had been able to peer through the window of the adjacent bunker complex and see Grahn beat four female inmates to death. Suspicious that von Posern could have sat on the roof of the kitchen without being seen, the defense asked him to elaborate on aspects of his story. Under pressure, von Posern changed his account, claiming that what he had initially described as a single incident involving the four women had in fact been four separate incidents observed over the course of five months.[55]

Once the defense found cracks in von Posern's testimony, cross-examination intensified. Drawing on the fact that von Posern had worked for Denson and his team, Lieutenant McMahon first asked him if he was familiar with Grahn only because he had had access to the evidence concerning each defendant in the weeks before the trial. In a series of increasingly pointed questions, McMahon sought to establish von Posern's close ties to the prosecution team, while drawing attention to the fact that von Posern had arrived at Dachau as a war crimes suspect for his role as a prisoner-functionary.

McMahon: How long were you a prisoner of the Americans here in Dachau?

Von Posern: I think it was from the 18th of October to the 21st of February.

McMahon: And did you then, after the 21st of February, go to
work for Lt. Guth of the Prosecution?
Von Posern: I lived over there in my witness barracks.
McMahon: Do you know Lt. Guth?
Von Posern: Certainly.
McMahon: Was he the officer who recommended your release to
the Americans?
Von Posern: I cannot say that . . .
McMahon: How many times have you been in Lt. Guth's office
since February 21st, the date of your release?[56]

Before von Posern could answer, the prosecution objected to Mc-
Mahon's line of questioning, insisting that work done by von Posern
for Guth was immaterial. Unable to discredit von Posern's testimony
on the grounds that he had helped Guth prepare the Mauthausen
case, McMahon attempted instead to discredit the witness on the
basis of the role he had played while a prisoner. After succeeding in
having von Posern admit that he "wasn't on bad terms with some
of the SS people," McMahon asked him if he himself had ever
beaten prisoners. "There is no doubt," von Posern responded, "that
some of them got slaps in the face by me." Satisfied, McMahon allowed von Posern to be excused, after having him affirm again for
the court that he had been a member of the Nazi Party. Though von
Posern's testimony was officially accepted by the court, McMahon
had succeeded in raising significant questions about its ultimate
credibility.[57]

Jewish Survivors on the Stand

Aside from the difficulties Denson and his team experienced with
von Posern, the prosecution had additional trouble presenting testimony from a series of young Jewish witnesses called to the stand
during the second week of the trial. Survivors Hermann Feuermann,

Meier Rosenfeld, Chaim Lefkowitz, Heinrich Schein, and Ephram Sternberg presented to the court some of the most disturbing testimony it would hear. First, they recounted sadistic beatings and killings in the tent camp at the hands of defendants Miessner, Frey, Kaiser, and Grahn; at Ebensee by Jobst and Kreindl; at Gusen by Billmann, Dörr, Rutke, Sigmund, and Fitschok; and at Melk by Ludolf. Most extreme, however, was the testimony of Feuermann and Rosenfeld concerning starvation conditions so severe that some had turned to cannibalism. In a particularly shocking exchange, Captain Matthews had Feuermann confirm that he himself had once been caught "attempting to eat the flesh from a dead body." "Why were you fixing to eat it?" Matthews asked. In a voice so quiet the court at first had trouble hearing him, Feuermann answered simply, "Because I was very hungry."[58] Although the ensuing disbelief expressed by defense counsel likely arose in part as a result of the relative youth of the witnesses, as well as the truly horrific nature of the evidence each gave, persistent questioning concerning the religious faith of each suggests that some degree of anti-Semitism may also have played a role.

When cross-examining these young survivors, the defense began by asking each to confirm they were Jewish and that they understood the meaning and responsibility of taking an oath. While such questions were not directly hostile, they were not put to other witnesses and therefore cast the backgrounds of these survivors into suspicion. Striking in this regard was the attempt made by the defense to dismiss witness Rosenfeld before he had given a word of testimony. Clearly nervous, the witness took the stand and stated his name as "Rosenfeld, Meier." "Is your name Meier Rosenfeld?" the prosecution asked. "We object to any testimony on the part of this witness," Hervey interrupted, "if he can't give his own name. He is not to be believed by anybody."[59] The cross-examination of each of these defendants included aggressive questioning that often required this group of witnesses to retell the smallest details of events they had recounted, while having to avoid traps set by defense counsel. The defense grilled witness Feuermann, for instance, about an incident he had seen in which former Melk commandant Ludolf had chased three prisoners into the electrified wire surrounding the camp. "Did their bodies fall to the ground immediately?" defense counsel asked. "Yes." "Don't you know," the defense continued, "that when a man is electrified on the electric fence, he hangs on that fence?" Though the court sustained the objections of the prosecution that such questioning was argumentative, the cross-examination of these witnesses nonetheless cast them as fundamentally unreliable.

Aside from attempting to discredit witnesses Feuermann, Rosenfeld, and others by bringing out contradictions in the details of their testimony, defense counsel suggested that the very nature of the Nazi persecution of the Jews made the testimony of any Jewish survivor unreliable. In a series of remarkably insensitive questions put to twenty-five-year-old survivor Heinrich Schein, for instance, McMahon attempted to illustrate that that the witness was motivated to give false testimony in order to take revenge on those who had destroyed his family.

McMahon: Do you have any brothers, Mr. Schein?
Schein: I did have. I don't have now . . . They were sent to
    Treblinka, and they were gassed and sent to the crematory.
McMahon: Were they killed by the SS?
Schein: Yes.
McMahon: Ever have any sisters?
Schein: Also.
McMahon: Are they alive?
Schein: No.
McMahon: Under what circumstances did they die?
Schein: Same as my brothers.
McMahon: Was your father and mother killed in the same way?
Schein: Yes . . .

McMahon: You hate the SS, don't you?

Schein: Not all of them.

McMahon: Are you trying to tell the court that you don't hate the SS after the way they treated your father and mother and the rest of your relatives?[60]

Though the objections of the prosecution to this line of questioning spared Schein from having to answer, the insinuations of the defense team were already clear: Jewish victims were inherently untrustworthy witnesses motivated by hatred and a thirst for revenge.

Although anti-Semitism may well have contributed to the exceptional level of hostility and suspicion that greeted the young Jewish survivors who took the stand, there were further factors in play. First, having testified after scores of witnesses who were older, more educated, and with various professional credentials, these witnesses were at once less well spoken, and yet required to recall incidents that virtually defied communication. Second, an embarrassing incident involving witness Efraim Sternberg certainly did not help alleviate the stereotypes promoted by the defense. On the stand, Sternberg grew increasingly agitated as he described the role of defendant Gützlaff in murders committed at Gusen. After telling the court how Gützlaff had often shot prisoners from a Gusen guard tower, Sternberg was asked to walk over to the dock and identify the accused. The court record reflects the ensuing explosion:

Sternberg: That is the one! That is he. That is the one that is spreading the new German culture! *(Sternberg throws a punch, hitting Gützlaff in the shoulder)*

President Prickett: Stop that!

Prosecution: Sit down![61]

Under cross-examination, the defense began its attack on Sternberg first by asking him whether or not he understood the meaning of an oath, and then whether his religious beliefs prevented him from taking an oath without wearing a hat. "I don't have to wear a hat," Sternberg told the court. "What would you say," the defense then asked, "if you were told that Gützlaff was not in Mauthausen during 1944 and 1945?"[62] While Sternberg insisted he had been, the details of Gützlaff's service illustrated that the defense was, in all likelihood, correct. To Denson's chagrin, Sternberg had helped legitimize the insinuations of the defense and cast further suspicion on the testimony given by the other Jewish survivors who had already taken the stand.

The Signed Confessions of the Accused

On April 13, 1946, Chief Prosecutor Denson called up his fifty-eighth and final witness, war crimes investigator Paul Guth. Though Lieutenant Guth was an active member of the prosecution team, he took the stand in order to introduce to the court the fifty-seven signed statements he had extracted from the accused in the weeks before the trial.[63] Testifying in army uniform, Guth identified each statement and detailed for the court the circumstances under which he had interrogated the accused. Under Denson's direction, Guth confirmed under oath that no inappropriate pressure had been placed on the accused in order to obtain these statements; that each was told that he was not required to make a statement, and that the accused were neither threatened nor offered any hope of reward to confess.[64] Before individual statements could be read, however, the defense introduced a motion aimed at mitigating the damning quality of these statements. Wilson and his team asked that the court dismiss any evidence by a defendant in his statement that concerned the activities of others in the dock—a limitation generally followed in American criminal law. As he had done on numerous occasions already, however, Denson reminded the defense that the rules of evidence for military commission courts were not synonymous with standard criminal practice in the United States, and that the court was free to accept any evidence it deemed to be of probative value.[65] Siding with Denson, the court allowed the prosecution to proceed.

The first statement identified and read into the record was that of former gauleiter Eigruber—a statement that reflected the interrogation strategy that had allowed Guth to extract a confession where other investigators had failed.[66] Though Guth permitted Eigruber, like a number of the other higher-ranking accused, to downplay his role in mass murder at Mauthausen, he succeeded in extracting a confession to a comparatively "lesser" offense. Like all the statements the prosecution would use, Eigruber's began with details of his place and date of birth, his status in various Nazi organizations, and his periods of service in the positions he had held throughout the war. Among his responsibilities, Eigruber admitted that he had overseen both the distribution of labor of Mauthausen prisoners into various war industries, as well as the district food office that provisioned the camp. Further, Eigruber stated that he had leased Reichsleiter Philipp Bouhler Castle Hartheim, so the latter could fulfill "an order of the Fuehrer that mental patients who were incurably ill or unable to work be killed."[67] Although these responsibilities helped to illustrate Eigruber's participation in the "common design" to commit war crimes at Mauthausen, it was his confessed participation in the execution of "ten prisoners of unknown nationality" that Guth had so vigorously sought and that most directly linked the former gauleiter to the specific abuses alleged in the charges.[68] As with each and every statement Denson would read into the record, Eigruber's concluded with a signature and a final sentence that affirmed he had written according to his own free will and without compulsion.

Among the most damning and disturbing admissions included in the statements that Denson read to the court were those of medical personnel at Mauthausen. Dr. Krebsbach confessed to having participated in the shooting of hundreds of prisoners, as well as the selection for the gas chamber of thousands of others. Krebsbach named camp pharmacist Erich Wasicky as chiefly responsible for the installation of the camp's gas chamber and identified fifteen fellow defendants who had participated in executions. He played down his own role by pointing to the orders of his superiors and to medical necessity. "Under my leadership," Krebsbach explained, "about 200 TB patients were selected," but only because they had "open, contagious TB of the lungs" and therefore threatened the welfare of other prisoners.[69] Dr. Entress, another former chief physician of Mauthausen, downplayed his murderous activities by explaining in his statement that he had selected for the gas chamber only "those patients with whom it was clear that they would not get well anyhow."[70] Doctors Henkel and Höhler, both camp dentists who had collected the dental gold from corpses in the gas chamber, used their statements to distance themselves from the killing process altogether, detailing instead the quantities of gold sent to Berlin each month, as if it had been drawn from a mine.[71] Defendant Willy Jobst, camp doctor at Ebensee, attempted to shift responsibility for the thousands of deaths that had occurred on his watch. Though Jobst admitted he had been responsible for the sanitary conditions in the camp, he "attributed the high number of death cases chiefly to the fact that the prisoners who were already weakened had to work hard in a damp underground cave."[72] As he had with Eigruber and so many other of the accused, however, Guth had succeeded in having Jobst admit to participating in an execution. Although this crime was dwarfed by the broader activities of Dr. Jobst and his peers, Denson hoped it would be sufficient for conviction.

The signed statements of the accused proved to be important for reasons aside from self-incrimination. In some cases, they provided details of crimes that had few surviving witnesses. Most striking in this regard is the step-by-step, matter-of-fact description of the killing procedure at Hartheim offered in the statement of Vinzenz Nohel:

> As soon as a group arrived which was destined to be gassed, we had them unloaded from the cars and undressed. It was my duty to see to it that none of them escaped before they were brought to the gas chamber. After they were photographed, we led them to the gas

chamber. Doctor Lonaner then threw the gas into the chamber. Then I fetched the corpses from the gas chamber and burned them in the crematory after the gold fillings and gold teeth had been removed by various dentists. Before they were gassed, the patients were examined for gold teeth and a cross was painted on their shoulders, chest and back.[73]

For each statement like Nohel's, there were also those of defendants like camp pharmacist Erich Wasicky, who was heavily implicated in the mass killing at Mauthausen and yet who admitted little knowledge of it. Numerous defendants and witnesses indicated that Wasicky had dispensed the necessary Zyklon B for all gassings at Mauthausen, yet Wasicky conceded only that he procured the lethal substance because it had been "necessary for all kinds of sterilizations."[74] Once again, however, any frustration that Denson may have experienced with Wasicky's attempt at obscuring his role in mass killing was compensated by his confessed participation in the execution of "20 or 30 Poles or Russians."[75]

Though the statements of some of the accused were pages long and constituted confessions to participation in horrific acts of cruelty and mass killing, many were brief, banal descriptions of a single event, often paired with some attempt at justification. More than any other group of defendants, this was true of the guards. Every one of the seventeen common guards that Denson had selected as defendants admitted to the shooting of at least one prisoner. Many emphasized that their victims were escapees whom they had repeatedly warned to stop before firing. Giese, for instance, stated that he had only shot his victim after he was "challenged three times according to regulation," whereas Dörr insisted that the Polish escapee he had shot "was already 15 meters outside of the barbed wire enclosure" and refused to halt.[76] Keilwitz and Barczay in part justified their actions by insisting that they shot so as to prevent other prisoners from attempting to flee. Further, Keilwitz claimed to have acted in response to a fear of punishment. "If I had not shot this Jew," Keilwitz stated, "then I myself would have been shot or hanged."[77]

The claim that one had acted out of fear of punishment was not limited to the statements made by the lowest-ranking of the accused. Defendant Hans Altfuldisch, responsible for the entire prison compound, admitted to directing the execution of 250 and the gassing of many more. Despite his high rank, however, Altfuldisch referred to himself as one of the "little people" in the camp, who "would have been sent to a concentration camp, or probably even would have been shot" if he had not assisted in these killing operations. The statements of two of the most notoriously cruel figures at Mauthausen—"rapport leaders" Niedermayer and Trum—echoed this sentiment. Niedermayer, who confessed to having participated in the execution of 400 and the gassing of an additional 1,400 sick prisoners from the hospital, explained he had "carried out this elimination because I was ordered to do so, and if I had not carried out the order I would have been killed myself."[78] To a large extent, the claims made by these defendants and others previewed the arguments they would make once on the stand. In this way, the signed confessions of the accused not only provided evidence of the crimes committed at Mauthausen, but aided Denson and his team in preparing for the fight to come. At the same time, however, questions concerning the methods used to extract these confessions were not put to rest with the assurances provided by Guth on the stand. Instead, casting doubt on the legitimacy of these statements would soon emerge as a major component of defense counsel's strategy.

On April 15, the prosecution rested its case, following the testimony of fifty-eight witnesses and the introduction of signed confessions that not only incriminated their authors and their comrades in the dock, but helped to confirm for the court Denson's contention that every member of the Mauthausen staff contributed to the overall functioning of the camp. Though the prosecution would now have to contend with efforts of the defense to challenge the testimony presented, Denson had learned that the court had little interest in excluding the evidentiary materials he introduced. Although the testimony of von Posern and Sternberg had provided embarrassing moments for Denson and his team and illustrated the pitfalls of relying on testimony alone, Denson's witnesses had collectively laid a substantial foundation of knowledge for the court concerning the Mauthausen camp system, while connecting each and every one of the accused to atrocities that had occurred there.

The Defense Case

On April 18, Major General Prickett called the Dachau court to order, following a mere two-day pause granted the defense to ready its case. In contrast to the significant source material both collected and generated by Chief Prosecutor Denson in the decades following the Mauthausen trial, no members of the defense team deposited materials or sat for interviews that grant the historian insight into the overarching approach of defense counsel to this case. As a result, one must glean the strategies of Lieutenant Colonel Wilson and his team from the trial transcripts alone. Whereas the prosecution sought to illustrate the commonality of purpose among all sixty-one accused, defense counsel employed a number of disparate strategies that do not neatly correlate to groupings of defendants categorized either by rank or duty. Instead, the former camp officers, doctors, guards, and even kapos drew variously upon six major defenses. They argued that they had acted under duress; that they had only followed the orders of a superior; that they had carried out legally constituted orders; that they had been falsely identified with the crime in question; that their signed confessions were inaccurate and/ or extracted improperly; and that they were unaware of the murderous nature of the Mauthausen camp system.

Defense counsel did not introduce its case with an opening statement but instead asked that the prosecution accept four stipulations designed to save time and reduce the amount of evidence Wilson and his team would have to present to the court. Defense counsel asked the prosecution to accept: that Allied military operations had created major difficulties and transportation delays throughout Germany, especially during 1945; that beginning in August 1944, members of both the German air force and army were ordered without choice into the SS; that it is "customary procedure" for guards at penal institutions to shoot fleeing prisoners of all types after due warning; and that the condition of prisoners prior to arrival at Mauthausen or its subcamps was not the responsibility of personnel from the Mauthausen camp system.[79] These stipulations, all of which the prosecution accepted, were designed to aid defendants who intended to argue that they had served at Mauthausen against their will; that they had acted within the law; or that they had held authority over prisoners who had died for reasons wholly beyond their control. These stipulations therefore revealed for the court a major part of defense counsel's strategy before a single witness had taken the stand.

Though the defense would call nearly 150 witnesses in the coming weeks, they did not do so in the linear fashion employed by the prosecution in order to gradually paint a single, cohesive picture of the camp system. Instead, the defense often called the accused and their supporting witnesses to the stand in no clearly discernible order. In this way, for instance, Mauthausen chief physician Waldemar Wolter was followed to the stand by Gusen guard Viktor Korger, and then by Melk mess sergeant Otto Striegel. Intended or otherwise, this helped give the impression that the Mauthausen camp system was not a cohesive institution with a singular purpose, but consisted instead of disparate locations, staffed by personnel of disparate backgrounds with little or no knowledge of each other's activities. Further, many low-ranking defendants spent only a matter of minutes on the stand, revealing very little about their broader role in the camp system beyond the incident or incidents in which they were allegedly involved. Many of the most notorious defendants—Riegler, Neidermayer, Altfuldisch, Krebsbach, Entress, Spatzenegger, and Trum—avoided taking the stand altogether, leaving prosecutors to reconstruct their crimes without the benefit of cross-examination.

Denials

The simplest and often least plausible of the strategies employed by various defendants involved outright denial of the evidence brought against them. Denial took various forms, the most common of which was the claim that the defendant was not present when a given incident had occurred. This often involved presenting the court with an alibi, the specificity of which sometimes bordered on the absurd. Camp pharmacist Wasicky, for instance, claimed he could not have participated in a certain gassing incident described by witness Podlaha, because "at seventeen hours on the 24th of October '42 I got into the Anhalt Station in Berlin." He could remember this so clearly, Wasicky explained, because it had been his son's birthday.[80] In a similar fashion, guard company commander August Blei challenged evidence that he had ordered his troops to shoot prisoners in the Wiener Graben, claiming he had left the camp that day in order to have his typewriter repaired.[81] To further counter various witnesses who placed him at the scene of executions within the camp compound, Blei insisted he had only entered it four times in all his years of service, "twice because of a show, once because of a boxing match, and once because of a wrestling match."[82]

A number of defendants made similar claims, either by arguing that they were victims of mistaken identity or of vengeful witnesses who intentionally fabricated the evidence they gave. Otto Striegel insisted that defendants Eckert and Blei, who placed him at various executions, had him confused with Karl Striegel, an unrelated member of the Mauthausen staff.[83] Willy Frey, the kapo accused of killings in the tent camp, claimed he never knew where the tent camp was, and that he was instead the victim of witnesses who sought to cover up their own misdeeds.[84]

A simple denial that one had not participated in a specific crime was not enough to free the defendants from implication in the "common design to commit war crimes" that the prosecution alleged. As Chief Prosecutor Denson reminded the court on various occasions, the accused needed only to have been aware of, and participated in the maintenance of, this system. As a result, some of the defendants attempted to deny such complicity by claiming to not have known of the murder or even the starvation that had occurred at Mauthausen and its subcamps on a daily basis. The higher the rank of the accused, the less plausible this defense appeared. Although there was a degree of credibility to the arguments of some low-ranking guards who insisted that as they were not permitted within the camp compound, they knew little of its inner workings, the denials made by a number of high-ranking staff verged on the absurd. Former adjutant Adolf Zutter, for instance, claimed he had never seen an emaciated prisoner in all his years at the camp, as did headquarters sergeant major Karl Struller.[85] Many of the defendants who were asked about the gas chamber and gas van claimed no knowledge of it. Rudolf Mynzak, who spent a year working in the very bunker in which the gas chamber was housed, claimed to have never known of its existence, while Zutter called the gas van "impossible."[86]

In a similar vein, many of the accused attempted to downplay their role or position of authority at the camp, while often shifting blame onto others. Both Zoller and Zutter claimed that as adjutants of Commandant Ziereis they had done "purely office work."[87] Zutter claimed that he simply had no time to have participated in atrocities, as he could "hardly keep track" of the mountains of mail that he was responsible for processing.[88] Like those who had worked in the office of the Commandant, defendants Müller, Leeb, and Diehl described their work in the camp's dreaded Political Department in similar terms. Diehl described himself as "a soldier, a clerk," and labeled the statements of Kresbach and Müller, which placed him at numerous executions, as "nonsense."[89] Werner Grahn, the sixty-two-year-old chief criminal secretary at Mauthausen, described himself as "merely a guest who was running a translation office."[90] Though he admitted to hearing screams in the prison compound where he worked, he explained that he had been "so busy with corrections and writing" that he had no time to concern himself with such things.[91] Dr. Wolter, implicated in the mass-killing process at the camp, described his role at Mauthausen as akin to "that of a priest in a prison," who provided aid to the needy.[92] Who then was responsible for the atrocities at Mauthausen? In a pattern similar to the one seen at Nuremberg, in which the defendants cast blame on those like Himmler, Bormann, and Hitler who were not present at the trial, the Mauthausen defendants cast responsibility for the atrocities at Mauthausen primarily on Commandant Ziereis, as well as leading camp officials Bachmayer and Schulze, neither of whom was in American custody.[93]

In order to bolster the versions of events put forth by the accused, defense counsel introduced dozens of witnesses, a move that revealed a major strategical dilemma for Wilson and his team. On the one hand, the denials and exculpatory explanations put forth by those in the dock required witness confirmation to hold any water whatsoever. On the other hand, the vast majority of those willing to give evidence on behalf of the accused were either other members of the camp staff fearing prosecution themselves or German prisoner-functionaries and kapos who had played dubious roles in the camp administration. As a result, the testimony of both groups tended to be exculpatory and self-serving, a fact the prosecution brought out with ease. In a typical example, the prosecution impugned the testimony of defense witnesses Richard Messner and William Schleth, called on behalf of defendant Gützlaff, simply by having them confirm that they were former Mauthausen guards currently under arrest in the Dachau war crimes enclosure.[94]

Even witness testimony concerning alleged acts of kindness on the part of the accused could be a liability to the defense case. Denson and his team used the testimony of witnesses like Erich Wiese, who told how defendant Dörr had risked arrest by aiding starving inmates, to prove that conditions at the camp must therefore have been every bit as bad as the prosecution case alleged.[95] Further, the few former inmates called as defense witnesses whose testimony could not be called into question because of their activities at Mauthausen were often coaxed during cross-examination into giving damning evidence against other defendants in the dock. Though survivor and defense witness Karl Peterseil testified that defendant Leeb had saved his life by having him transferred out of the punishment company in the Wiener Graben, the prosecution succeeded not only in having him confirm that beatings and killings were a common occurrence in the quarry, but also to describe defendant Spatzenegger as "the worst pig known to this world."[96] To a large extent, therefore, the witnesses called to confirm the accounts of those in the dock often did little to help Wilson and his team make their case.

The prosecution's most useful tools in exposing the fraudulence of the alibis of the defendants and their supporting witnesses were the camp's death books, which provided unimpeachable evidence directly connecting many of the accused to specific killings. Guard Heinrich Fitschok was the first on the stand to be confronted with entries in the death books that directly contradicted his testimony. In what would become a common pattern when cross-examining former camp guards, the prosecution first had Fitschok confirm the testimony given—that he had killed one Italian prisoner in April 1944. Denson then handed Fitschok the death book and asked him to read out various entries. When entry number 468 confirmed

Fitschok's testimony, the prosecution then had him read out entries 472 and 951—each of which recorded the killing of a prisoner, and each of which identified Fitschok as the shooter.[97]

Denson further used the death books to dispel the erroneous claims of higher-ranking defendants. Viktor Zoller claimed, for instance, that in the two years he had served as adjutant to Commandant Ziereis, only "two or three" executions had occurred at Mauthausen. Forcing Zoller to read from the death books, Denson showed how executions had been a regular occurrence at the camp during the time in which he served.[98] In a similar fashion, Denson used the death books to challenge former Political Department clerk Hans Diehl's claim that "shot trying to escape" had meant only that. Handing Diehl the death book, Denson had him read the names of eleven Jews all "shot trying to escape" at exactly 8:15 A.M. on February 20, 1942; another twenty names followed at exactly 1:45.[99] In this case, as in others, the death books revealed a pattern of atrocity that dramatically contradicted the sanitized depictions of Mauthausen presented by a number of the accused. The denials of defendants unlucky enough to be named within the pages of the death books were effectively rendered null and void.

Justification and Mitigation

For many defendants, outright denial of the often substantial evidence brought against them was not a viable strategy. Instead, many of the accused attempted to justify their actions on the grounds that they had only followed the orders of their superiors. Though a 1944 amendment to the U.S. Army's *Rules on Land Warfare* had rendered this defense invalid in war crimes cases, superior orders could be considered by the court as a mitigating circumstance in sentencing.[100] In a play to gain the sympathies of a military court, many of the defendants therefore cast themselves as unlucky soldiers, too honor-bound to disobey the orders handed down to them. Dr. Jobst conceded on the stand that "the fact of the existence of the camps as such was wrong" but argued that, once posted there, obeying the orders of his superiors remained the noble thing to do.[101] Hans Diehl reserved his final words on the stand for the members of the court, declaring, "I was a soldier and according to the soldier's oath, I had to carry out the orders that were given to me."[102] Others claimed that while they had followed orders, they had tried to diminish their negative impact. Defendant Hans Hegenscheidt explained for instance that when ordered by Commandant Ziereis to take part in an execution, he had "fired to miss."[103] Such statements were as close as any of those in the dock would get to an expression of contrition.

Closely related to the superior-orders defense was the claim that legitimate state authorities had ordered the beatings and executions carried out by the accused. These acts, Wilson and his team argued, had therefore been legal under German law. Emil Müller, a Mauthausen block leader, claimed he had only taken part in "proper executions," of prisoners sentenced to death by "proper German courts."[104] Willy Jobst and Adolf Zutter claimed the same, the latter adding that participation nonetheless remained "one of the most severe spiritual burdens."[105] In cross-examination, the prosecution often asked defendants how they could have known if a given execution had been officially sanctioned. Whereas some claimed to have seen the written order itself, chief physician Wolter told the court he had spoken to the victims before death and determined that they were properly sentenced.[106] As the prosecution showed, however, such details were largely irrelevant in light of existing international law. Accordingly, those who violated the laws and usages of war were deemed culpable, whether or not such acts had violated the domestic laws of the country where the crimes had taken place.[107]

Though arguments for the legality of state-sanctioned executions and beatings were unlikely to sway American judges, many of the eighteen common guards in the dock offered a variant of the "legality of orders" defense that was less susceptible to invalidation through international law. At the outset of the defense case, the prosecution had accepted the stipulation that it was "customary procedure" for guards to shoot prisoners fleeing from penal institutions, after issuing due warning. As a result, thirteen accused former guards contended that those they had shot were escapees whom they had repeatedly warned before firing upon. After telling the court how he had warned his victim three times and shot him as a last resort, Karl Billmann insisted that he was simply a "little man" who acted according to "International Guard Regulations which are applicable to all camps, including American [ones]."[108] In a show of solidarity, defendants who had worked in the same guard companies often reinforced the claims of their comrades, confirming the accounts of their fellow defendants.

A related strategy employed by defendants who chose not to dispute the fact that a specific atrocity had occurred was to claim that the crime in question had been committed under duress. As with superior orders, the court did not accept duress as a legitimate defense per se, but instead considered it a mitigating factor to be considered possibly in sentencing.[109] In pursuit of such mitigation, a number of defendants claimed that their superiors had threatened them in order to secure their participation in atrocities. Guard Willy Brünning admitted he had killed five people during an evacuation march from subcamp Hinterbrühl, but only after his superior officer had killed a guard who had not obeyed an order to shoot those too weak to continue the march. Those not willing to kill, he was told, would be guilty of "cowardice in front of the enemy."[110] Defendant Huber, who admitted killing nine people during the same march, backed up Brünning and testified that the guard company was to kill the weak, or "bear the consequences."[111] Defendant Korger went so far as to describe the duress under which guards at Mauthausen lived as sufficient to render them "prisoners of the second category" who "any day would be in the concentration camp."[112] Few defendants could back up their claims, however, and none but the accused testified that any Mauthausen staff were killed for refusing to obey orders.

To further mitigate the degree of culpability of the accused, the defense also tried to show that a number of the defendants were draftees who had sought to escape concentration camp service. As stated in the stipulation offered up by defense counsel at the opening of their case, concentration camp staff had sometimes been drawn from the Luftwaffe and Wehrmacht and drafted involuntarily into the SS. Many of the guards in the dock claimed to have arrived at Mauthausen and its subcamps under such circumstances. Among those claiming to have been drafted, some, like defendants Dörr and Mack, tried to illustrate their opposition to the camp system with claims they had risked arrest to aid prisoners by giving them food. Johannes Grimm, also drafted into the SS after serving as the civilian production manager of the Wiener Graben, claimed that the aid he had extended to the prisoners who slaved under him was such that at liberation, they had "lifted me up on their shoulders and yelled, 'May he live long.'"[113]

The problems the defense faced in presenting a defendant's draft history were twofold. First, a 1941 decree stipulating that concentration camp personnel could be relieved of their camp duties if they volunteered to fight at the front led the Dachau courts to consider those who had not asked for transfer as volunteers.[114] Second, the very charge of participating in a common design to commit war crimes did not require illustration of a motive. In this way, the circumstances that brought the various defendants to Mauthausen had little bearing on the role they had played in helping an inherently criminal enterprise to function.

The circumstances that led to each defendant's entry into the Mauthausen camp system were more relevant in the cases of the three kapos. Defense counsel portrayed Gössl, Fiegl, and Frey primarily as victims of the Nazis, incarcerated at Mauthausen as antifascists. Though Gössl was himself from Munich, the defense asked him first to tell the court about when he was first arrested by "the Germans."[115] In the testimony that followed, Gössl detailed his service in the leftist Reichsbanner and in particular his participation in open skirmishes with the SA and with a 1936 leaflet campaign that led to his arrest. In a similar vein, Frey referred to himself as an "enemy of the state" who had worked with Socialist and Communist resisters and who had slashed his wrists in order to get out of the SS.[116] The defense further sought to cast the kapos not as dreaded figures who wielded authority over others but fellow prisoners who used their position to aid other inmates. Fiegl testified, for instance, that though prisoners had killed scores of kapos in the wake of the liberation of Gusen, he had remained there unharmed because he was "too well known and too much beloved by the prisoners." To counter the specific and damning evidence that linked all three kapos to horrific atrocities, each denied participation in killings outright, while claiming to have acted according to the best interests of the prisoner population, even when this had involved beatings. Having already gained an understanding of the difficulties related to prosecuting former prisoners, however, Denson had chosen three kapos whose notorious deeds had many witnesses.

Challenges to the Jurisdiction of the Court

Although defense counsel abandoned efforts to categorically challenge the jurisdiction of the Dachau court once judges had ruled against the motions put forth on the first day of the trial, jurisdictional issues continued to play a role in the defense of a number of the accused. In the case of guards Priebel and Mayer, defense counsel Lieutenant Deibel seized on the evidence preserved in the death books to show that the victims shot by these men had been Germans. On the grounds that these killings were therefore beyond the purview of the charges, the defense asked that all testimony concerning these crimes be stricken from the record—a motion that the court quickly denied.[117] As it had done in the past, the court accepted evidence for crimes outside its jurisdiction on the grounds that such evidence nonetheless helped to illustrate the nature of the common design the prosecution was attempting to show.

To affirm the charges brought against these men, Denson simply asked each guard whether or not he had seen abuses or killings at the subcamps where he was stationed. In so doing, the prosecution sought to remind the court and the defense team that whether or not Mayer, Priebel, or any other defendant had actually killed a non-German national, they had nonetheless participated in the common design to commit war crimes by preventing prisoners from escaping the clutches of a murderous system. Here the ruling of the court revealed the great difficulty associated with defending these men against the common-design charge. Though Wilson and his team could disprove the evidence given by a certain witness or illustrate that the specific crimes of certain defendants lay outside the jurisdiction of the court, in the theory of the prosecution, each of the accused remained implicated in the central charge by virtue of his service at Mauthausen. For defense counsel and those they represented, the charges must have appeared virtually unshakeable.

Though defense counsel raised jurisdictional issues on behalf of some defendants, former gauleiter August Eigruber was the only one of the accused to challenge the common-design charge directly and to question the authority of the court to judge his activities. Owing to Eigruber's rank as well as his uncooperativeness during pretrial preparations, Denson and his team were particularly determined to secure a conviction. On the stand, Eigruber was "cocky, disrespectful and crafty" and sought to undermine his opponents in the courtroom with every chance he got.[118] Asked whether he had authorized the building of a small Austrian concentration camp called Wiedermoos, Eigruber refused to answer, declaring that the camp had been closed in 1941 and was therefore "before the period of time which is included in the charges." When handed a document by Denson concerning the camp, Eigruber refused to read it, insisting this was "purely an internal German matter," which had "nothing to do with the charges." Rather than attempt to rein in Eigruber, however, Denson instead turned the cockiness of his opponent to his advantage, a strategy he still recalled with pride fifty years later. Recognizing Eigruber to be "without doubt the most obnoxious individual" he had ever prosecuted, Denson encouraged his arrogance on the stand. "I wanted the court to drink deeply at that well," Denson recalled, "and he filled the bill."[119] Unwittingly, Eigruber tightened the noose around his own neck, showing himself to be every bit the fanatical, unrepentant Nazi that Denson insisted he was.

Retracting Statements

Though some defense strategies could be applied only to certain defendants, Wilson and his team contested the credibility of the confessions of the accused on behalf of every man who had signed one. First, the defense claimed that war crimes investigator Guth had extracted untrue statements from a number of defendants through the use of threats. Adjutant Viktor Zoller testified that during his interrogation, Guth had called him a "degenerate pig," forced him to undress, and told him he would be shot if he did not sign the statement dictated to him.[120] Hospital kapo Georg Gössl claimed he had signed only after Guth had "put his hand to his neck and turned his eyes upward and snapped his fingers."[121] Similarly, Political Department functionary Wilhelm Müller claimed Guth threatened to hang him.[122] More common than claims of death threats, however, was the contention that defendants had signed because of the privations they were subjected to. Defendants Struller and Striegel both claimed to have signed simply to find relief from sleepless, hungry nights spent in the cold arrest bunker.

More common than the allegation that statements had been extracted under threat of death or pain of deprivation was the claim that defendants had not understood either the meaning of the oaths they had taken or the substance of what they had written. Willy Eckert explained that his "mental and physical condition" at the time of interrogation had clouded his judgment when signing, whereas defendant Hans Eisenhöfer referred to the "spiritual depressions" he suffered to explain a similar phenomenon.[123] Leopold Trauner, the oldest defendant in the dock, tried to use his age to explain away what he had signed in Guth's presence. "I don't remember things so well," he testified. "I am so old . . . I didn't understand what I had written."[124] In a similar vein, Hartheim "fireman" Vinzenz Nohel, for whom the defense had unsuccessfully petitioned for a finding of insanity, claimed that a head injury in his youth had deeply affected his comprehension. "My thinking processes are slowed down in such a manner that I cannot understand things as well as others," Nohel claimed. Like Trauner and Nohel, former kapo Willy Frey attempted to use his alleged shortcomings to explain away the fact that he had sworn to the truth of his statement. "I am a layman and a school boy," Frey insisted—one who did not understand the meaning of an oath.[125]

Rather than ascribing their signed confessions to the threat of violence or to misunderstandings, some claimed instead to have signed because of the great degree of faith they had either in Guth or in the American administration of justice as a whole. Several defendants claimed they had signed without first reading their statements. "I signed upon trust," August Blei testified. "I thought well, it will probably be correct."[126] Likewise, former Melk commandant Julius Ludolf explained to the court that he had had "so much good faith" in Guth that he had also signed without reading.[127] Defendant Miessner claimed to have been lulled into signing an allegedly false confession, telling the court "Lt. Guth was so friendly . . . If I was in a hypnotic state or something, I don't know."[128] Most defendants, like Franz Huber, explained that although they had knowingly signed an inaccurate document, they had done so on the understanding that they would be able to clear up inaccuracies when "put before a regular court."[129]

Aside from drawing the accuracies of their own statements into question, some defendants went so far as to try to explain away damning evidence that had emerged in the statements made by others in the dock. In particular, some claimed that during the trial, they had had the opportunity to speak with the other defendants who had implicated them in their statements. Detail leader Rudolf Mynzak, for instance, claimed that private conversations with Niedermayer, Grimm, and Dr. Krebsbach prompted the three to reveal that their testimony concerning Mynzak's participation at executions was patently untrue and the result of pressures faced during interrogation.[130] Leeb offered similar explanations for the testimony of Trum and Drabek, both of whom identified him as having participated in executions. Leeb claimed that in conversation at Dachau, Trum admitted "not remembering ever having seen me at an execution," while Drabek claimed "that he never knew me."[131] Ex-gauleiter Eiguber offered the broadest theory to account for the damning evidence that many other defendants gave against him in their statements:

> Criminals, men such as Trum, Neidermayer, Häger and Grimm were asked by the prosecution, "Do you want to be hanged for the Gauleiter, State Leader Eigruber?" Since everyone wants to live, all of them thought "no," and then they were told, "Well, write," and this is how these statements which were read came about.[132]

Following the testimony of dozens of witnesses who challenged in various ways the legitimacy of the confessions they had signed, Wilson and his team sought again to draw the entire interrogation process into question by recalling Paul Guth to the stand. As he had done when questioned by Denson in the first half of the trial, Guth reaffirmed that no one was threatened, and added that although many now challenged the information they gave, each of the accused had had the opportunity to read and correct each typed statement before signing. Unsatisfied with Guth's explanations, however, Defense

Counsel McMahon read to the court passages from numerous statements in order to illustrate "that there is not only striking similarity in these statements, in the language used, but identical language and phrases and sentences and assurances throughout."

When scrutinized and compared, the statements signed by the accused do include some curious similarities—similarities that McMahon hoped would raise the suspicions of the court. In strikingly similar terms, some passages even appeared to confirm the central pillar in the prosecution's case: that a common design to commit war crimes existed at Mauthausen, one that required the active participation of all who worked there. Altfuldisch stated, for instance, that

> there is no point in ascribing to any non-com under my supervision the responsibility for certain dealings or ill conditions, since their field of work, as well as their practical activity, continuously overlapped . . . The bad, inhuman conditions in the Mauthausen concentration camp cannot be made the responsibility of a single leader or non-com, but all who worked in the Mauthausen concentration camp added to them in their field of work.[133]

Altfuldisch's statement, which virtually parrots the contentions put forth by the prosecution, is all the more remarkable when compared to the statements of others in the dock. Rapport leader Andreas Trum described those who held varying degrees of authority in the camp, explaining that

> There is no point in defining their direct field of work, since all of them influenced all affairs of the camp, gave direct orders, and, for example, selected prisoners who were unable to work for the gas chamber. . . . All of us participated equally in the camp leadership.[134]

In virtually the same language as Altfuldisch and Trum, Willy Eckert declared that there was "no point in ascribing the responsibility for the terrible conditions in Mauthausen to any one leader or non-com, or any groups of leaders or non-coms."[135] Similarly, Dr. Entress explained in his statement that "each of the many dealings which occurred daily in the camp required the cooperation of all departments."[136] Curiously, many of the accused also refer to Mauthausen as an "extermination camp" in their statements, though this was a postwar term.[137] Some insisted later that they had never heard the expression before facing Guth during interrogation.

McMahon's chosen passages had their desired effect, piquing the interest of the judges. Guth now faced examination by the court. "To what do you ascribe the amazing similarity of language and sentence construction?" President Prickett asked.

> Well, sir, in all these cases you have simple people and they write very short sentences. They were together all afternoon long writing these things, and I don't know—if you have a group of men who haven't much schooling in one room . . . [138]

According to Guth, the specific similarities in the statements extracted from the accused were not the result of undue pressures, but rather emerged because he had asked each defendant similar questions and because army personnel had then reduced to writing and translated each statement using a similar format. Guth assured the court that he had granted each defendant plenty of time to read over these written statements and to make any necessary changes before they were asked to sign them. Having largely repeated the explanations he had given when the prosecution had him introduce these statements, Guth seemingly satisfied the court and was excused.

Despite defense counsel's efforts, challenging the legitimacy of the confessions did not pose the problems for the prosecution Wilson and his team had hoped for. Nevertheless, though the judges were willing to accept these statements in their entirety, McMahon's questioning revealed that, at the very least, there existed some form of template for these interrogations, which at times involved leading the accused to confirm the conceptions of their captors. At worst, there was the possibility of outright abuse, a prospect that defense counsel in this case, as well as at numerous Dachau cases in the future, would again raise when given a final opportunity to address the court.

As president Prickett brought the court to order on May 11 to hear the closing arguments of the prosecution and defense teams, the fate of sixty-one men hung in the balance. In the preceding thirty-six trial days, Chief Prosecutor Denson had introduced dozens of witnesses in an attempt to inform the court on the function of the Mauthausen camp system, match perpetrators with their crimes, and condition the judges to believe testimony concerning atrocities of the most horrific nature. To challenge the prosecution's case, defense counsel responded with vigorous attacks on the charges and the jurisdiction of the court, while drawing into question the reliability of the testimony and the statements signed by those in the dock. With only one chance remaining to address the court before it ruled on the guilt or innocence of the accused, prosecution and defense counsel prepared to make their final appeals and discover whether their chosen strategies would be vindicated by the verdicts. For the sixty-one men in the dock, the shadow of the gallows must have appeared unbearably close.

CHAPTER 5

Judgment at Dachau

The final two days of the Mauthausen trial were its most eventful. Not only did the prosecution and defense present their final arguments to the court, but the Dachau judges announced their verdicts, sentences, and a series of special findings designed to facilitate the more rapid prosecution of other Mauthausen personnel in subsequent proceedings. The brevity of this final trial phase typified the military trial process, while raising questions about its ultimate fairness. To summarize a case brought against sixty-one defendants, the prosecution spoke for a mere half hour, and the defense for even less. To arrive at sixty-one verdicts, the judges adjourned for only an hour, roughly the same amount of time they devoted to considering sentences for the guilty men. To be sure, the evidence that the prosecution had produced both through the use of survivor testimony and key documents such as the camp's death books left little doubt that the men in the dock were party to heinous acts of violence. It remained to be seen, however, whether a trial system that increasingly revealed its inadequacies had adequately rendered justice.

Closing Arguments

The purpose of a closing statement, Denson told the court, was to assist the judges in determining "the true facts" and to point out the applicable law so that the court might "arrive at a righteous judgment."[1] The court's greatest challenge, Denson explained, would be to weigh the testimony of dozens of witnesses and consider the questions of credibility the defense team was sure to raise. Reflecting the risk inherent in a trial strategy based almost solely on witness testimony, Denson moved first to mitigate the damage done by witnesses Sternberg, von Posern, and others whose questionable accounts threatened to bolster defense counsel's claim that survivors took the stand predominantly to seek revenge against their former captors.

> It may be pointed out . . . that some of the witnesses for the Prosecution have testified falsely because . . . Gützlaff testifies that on a particular date he was not in Mauthausen or any of the by-camps of Mauthausen . . . Now, it may be that the witness who testified concerning Gützlaff was mistaken in the date, but this court should not concern itself solely with dates.[2]

Instead, Denson argued that inaccuracies in the testimony of those he had called to the stand resulted from the fact that inmates had had no access to calendars and had endured "tortures in more inhuman forms than had ever before been devised by mankind up to this time."[3] Determined to keep the judges focused on the bigger picture, Denson declared that events rather than dates were central, and only in so far as such events went toward illustrating the common design to commit war crimes that the charges alleged.

"It is sincerely hoped," Denson continued, "that this court has not lost sight of the gravity of the charge that is before the court because of the type of evidence that was adduced." Though Denson insisted that the evidence presented in the previous five weeks had shown defendants like Eigruber, Riegler, Trum, and Huber to be brutal and sadistic murderers, he told the court that the specific acts attributed to each had been presented merely to illustrate the nature of the common design in play at Mauthausen. "We are not trying Altfuldisch or Niedermayer or Trum for their mistreatment of American prisoners of war, of the Dutchmen, or the Russians," Denson explained, but for their participation in the overarching scheme to commit war crimes, which produced such acts. As a result, inaccuracies in testimony relating to the individual acts of the defendants were cast as largely immaterial to the bigger question on which the court had to rule.

Denson claimed that determining the full extent of the participation of each of the sixty-one defendants in the deaths of the tens of thousands who had perished in the Mauthausen camp system had never been the intention of his team. Rather, Denson had introduced evidence to demonstrate "beyond all peradventure of doubt" that there existed in Mauthausen a common design to kill, to beat, to torture, and to starve the prisoners incarcerated there.[4] Here, the unorthodoxy of the prosecution's case was laid bare: by casting evidence of specific atrocities as relevant only insofar as it helped paint a picture of the camp system as a whole, Denson made the testimony of his witnesses virtually unchallengeable. So long as the evidence impressed upon the court the nature of Mauthausen and its subcamps, Denson asked the judges to overlook inaccuracies that would have impeached the testimony of a number of his witnesses in regular American criminal proceedings.

Once he had instructed the court on how the masses of testimony concerning the atrocities at Mauthausen were to be interpreted, Denson turned to the specifics of the common-design charge. Reading from *Black's Law Dictionary*, Denson reminded the court that common design referred simply to "a community of intention between two or more persons to do an unlawful act."[5] It was the task of the Dachau court judges to decide whether or not such a community of intention existed. Denson took great pains to impress upon the court that this community of intention was not synonymous with the charge of conspiracy and did not include the same evidentiary burden.

It is not contended that the accused in that dock got together at a single time and decided upon an extended plan of persecution of these prisoners . . . Nor is it necessary to show that there was a meeting that was common among all of them where such a plan was discussed.[6]

In fact, Denson maintained, such a contention "would be absurd on its face," if one considered that Mauthausen staff came and went at various times, held varying positions of authority, and were often not acquainted with each other. To instruct the judges on what was necessary to prove the existence of a common design to commit war crimes, Denson turned to another volume, *Underhill's Criminal Evidence*. "The existence of the assent of minds," Denson read aloud, "must be inferred . . . from proof of facts and circumstances which, taken together, apparently indicate that they were merely parts of some complete whole."[7] No explicit agreement to enter into such a common design was necessary.

What then illustrated the existence of such a "community of intention"? First, Denson pointed both to the size of the Mauthausen inmate population and of the system as a whole. "It is absolutely inconceivable," Denson argued, "that anyone could argue that [the crimes at Mauthausen] could be conducted and executed without the close cooperation of all those . . . who sit in the dock."[8] Second, Denson reasoned, the length of time over which the atrocities occurred, as well as the dozens of subcamps where they were perpetrated, precluded arguments that such horrors were the product of one man's plan, or were carried out by a single individual or small group of individuals. The administrative setup of Mauthausen, Denson argued, illustrated the relationship each of the defendants had to the common design and to each other. The mass killing at Mauthausen, Denson contended, required the participation of all departments, from the labor office, to the medical and political departments, and on to the guard companies. Drawing on the signed confessions that defense counsel had so rigorously challenged, Denson argued that the statements of higher-ranking defendants such as Niedermayer, Trum, and Altfuldisch illustrated the interdependence of all personnel, "that the problems that arose were the problems of all," and that the conditions that existed in Mauthausen were the product of all.[9] The simple fact that each of the sixty-one defendants had been stationed at Mauthausen or one of its subcamps, Denson argued, made them a party to war crimes. Once the prosecution had proven the existence of a common design at Mauthausen and had identified each defendant, the burden of proof shifted onto the accused. So long as the defendants had served at Mauthausen, they were, Denson implied, guilty unless proven innocent.

"There was no other camp under the German Reich," Denson continued, "where the conditions were as terrible, where beatings were more severe, where the prisoners received less food, than at Mauthausen." Accordingly, Denson reaffirmed to the court his contention that Mauthausen was a "Class III extermination camp," a designation he deemed "utterly consistent with the existence of a common design to beat, to kill, and to torture the prisoners."[10] As evidence, Denson pointed to the existence of the camp's gas chamber and crematoria, entries in the death books that illustrated killing at regular intervals, and the registration cards of prisoners marked "Return Undesirable."

Although such evidence may have illustrated Mauthausen's role as a killing center, it did nothing to back Denson's erroneous claim that the camp was the worst "under the German Reich," presumably outranking death camps such Auschwitz-Birkenau and Treblinka, where the Nazis had murdered more than two million people. Interestingly, Denson backed this claim with reference to an estimated death toll at Mauthausen and its subcamps "in excess of 70,000," a stark departure from the much larger statistics presented to the court in his opening statement.[11] Originally, Denson had drawn on the report of war crimes investigator Eugene S. Cohen, estimating the persons killed within the Mauthausen camp system to number "somewhere between 165,000 and a million and a half."[12] Although it is unclear whether Denson continued to believe in these grossly inaccurate statistics, he now opted for the much lower and more accurate figure likely because the death books accounted for only 72,000 dead and were the only evidence presented at trial to illustrate the mortality rate at Mauthausen. It is remarkable to note that the court made no mention of this dramatic change, despite the fact that the number of dead at Mauthausen was a fundamental marker of the extent of the crimes committed there.

Having defined the role of Mauthausen and the common design that allowed it to function, Denson now turned to the defense strategies. Some of them Denson dismissed out of hand, making no attempt to illustrate their flaws to the judges. First, he insisted that the arguments of some defendants, who claimed that resisting orders to participate in atrocities would have been futile because hundreds of others were on hand to commit them, did not constitute a defense. "The law," Denson explained, "requires each man to take the obligation upon himself not to commit a crime."[13] Just as briefly, Denson dismissed defense counsel's contention that some of the accused had not participated in, encouraged, or abetted the common design because they had no knowledge of it. This, Denson maintained, was totally untenable in light of the evidence presented to the court, and because "the very magnitude of the operations [within the Mauthausen camp system] was bound to have created notoriety."[14] Denson reserved a little more time to the question of the eighteen common guards in the dock, most of whom had served in the towers around the camp without access to the prisoner compound. According to Denson, the very act of having kept these prisoners behind electrically charged fences under armed guard was "a most heinous felony in itself."[15] Drawing upon *Wharton's Criminal Law* for authority, Denson explained to the judges the fact that the law considered those "outside keeping watch" as principals in the commission of the crime in question.[16]

Finally, Denson addressed the issue of superior orders, and how the claim that certain defendants had acted only as soldiers obeying the instructions of their commanders should be considered when assessing the guilt of the accused and during sentencing. First, Denson warned the judges of the danger implicit in shifting responsibility for war crimes solely onto those in command. Quoting from *Wheaton's International Law,* Denson argued that acting under orders "cannot furnish a valid excuse," for if it were considered so, "we arrive at a common conclusion that millions of men, including the responsible officers of the high command are to be held free from blame no matter what atrocious deeds they may have perpetrated," leaving responsibility solely with "the monarch or president of the belligerent state."[17] As for considering superior orders as a mitigating factor during sentencing, Denson argued that any lessening of punishment would be an affront to Mauthausen's thousands of victims.

> Those men who were prisoners had the intestinal fortitude to stand up for those things they thought were right . . . If the prisoners were willing to endure the killings, beatings, tortures and starvation to prove the courage of their convictions, why should this court permit a lesser standard of courage to be applied to these murderers and sadists, in order that they may be acquitted or receive a lesser punishment for their inhuman offenses? . . . It was up to every man in that dock to say "No. I will not take part in this nefarious scheme."[18]

According to Denson, there were only two simple questions before the court: had there been a common design to commit war crimes at Mauthausen, and had each and every one of the accused aided, abetted, or participated in that common design. "If the answer to both these questions is Yes," Denson insisted, "then they are guilty as charged . . . [and] may be punished by death."[19] Now pushing to have the death penalty applied to each of the sixty-one men in the dock, Denson warned the court what effect lenient sentences would have. "Unquestionably," Denson asserted, "the conduct of these accused will have turned back the clock of civilization at least one thousand years if this court, by its findings or by its sentences condones this misconduct . . . Every man in that dock . . . has forfeited his right to live in a decent society." It is interesting to note here the vision of Nazism and the role of the law that Denson invoked in order to conclude his case. Denson cast the ruthless murder of the political, social, and racial enemies of the Third Reich as a terrible deviation from the forward march of Western civilization. He did not recognize the essentially modern, bureaucratic, and systematized nature of the Nazi program of terror.[20] In his view, the crimes committed at Mauthausen were symptomatic of a return to barbarism. The rational and righteous authority of those behind the bench, Denson implied, had the power to prevent rupture.

Closing Arguments of the Defense

Lead defense counsel Lieutenant Colonel Robert W. Wilson was sick in hospital when court president Prickett called upon his team to present its closing arguments. As defense counsel had chosen to make no opening statement at the outset of the trial, its final comments to the court represented the first and only time that Wilson's team systematically laid out the central pillars of its case for the judges. With Wilson absent, however, the defense team's statements offered little impression of a cohesive strategy. Instead, Lieutenants Charles B. Deibel and Patrick W. McMahon, and then Major Ernst Oeding, proceeded to challenge, in no particular order, aspects of the legal and conceptual foundations on which the prosecution had built its case. Like Denson, Wilson's men referred to few of the accused individually, choosing instead to cast them collectively as victims of the Nazi state and as prisoners of an unjust occupying power.

Lieutenant Deibel was the first to address the court, briefly challenging the claim that Mauthausen was in fact an extermination camp, and that all who served there were complicit in mass killing. That the Mauthausen camp system was not created chiefly to exterminate people was "obvious," Deibel maintained, given the reliance the Nazis had on the "skilled workers" who slaved, for instance, in the tunnels of subcamp St. Georgen, deemed "one of the most modern plants in the whole Reich."[21] Deibel was not wrong in pointing to the masses of slave laborers who toiled in the broader camp system, but certainly stretched the truth by suggesting that the experiences of these workers was typical. According to Deibel, the guards who had worked at such subcamps were chosen as defendants not because they could be connected with an alleged common design to commit war crimes, but instead because their names appeared in the death books as having shot an escapee. If this were the case, Deibel suggested, the court could not convict these men, given that the prosecution had accepted the stipulation that it was customary procedure in penal institutions the world over to shoot those attempting to flee. "If it were merely a matter of Common Design," Deibel continued, the prosecution could have joined to the case "the 1,200 other men who are presently sitting in our *Sonderlager*."[22] Although there was certainly truth to Deibel's contention that the prosecution had selected guards for trial most directly connected to acts of killing, the suggestion that the 1,200 remaining personnel from Mauthausen currently in American custody could somehow have been joined in the current proceeding was absurd. Further, American authorities at Dachau had every intention of using the findings of the court in this first Mauthausen case to prosecute many of the very detainees referred to by Deibel with the common-design charge.

Lieutenant McMahon presented most of defense counsel's closing arguments and primarily sought to draw the legitimacy of the common-design charge into question. "Nowhere in the civilized world," McMahon began, "is an act committed without actual or implied consent to do wrong considered a crime."

> Under the prosecution's theory . . . any man[,] even you or I[,] would be guilty of the murder of thousands of Allied Nationals if perchance we had been born on this side of the Atlantic and had been ordered to Mauthausen or some other concentration camp merely because we were physically unfit soldiers. Well, you say to that, we would not have been members of the SS, and I answer you back, perchance we might have been.[23]

According to McMahon, the SS was "just another protective, uniformed organization, like all other parties had at the time," which had originally shown no "militaristic or criminal attitude." By the time Hitler came to power and revealed his evil intentions, McMahon argued, it was then too late for those who had initially supported him, for they lived "in imminent danger" of being deemed an enemy of the state.[24] Here, McMahon's depictions are misleading. As McMahon must have known, the SS was a paramilitary organization from its inception, founded as Hitler's personal bodyguard and composed of Nazi loyalists who could prove their racial purity. Further, defense counsel presented no evidence at trial that illustrated any mortal danger of leaving the SS. Nonetheless, McMahon insisted that the accused had been virtual prisoners of the Third Reich and that it was preposterous that they be considered culpable for acts to which they had not freely consented. To "judge the intimidated acts of the unfree German by the standards of free men" would be a grave error, he told the court. If his clients lacked freedom, McMahon contended, "they lacked also the obligations of free men."[25]

Next, McMahon expressed his "grave doubts" that the signed confessions of the accused had been freely given, or reflected anything other than what was "desired by the prosecution interrogator." As defense counsel had already done during trial, McMahon read the strikingly similar statements of defendants Altfuldisch,

Niedermayer, Drabek, Eckert, Häger, Trum, and Blei concerning the setup of Mauthausen and how each member of the staff contributed to the upkeep of the institution as a whole.[26] McMahon also read portions of statements concerning Mauthausen's role as an extermination camp. Niedermayer described Mauthausen as "a camp in which as many inmates were to die as possible," while Trum stated that "the purpose of Mauthausen was to kill as many prisoners as possible."[27] In search of further similarities, McMahon read out common passages from the statements of guards confessing to the shooting of escapees, as well as virtually identical passages from various defendants declaring their statements to be freely given. In an attempt to raise doubts again about the nature of his clients' confessions, McMahon labeled the contents of their statements "unbelievable." "People just don't talk about themselves that way," McMahon insisted. To confess freely to such atrocities and describe the cruelties inflicted by one's comrades was "contrary and contradictory to normal human standards." For this reason alone, McMahon argued, the contents of the statements clearly show "beyond any doubt that threats and duress were used to induce the signing of the untruthful statements."[28] Perhaps because the court had already heard the testimony of Paul Guth, the interrogator responsible for extracting these confessions, and had appeared to accept it as truth, McMahon made no reference whatsoever to Guth, nor to the specific allegations of abuse raised by many of those in the dock. The similarities in the statements, McMahon hoped, would speak for themselves.

Before giving the floor to Major Oeding for closing remarks, McMahon asked the court to give "due and serious consideration" to the dissenting opinion of U.S. Supreme Court Associate Justice Frank Murphy in the failed appeal of the guilty verdict reached in the trial of Japanese general Tomoyuki Yamashita. Murphy had argued that despite Yamashita's Japanese citizenship and commanding role in the slaughter of Filipino civilians, he was due all the legal rights and protections spelled out in the American Constitution when tried by a U.S. military commission court for war crimes. Quoting Murphy at length, McMahon insisted that

> the Fifth Amendment guarantee of due process of law applies to "any person" who is accused of a crime by the Federal Government or any of its agencies. No exception is made as to those who are accused of war crimes . . . Indeed, such an exception would be contrary to the whole philosophy of human rights which makes the Constitution the great living document that it is . . . To conclude otherwise is to admit that the enemy has lost the battle but has destroyed our values.[29]

McMahon chose lengthy passages from Murphy's opinion to cast further doubt on the legitimacy of the common-design charge, a charge that "the annals of warfare and the established international law afford not the slightest precedent for." McMahon further used Murphy to raise doubts about the fairness of a trial process lacking fundamental elements otherwise guaranteed under American law. Murphy had bemoaned the relaxed rules of procedure at the Yamashita trial, which, like those of the Dachau trials, heavily favored the prosecution. McMahon pointed out that unlike at the Yamashita trial, defendants convicted by military courts at Dachau did not even enjoy the right to appeal their convictions. However, while Murphy's eloquent opinion may have helped McMahon establish the problematic nature of the law followed by jurists at Dachau, the very act of drawing on a dissenting opinion illustrated that McMahon's concerns were in the minority.

The last member of the defense team to address the court was Major Ernst Oeding. First, Oeding challenged the nature and credibility of the evidence presented by the prosecution. Denson had relied almost entirely on witness testimony, a strategy Oeding now sought to cast as deeply problematic. According to Oeding, the fact that the vast majority of witnesses were former prisoners raised serious questions about the credibility of their testimony. Oeding contended that many camp survivors had used the chance to testify to get even with those responsible for holding them captive. Second, Oeding challenged the contention that the low-ranking accused could be held accountable for carrying out policies of which they had no part in the formulation. As Denson had done when drawing his own statement to a close, Oeding concluded his address to the court with a warning to the judges. If the court were to rule that low-ranking guards such as Korger or Gützlaff were guilty simply for carrying out the orders of their superiors, Oeding reasoned, it would be incumbent "upon all fathers to instruct their sons that if they are ever called to active duty . . . they refuse to obey any order until they have had a chance to determine whether or not it is legal . . ." "Yours is a heavy responsibility," Oeding continued. "What you do here will influence military people for generations to come and this law that you are asked to enforce and interpret may very well make an army an impossibility."[30] With that, Oeding drew the defense case to a close and returned to take his chair behind the large wooden table occupied by the rest of the members of his team. Shortly before 3 P.M., Court President Prickett called the session to a close.

The Judgment

At four o'clock, after only an hour's recess, Prickett called the Dachau court back to order to announce the verdicts. In deliberating against sixty-one men of widely varying rank and responsibility from Mauthausen and its disparate subcamps, the eight judges had spent no more than sixty-five seconds on average assessing the guilt of each defendant. Given the brevity of deliberations, it is clear that the judges spent no significant amount of time reviewing the evidence, examining legal precedent, or evaluating the issues surrounding the common-design charge that defense counsel had raised. In all likelihood, the judges had begun deliberations with their minds made up. Without pause or exception, Prickett read the names of the accused in alphabetical order, instructed each to stand, and informed each of the defendants individually that

> the Court, in closed session at least two-thirds of the members present at the time the vote was taken concurring in each finding of guilty, finds you of the Particulars of the Charge guilty.[31]

Again the court adjourned.

On the following Monday morning, Prickett opened proceedings at the Mauthausen trial for a final forty-five-minute session in order to announce sentences to each of the sixty-one guilty men. As with the verdicts handed down the previous day, the process of arriving at sentences for each defendant had not been a lengthy one. As Sunday was treated as a holiday at Dachau and proceedings had ended late on Saturday afternoon, it is unlikely that the assembled judges spent more that an hour discussing the fate of the war criminals they had just convicted. With no introduction save for a call to order, Prickett asked former compound commander Hans Altfuldisch, alphabetically first among the defendants, to stand before the bench.

> Hans Altfuldisch, the Court, in closed session at least two thirds of the members present at the time the vote was taken concurring, sentences you to death by hanging, at such time and place as higher authority may direct.[32]

In rapid succession, defendants Barczay, Brünning, Billmann, and Blei followed each other to the bench and received their death sentences. The monotony of sentencing was broken only three times, first by defendant Michael Cserny and then by Paul Gützlaff and Josef Mayer, who, likely to their own great surprise, did not receive the death penalty but "life imprisonment commencing forthwith."[33] According to brief reports in the press, many defendants paled upon hearing their fate. Two collapsed and had to be helped from the courtroom by guards. Former gauleiter August Eigruber, the *New York Times* noted, did not show any emotion whatsoever.[34]

Once sentencing had concluded, Prickett announced the so-called special findings of the court. Designed to serve as the basis for further proceedings against Mauthausen personnel then in American custody, these findings represent distilled conclusions that the military judges had drawn from the previous six weeks' proceedings.

> The Court finds the circumstances, conditions and very nature of the Concentration Camp Mauthausen, combined with any and all of its sub-camps, was of such a criminal nature as to cause every official, governmental, military and civil, and every employee thereof, whether he be a member of the Waffen-SS, Allgemeine SS, a guard, or civilian, to be culpably and criminally responsible.
>
> The Court further finds that it was impossible for an . . . employee of the Concentration Camp Mauthausen . . . to have been [at Mauthausen] . . . at anytime during its existence, without having acquired a definite knowledge of the criminal practices and activities therein existing.
>
> The Court further finds that the irrefutable record of deaths by shooting, gassing, hanging and regulated starvation, and other heinous methods of killing, brought about by the deliberate conspiracy and planning of Reich officials, either of the Mauthausen Concentration Camp . . . or of the higher Nazi hierarchy, was known to all of the above parties, together with the prisoners . . .
>
> The Court therefore declares: That any official, governmental, military or civil . . . in any way in control of or stationed at or engaged in the operation of the Concentration Camp Mauthausen, or any or all of its by-camps in any manner whatsoever, is guilty of a crime against the recognized laws, customs, and practices of civilized nations and the letter and spirit of the laws and usages of war, and by reason thereof is to be punished.[35]

With that, Prickett brought the trial to an end.

Fifty-Eight Death Sentences and the Mauthausen Trial "Jackpot"

Given the gravity and inclusive nature of the charges, the authority of the court to assign the death penalty, and the previous Dachau concentration camp trial judgment that had sent thirty-six of forty defendants to the gallows, the penalties imposed by Prickett and the other members of the court must not have taken Denson and his team by surprise. Further, the weight of the evidence against many of the condemned men had been damning. Although defense counsel raised significant questions about the legitimacy of the signed confessions of the accused and cast doubt on the testimony of some trial witnesses, the court appeared generally unreceptive to these issues. In this light, therefore, the most curious question when assessing the sentences is not why the Dachau judges handed down so many death penalties, but rather why they chose to spare three men from this ultimate punishment. Unfortunately, the reasons that defendants Cserny, Gützlaff, and Mayer received life imprisonment instead is a matter of speculation, given that Prickett and his team did not provide explanations for their decisions in court, nor were they required to publish reasons for their verdicts and sentences after the trial came to a close. Instead, one must compare and contrast the sentences to shed light on this question.

In many respects, the cases of Cserny, Gützlaff, and Mayer share features that help to account for the relative leniency of their sentences. First, all three men were common guards, stationed outside the fences of the camps at which they served. Cserny and Mayer were both draftees to the SS and to concentration camp service and were, at twenty-two, among the youngest defendants in the dock. Neither was German. Though Gützlaff was both older and German, he was implicated in killings of the same sort as Cserny and Mayer: all three had admitted to shooting escapees who had refused to halt when ordered. Given defense counsel's stipulation, accepted by the prosecution, that it was "customary procedure" the world over to shoot escapees from penal institutions, it is likely that the judges took the circumstances of these shootings into consideration. The fact that the judges nonetheless found the three men guilty and sentenced them to life in prison therefore reflects the fact that the Dachau court was won over by Denson's contention that even those who worked outside the fences of the camp remained culpable by preventing the escape of prisoners from a murderous system. They were guilty by virtue of their service alone.

The nature of the testimony and evidence brought against Cserny, Mayer, and Gützlaff also played a role. Konrad Wegner, the sole witness to testify against Cserny, had considerable difficulty identifying him in the dock, accidentally choosing Rudolf Mynzak first. Questioned about what he had seen, Wegner had been vague. He described seeing Cserny at executions behind Block 20 in 1942 but said he couldn't remember whether this had occurred "two times . . . or twenty times."[36] On the stand, Cserny insisted he had only arrived at Mauthausen in 1943, a contention Denson could not disprove.[37] Mayer's case was similar: aside from his confessed killing of an escapee, the evidence against him was exceedingly thin. Witness Jusef Suchonek claimed Mayer had taken part in the beating of Russian prisoners at Wiener-Neudorf, but admitted under cross-examination that he had not seen the beating but had only heard screams.[38] Witness Hulak Tadensz testified that Mayer had shot a Pole too weak to work in November 1944 at Wiener-Neudorf, but Mayer, as well as a number of witnesses called on his behalf, stated that he had been transferred to Ebensee in March of that year.[39] The testimony against Gützlaff was most problematic, given that witness Sternberg had attacked and insulted him when asked to identify him in the dock. Sternberg's outburst gave credit to defense counsels' contention that some witnesses testified simply to take revenge on their former captors. That Denson mentioned in his closing statement the flawed testimony against Gützlaff betrayed the fact that the Chief Prosecutor must have had concerns about the impression his witness's actions had had on the judges.

Although these factors help to explain the logic of the sentencing process, a comparative look at the sentences of other defendants in similar positions to Cserny, Gützlaff, and Mayer raises more questions than it answers. Of particular interest in this regard are the cases of defendants Billmann, Dörr, Grzybowski, and Höhler, among others, all of whom were sentenced to hang. Like Cserny and Mayer, Billmann was drafted both into the SS and into concentration camp service. Like all three, Billmann had admitted to shooting an escapee. The only other evidence brought against him concerned a beating carried out in Gusen—testimony he vigorously denied. Further, numerous former guards testified he was good to prisoners and often expressed his hatred of concentration camp duty.[40] The cases of guards Dörr and Grzybowski are remarkably similar. Both were implicated in the shooting of an escapee, though in the case of the latter defendant, the incident had not resulted in death. Nonetheless, the Dachau court condemned both to hang. An interesting comparison can be made also to the case of former chief dental officer Walter Höhler. Höhler had not been a guard, but was condemned to death instead for his role extracting the gold teeth of dead inmates in the crematoria complex. In this case, the prosecution had presented no evidence to implicate Höhler in the killing or even abuse of a single living prisoner. Nonetheless, he and the others were condemned to die. Such comparisons show that the Dachau judges followed no hard-and-fast template for assigning sentences to the trial defendants. Judges may have justified individual sentences as resulting from a particular defendant's role in the common design to commit war crimes at Mauthausen, but the apparent inconsistencies in the sentences handed down by the Dachau court would raise the eyebrows of more than one of the officers charged with reviewing the Mauthausen case in the coming months.

Fairly allotted or otherwise, the court's stiff punishments gave Denson and his team reason to celebrate. Reflecting on the verdicts some fifty years later, Denson remembered feeling that he had "almost hit the jackpot with the Mauthausen trial."[41] Though unknown to Denson at the time, the Mauthausen trial would in fact result in the largest number of executions stemming from a single trial in American history. Despite the fact that the Dachau court had given an average of only four hours' consideration to each defendant's case during trial, Denson felt the accused had been dealt with fairly and had received their just deserts. Though some defendants, Denson reflected, had been "more guilty than others," his only disappointment had been that the Dachau court had not condemned all sixty-one to hang.[42] The judgment of the court, Denson maintained, had illustrated that his attempt to condition the Dachau judges to truly understand the level of atrocity within the Mauthausen camp system had paid off. The members of the court, Denson noted with pride, had become "believers," just as he had when preparing his case.[43] Denson concluded that his greatest achievement was to help put "teeth into the written word," making it "apparent to those who violate the Laws and Usages of War that they would be punished."[44] For Denson, justice, at least for the time being, had been served.

The Judgment of the Court and Visions of Criminality at Mauthausen

Though the verdicts and sentences provide a quantitative basis for the measurement of the success of the Mauthausen trial, the special findings of the court offer an alternative and more subjective lens through which to assess the trial's outcome. At their most basic, the special findings had confirmed the contention at the heart of Denson's case: that simple service at Mauthausen or any of its subcamps constituted a war crime.[45] According to Denson, the purpose of the Mauthausen trial, aside from punishing the perpetrators, had been to "obtain a judicial determination that these camps were criminal operations in their entirety, from the commandant on down to the Kapo."[46] In this regard, the trial must again be considered a success.

In Denson's estimation, the court's judgment provided the basis "for disposing by trial of the issues of guilt or innocence of some 3,500 alleged war criminals that we were holding."[47] Indeed, the special findings of the court had certainly greased the wheels for the prosecution of additional personnel in American custody.

But how did the judges perceive the crimes they had judged? The answer to this question may lie chiefly in understanding the limitations of American military law. Dachau prosecutors were empowered to try enemy nationals for violations of the laws and usages of war, a preexisting framework that gave the proceedings their fundamental shape. As a result, the crimes at Mauthausen were necessarily presented as extreme manifestations of the excesses of war, rather than as unprecedented atrocities that both required and justified the creation of new legal concepts in order to prosecute successfully. At Nuremberg, the "crimes against humanity" charge, defined as "murder, extermination, enslavement, deportation, and other inhumane acts . . . or persecutions on political, racial or religious grounds," had allowed for the introduction of evidence concerning prewar persecution of victim groups and the policies and logic that set programs of ill-treatment and killing into motion.[48] Unlike the International Military Tribunal at Nuremberg, which attempted to get at the root of Nazi crimes, the Dachau courts functioned with the more limited objective of prosecuting low-level perpetrators for their participation in atrocities that had occurred at specific locations. In this context, it was neither necessary nor relevant to produce evidence concerning the bases or extent of the persecution of any particular group. In fact, even the most heinous manifestations of Nazi criminality remained outside the jurisdiction of the Dachau courts if committed prior to January 1942. If one were to understand the role of Castle Hartheim only through the Mauthausen trial, one would scarcely know that the vast majority of victims of the notorious "euthanasia" facility were not camp prisoners but handicapped Reich citizens murdered as part of the T4 program in

1940 and 1941. As the special findings of the Mauthausen trial judges reflect, it was the nature of the acts committed by the perpetrators within the camp system that was of central importance— the particular identity of their victims had little relevance in the judgment the court rendered.

Partly for this reason, Lisa Yavnai, in her study of the Dachau trial program as a whole, concludes that the American army missed a unique opportunity when prosecuting the concentration camp cases, despite the impressive rates of conviction and stiff sentences the courts assigned.[49] In particular, Yavnai argues that the courts neglected to foster historical understanding among the German and American publics concerning the Nazi genocide of the Jews. American military prosecutors and judges such as those at the Mauthausen trial, Yavnai argues, failed to deal with victims of the camps in a fashion that reflected "the gradations of cruelty that were fundamental to Nazi policy."[50] A cursory look at the Mauthausen case, and in particular the court's judgment, appears to confirm this conclusion. Although the special findings of the court emphasize the program of mass murder instituted in the Mauthausen camp system, no mention is made of the victims who perished there, nor the reasons they were singled out by the Nazi state. Although Chief Prosecutor Denson identified victim groups at various stages of the trial, he seldom mentioned Jews and failed to list them either in the indictment or in his opening statement to the court. Further, though Denson did introduce a number of Jewish witnesses in the second week of the trial, he never sought to present their suffering as qualitatively different. Not surprisingly, therefore, the court placed no special significance on the suffering of the Jews.

But why was it that the destruction of European Jewry was largely absent from a case that dealt with an important site of the "Final Solution"? Aside from the nature of the legal framework, consideration must be given to the context in which the trial occurred. At the most elemental level, there is the possibility that anti-Semitism, or at least the anticipation of anti-Semitism harbored by trial observers, played some role. As Lisa Yavnai has argued, the army feared that focus on crimes against Jews might lead to accusations that the trials were motivated by a thirst for revenge.[51] In his study of postwar justice and the Nuremberg proceedings, Donald Bloxham describes a similar phenomenon, in which an "unwritten rule" dictated that American war crimes trials could in no way be seen to be influenced by Jewish interests. According to Bloxham, this attitude was rooted in the "long-standing mistrust of the 'objectivity' of 'Jewish' evidence and the traditional Christian stereotype of the vengeful Jew."[52] Certainly Denson's introduction of Jewish witnesses during the Mauthausen trial raises some questions. Although Jews represented roughly one-quarter of Mauthausen's dead, Denson introduced scores of witnesses before calling a single Jew to testify. Once on the stand, these young Jewish witnesses appear to have been treated with extraordinary hostility and suspicion when facing cross-examination by defense counsel, a phenomenon I described in Chapter 4.

Though Denson may well have been swayed by the aversions others had toward Jews as described by Bloxham and Yavnai, there is no evidence that anti-Semitism played a role in the Chief Prosecutor's trial strategy, nor in the thinking of Prickett and the other judges. Instead, it is possible that Denson's placement of Jewish witnesses had a far less sinister logic. Because Denson insisted on the need to "condition" the court to hear testimony of an increasingly disturbing nature, he may have waited some time before introducing Jewish witnesses simply because their testimony was sure to be among the most horrific the court would hear. Further, in the immediate aftermath of the war and before the Trial of the Major War Criminals had drawn to a close at Nuremberg, the weighty significance of the Nazi genocide of the Jews had yet to be grasped. Given the high volume of cases Denson worked with, the masses of evidence he had to sort through, and the scant resources and personnel he had to assist him, it is of little surprise that he was not among the first to perceive its broader implications.

When assessing the vision of Nazi crimes presented at trial and ultimately laid out in the court's judgment, the role of Mauthausen in the Jewish genocide must also be kept in perspective. Although more than 25,000 Jews died in Mauthausen as well as in subcamps such as Ebensee and Melk in the final months of the war, they did not constitute a major portion of the camp's population prior to 1944. Beginning in 1942, Mauthausen personnel starved and murdered Soviet prisoners of war with every bit of the cruelty and determination they would employ for the camp's Jews. Seen in this light, a major emphasis on Jewish suffering during the trial or in the judgment of the court would have skewed the historical record, given the horrific suffering endured by various categories of prisoners at Mauthausen. As a result of these realities, it is most likely that Dachau jurists simply did not understand the special vigor with which the Nazis exterminated the Jews of Europe, or the programmatic differences between Mauthausen and Treblinka and Auschwitz-Birkenau.[53]

If one laments the ways the trial, and in particular the judgment of the court, failed to create broader historical understanding about the crimes committed in the camps, one must also consider public interest in the trial program before concluding that the U.S. Army had missed a "unique opportunity" to educate the world about the Nazi extermination program. Although the Dachau concentration camp trial opened to a courtroom packed with members of the press and high-ranking military officials, the audience soon evaporated as proceedings against the major figures of the Third Reich began at Nuremberg on November 20, 1945. At the Mauthausen trial, William Denson and his team of prosecutors delivered their case to an empty courtroom almost from the start. Photographs from the trial reveal rows of empty seats, punctuated only occasionally by a curious observer or a witness awaiting his day on the stand.[54]

Articles in the press were as sparse as the audience. In fact, the press appears to have reported only on the opening day of proceedings, on the judgment of the court, and later on the executions of the condemned men. Brief and sensational, such reports could hardly have been the medium by which the broader public would be enlightened about the horrors committed in the camps. To all intents and purposes, therefore, the court's vision of Nazi crime, while interesting to the historian, not only lacked depth but lacked the means by which to convey a pedagogical lesson.

Reviews, Reprieves, and Executions

Immediately following the close of the Mauthausen trial, military authorities transferred the sixty-one defendants to Landsberg Prison, sixty-five kilometers west of Munich. The Gothic prison, where Hitler had spent nine months writing *Mein Kampf* in the wake of his failed 1923 putsch attempt, was certainly a foreboding place from which to contemplate execution or a life spent behind bars. The grim reality facing the prison's new inmates must have appeared all the more stark as the executions of those condemned at the Dachau concentration camp trial began in the prison courtyard only days after they had arrived. While counsel prepared petitions for review and appeals for clemency, the Mauthausen trial convicts could do little but sit and wait.

Review and Recommendations

Defendants tried by military commission courts at Dachau could not appeal their convictions, but instead received the benefit of a series of automatic reviews carried out by military authorities. The first and most substantial review was prepared by the Deputy Judge Advocate for War Crimes and his team of reviewing officers. The Deputy Judge Advocate's "Review and Recommendations" summarized the evidence and findings in the case while suggesting any possible sentence reductions or reversals of conviction. In turn, the Judge Advocate (European Command) received his deputy's report and confirmed or rejected the recommendations it contained, while adding any further reversals or reductions he saw fit. In cases that did not involve the death penalty, the Judge Advocate held final authority. In those cases involving the death penalty, the Judge Advocate forwarded his report on to the theater commander, General Lucius Clay, who had final authority to confirm or commute a pending execution.[55]

More than nine months had elapsed since the close of the Mauthausen trial when Deputy Judge Advocate Colonel C. E. Straight submitted his Review and Recommendations for the case on February 25, 1947. As with the investigation phase, a combination of chronic understaffing and the sheer volume of cases requiring examination had caused major delays in the review process.[56] The bulk of Straight's report summarized the evidence presented at trial and included sections on the demographics of the prisoner population at Mauthausen, the food, shelter, and medical attention provided to inmates, the horrific experiments carried out on prisoners, and the various methods of torture and killing that made Mauthausen an "extermination camp."[57] Further, Straight's team explored legal issues such as the jurisdiction of the court and the sufficiency of the "common design" charge, and scoured the trial record for errors in procedure that may have affected the rights of the accused.[58] In addition, they scrutinized the sentences imposed by the court in order to guarantee that punishments were not excessive and fit the crimes in question.

Aside from the trial record, the Deputy Judge Advocate's Office also assessed petitions for review submitted by defense counsel on behalf of various defendants, as well as petitions for clemency submitted by the families and friends of the convicted men. For the majority of the sixty-one convicts, including notorious figures like Altfuldisch, Entress, Eigruber, Grahn, Krebsbach, Niedermayer, Riegler, Spatzenegger, Trum, Wasicky, Zutter, and Zoller, counsel submitted no petition. Instead, the attorneys reserved their efforts for the former defendants—predominantly guards—who were least implicated in atrocities at the camp. For those who did not fall into this category, letters from wives, parents, siblings, friends, and occasionally former employers or clergymen were the only supporting documents available. Some convicts, for instance former chief dental officer Wilhelm Henkel, managed to accumulate a remarkable number of clemency petitions nonetheless. Henkel's petitioners included his wife, mother, mother- and father-in-law, seventy-two citizens of Obenhausen, and seventy-five citizens of Offenbach am Main.[59]

Whereas personal pleas from family and friends had negligible influence on reviewing authorities, lawyers filed a number of lengthy petitions for review, which methodically challenged both the verdicts and sentences in the cases of twenty-six Mauthausen defendants. Lawyer Franz Bücherl, petitioning on behalf of guards Billmann and Grzybowski, insisted that his clients had not participated in the common design alleged by the prosecution because participation, he argued, required intent.[60] Given the fact that his clients were drafted into both the SS and into concentration camp service, they had participated against their will. Bücherl further challenged the evidence brought against his clients and insisted that the fleeing inmates killed by each had been shot according to protocol and for good reason. Common design, Bücherl warned, could not be used "like an atomic bomb," designed to kill masses without determining their individual guilt.[61]

Aside from mounting similar challenges, Lieutenant Charles B. Deibel's petition for review for defendants Mayer, Gützlaff, Priebel, Mynzak, Lappert, Korger, Dörr, Mack, Sigmund, and Rutka focused on the nature of the witness testimony brought against his clients.[62] Deibel alleged that the prosecution had had a great deal of trouble finding witnesses who could identify these low-ranking guards, and resorted to lineups in which these defendants were repeatedly referred to by name and marched by witnesses before anyone could identify them. German defense counsel Alexander Wolf's petition on behalf of Michael Cserny was more blunt than either Bücherl or Deibel. Wolf attacked the very underpinnings of the trial program, concluding in bold print that "THE COURT ERRED IN ITS CONDUCT OF THE TRIAL, IN ITS RULINGS, IN ITS CONSIDERATION OF THE EVIDENCE, IN ITS FINDINGS AND IN ITS JUDGMENT."[63]

Despite the efforts of counsel and the families and friends of the convicted men, the Deputy Judge Advocate's 105-page Review and Recommendations did not bring good news. In a pattern common to the cases of almost all the former defendants, a one- or two-page summary of evidence followed each name, as did the single phrase "Approval of findings and sentence." As an examination of the report makes clear, the most important factors for reviewing officers had been the severity of the crime in question and the weight of the evidence brought against each. Further, those reviewing the case had considered the age and nationality of each defendant, their status in various Nazi organizations such as the SS, and their position and period of service within the Mauthausen camp system.[64] Generally speaking, the Deputy Judge Advocate saw little grounds for sentence modification. Like the Dachau judges themselves, the Deputy Judge Advocate was largely unswayed by arguments that aspects of the proceedings had been unfair. "An examination of the entire record of trial," he concluded, "fails to disclose any error or omission which resulted in injustice to the accused." The evidence presented by the prosecution, the review declared, was "legally sufficient to support the findings of the court."[65]

There were, however, exceptions. Although he had accepted that the trial was fundamentally fair, the Deputy Judge Advocate recommended that the death sentences of guards Billmann, Dörr, Grzybowski, and Mack be commuted to life imprisonment. "It is not believed," Straight concluded, "that the nature and the extent of [their] participation in the common design warrant the death penalty." Apparently, the Deputy Judge Advocate was influenced both by the arguments presented by defense counsel in their petitions for review, as well as by the evidence in the court record. As defense counsel Deibel had pointed out, the evidence presented against the four guards was comparatively thin, as no more than two witnesses had testified briefly against each. Further, all four had shot escapees—an act the prosecution had agreed was in keeping with protocol at American penal institutions. While the Deputy Judge Advocate upheld the conviction of these four men, he did not accept Denson's argument that camp personnel standing guard from outside the fences were equally culpable as those who worked in the dreaded Political Department or carried out medical experiments on prisoners. Although counsel did not succeed in having review authorities cast aside the common-design charge, they may have nonetheless helped to reveal its limits.

Judge Advocate Colonel J. L. Harbaugh's review, which followed three weeks after that of his deputy, was brief and to the point.[66] In order to reach his conclusions, Harbaugh drew up a chart that listed each of the sixty-one condemned men, alongside their age, rank, membership status in the SS, and their role at Mauthausen. The chart included the atrocities each had committed, the number of witnesses who had testified against each, the sentence each had received, and any commutation of sentence suggested by the Deputy Judge Advocate in his review.[67] Only two pages in length, Harbaugh's review provided a condensed version of the trial proceedings and included recommendations for a number of further sentence reductions. Aside from confirming the commutations suggested by his deputy, Harbaugh recommended that the death sentences of guards Giese, Korger, Lappert, and Rutka be commuted to life imprisonment, as well as that of chief dental officer Höhler. According to Harbaugh, the evidence brought against the guards in question did not differ substantially from that against Cserny, Gützlaff, and Mayer, the three whom the Dachau judges had spared from the death penalty. As for Höhler, Harbaugh saw no evidence that linked the dentist to atrocities at the camp, despite his responsibility for removing gold from the teeth of dead prisoners.[68]

Harbaugh's notes also reveal commutations he had considered but decided against. Though Harbaugh generally found the participation of guards in the common design to commit war crimes at Mauthausen insufficient to warrant the death penalty, certain guards remained slated for execution. A separate comparative chart drawn up by Harbaugh shows personnel under consideration for clemency, with the names of Klimowitsch, Priebel, and Kautny scratched out. Although each had been a guard, the three were implicated in more vicious atrocities, such as the beating to death of prisoners on work details and in the Wiener Graben quarry. Another handwritten sheet lists the non-German guards. Remarkably, the foot of the page includes a note that appears to reveal a lack of familiarity with war crimes law on the part of Judge Advocate Harbaugh. "Ask Col. Fleischer to look up law concerning jurisdiction over non-Germans employed in Concentration Camps. And whether the above nationalities were allies of Germany during the war."[69] Such unfamiliarity with basic jurisdictional issues that courts at Dachau dealt with repeatedly helps to reveal the insufficiencies of a review process that put life-and-death decisions into the hands of military authorities who often lacked sufficient knowledge of, or experience with, war crimes prosecution. Further, the fact that Straight and Harbaugh were Denson's direct superiors illustrated the total lack of independence that defined the review process.

Executions

By the time the Judge Advocate's review reached the desk of theater commander General Lucius Clay, a mere rubber stamp stood between those Mauthausen personnel on death row and the gallows in the courtyard of Landsberg Prison. Although General Clay had the authority to confirm death sentences or grant reprieves, he generally took the advice of his Judge Advocate, giving force to the recommendations his better-informed subordinate had made. On April 30, 1947, Clay approved the death sentences of the forty-nine men for whom the Judge Advocate had not recommended clemency:

> Whereas the case has now come before me by way of review and after due consideration and in exercise of the powers conferred upon me, I hereby order that the findings and sentences are approved. The Commanding General, First Military District, will carry the sentence into execution at War Criminal Prison No. 1, Landsberg, Germany, at a time to be determined by him.[70]

For those Mauthausen trial defendants not reprieved from death row, the clock had finally run out.

On May 27, 1947, the largest mass execution in the history of the American war crimes trial program began in the courtyard of Landsberg Prison. Mounted atop two-and-a-half-meter platforms skirted in black curtain, two gallows operated in tandem, allowing for an execution every seven minutes.[71] Starting at 9 A.M., military police officers escorted the condemned men one at a time from their cells and out into the courtyard, flanked by army officials and a chaplain. Before mounting the gallows, each man was handcuffed and read the execution order. Once the condemned was atop the platform, executioners Norvill, Julion, and Goode bound his feet and asked if he had a last statement to make. Seconds later, a black hood was placed over his head, while the chaplain rendered a prayer. The moment the chaplain finished, the executioner sprang the trap door, sending the prisoner to his death. Minutes after each execution, military personnel emerged from beneath the gallows, carrying plain wooden coffins they placed in the corner of the courtyard. By the time the first day's executions stopped, shortly before noon, twenty-two pine boxes lay stacked and awaiting disposal.

For the most part, the forty-eight executions, completed the following morning, went smoothly.[72] Only a few incidents broke the morbid rhythm of the mass hanging. The first occurred when former Mauthausen mess sergeant Otto Striegel learned that military authorities had granted him a last-minute stay of execution in order to consider new evidence in his case. Defiantly, Striegel demanded to know why he could not be hanged alongside his comrades.[73] A second and more disturbing incident occurred when Anton Kaufmann, former Gusen quarry manager, broke his wrist bindings as he fell through the chute. Grabbing onto the executioner's rope, he held off death for eighteen minutes.[74] Generally, however, most appeared composed before the executioner's hood veiled their final expressions. Only dentist Wilhelm Henkel cracked under the strain, shaking, crying, and begging God for help.[75] More common was defiance. Hans Diehl, former clerk from Mauthausen's dreaded Political Department, sang the German anthem *Deutchland über alles* as he was taken from his cell, and inspired a number of his fellow prisoners to join in.

The last words of the condemned men reveal above all a stunning lack of contrition for the crimes committed at Mauthausen and its subcamps. Many used the gallows as the final platform from which to protest their innocence and decry the treatment they received before the American military court. "Dear Lord I am innocent," Willy Brünning declared. "The punishment is not just."[76] Heinrich Fitschok, who had guarded various subcamps including Gusen, Wiener-Neudorf, and Ebensee, insisted he would "die innocent," as he had done his duty "like any American soldier."[77] Others voiced a greater defiance. Kapo Willy Frey shouted out that he and his comrades were victims of "murder by order." Former chief physician Waldemar Wolter insisted that the executions represented "power before justice."[78] "May the Lord save my Fatherland from future rape," Wolter finished.

In typical fashion, former gauleiter August Eigruber's final words were filled with the same bravado that had defined his testimony on the stand. "I regard it as an honor," Eigruber declared, "to be hanged by the most brutal of victors. Long live Germany!"[79] Mess sergeant Otto Striegel revealed an even greater fanaticism in his final words:

I am no war criminal, but the revenge and hatred against the Jews will never end, for they are guilty of the suffering and hardships here in Landsberg. I am greeting my poor Fatherland. May God bless my wife and children. Now perform the order which was given to you by the Jews.[80]

In contrast to Striegel's vicious anti-Semitism, work detail leader Willy Eckert praised his American captors. "My sincere thanks to these respectable Americans who at all times have treated me fair and correct, especially to Major Denson. I hope the world finds its peace."[81] Of all the condemned men, guard Stefan Barczay was the only one to express contrition, asking that the Lord forgive him.[82] Many spoke no words at all.

Ironically, the macabre scene at Landsberg received far more attention in the press than the trial itself. As with the brief reports on proceedings at Dachau, reporters favored graphic and shocking details over historical context. One particular piece in the *New York Times* entitled "Doomsday at Landsberg" detailed not only the executions, but listed also the most brutal methods of killing at Mauthausen. The executions, the author wrote, were a part of the antidote to the "venom bred in the Nazi snake" that "did its best to poison the whole world." "Some day, God Willing," the article continues, "a generation of Germans may arise who will understand from what we saved them."[83] The executions, the article suggests, were the just answer to crimes that virtually defied the imagination.

In the months following the executions of the condemned Mauthausen personnel, the Dachau trial program would come increasingly under the scrutiny of a critical German public that began to see those who mounted the gallows as victims of a vengeful occupation. The mass hanging of the Mauthausen defendants at Landsberg— the largest in American history—represented the peak of the U.S. Army's zealous pursuit and punishment of Nazi war criminals. Although the prosecution of personnel from camps such as Flossenbürg and Buchenwald followed the Mauthausen trial and resulted also in dozens of death sentences, far fewer were carried out. Rapidly decaying relations between the United States and the Soviet Union increasingly made the emergent West German state an essential ally America could not afford to alienate. As a result, military authorities soon lost their taste for such dramatic expressions of power. Though those condemned to death at the Mauthausen trial were convicted too soon to benefit from the softening of American resolve and the growing protest against the war crimes program mounted by various sectors of the German population, those sentenced to life in prison lived to reap its rewards. Without exception, all those Mauthausen personnel sentenced to life in prison by the Dachau court would be free men by the end of 1951.

Conclusion

In the months following the close of the Mauthausen trial, proceedings at Dachau continued at full steam. Almost immediately, the Deputy Judge Advocate for War Crimes assigned Chief Prosecutor William Denson his next major task: preparing the Flossenbürg concentration camp parent case following the death of the original prosecutor.[1] Building on his experiences with both the Mauthausen and Dachau cases, Denson had a preexisting, efficient trial strategy with which to approach the Flossenbürg case—a strategy that would again provide a 100 percent rate of conviction.

Despite his impeccable prosecutorial record, however, the immense workload placed upon the shoulders of the young prosecutor, coupled with the nature of the crimes with which he dealt, began to take its toll. By the time the court announced verdicts at the Flossenbürg trial, Denson was complaining of headaches, insomnia, and nightmares. His hands shook so much that he had trouble holding a glass.[2] Reduced to 117 pounds from his original 160, Denson collapsed in his room in January 1947 and remained bedridden for two weeks.[3] Remarkably, this brief period of recovery was not followed by his return home or a reduction in workload, but instead by preparations for yet another concentration camp parent case—that concerning the personnel of Buchenwald. Prior to his return to the United States in late October 1947, Denson worked tirelessly to see as many concentration camp personnel as possible face justice. When he left Dachau, Denson had not lost a case. Of the 177 men he prosecuted, not one was acquitted.

Although Denson did not take part in the subsequent proceedings that his concentration camp "parent cases" spawned, military personnel at the end of 1946 began to use the findings of the court in these cases to prosecute perpetrators not included in the main camp trials.[4] In mid-1947, eight separate tribunals operated simultaneously at Dachau.[5] By year's end, 219 subsequent concentration camp trials involving 812 accused from Dachau, Mauthausen, Flossenbürg, Buchenwald, and Nordhausen had taken place.[6] The efficiency of these subsequent proceedings—some of which lasted only a day—lay in their design. A court that was to hear a subsequent concentration camp case would be furnished with the charges and particulars from the original parent case, as well as the special findings and sentences that the judges had announced. Once the court had taken judicial notice of these findings, no examination of the original trial record was deemed necessary. A defendant in a subsequent proceeding could only contend that he had not participated in the common design to commit war crimes at the camp; that he was a victim of mistaken identity; or that he had been at the camp for such a short time as to make his participation undeserving of severe punishment. In such trials, William Denson later explained, "the burden of proof shifted onto the accused to establish either that he was not there [or] that he did not act in the capacity alleged." Though defense counsel labeled these proceedings "trials in absentia" because the accused were not present at the original trials where much of the evidence was introduced and many of the witnesses examined, Denson nonetheless maintained that such trials were fundamentally fair.[7]

Between March and November 1947, sixty proceedings based on the findings of the Mauthausen parent trial and involving a total of 238 defendants took place at Dachau.[8] Though the efficiency of this trial system allowed for the punishment of dozens more Mauthausen personnel involved in the commission of war crimes, the sentences handed down by the courts in these proceedings tended to be far milder than those given by the judges at the parent trial. Of the 238 defendants, 58 were sentenced to death, 44 to life imprisonment, 115 to prison terms ranging from thirty-one months to thirty years, while 21 were acquitted.[9] Despite more lenient sentences, the crimes in question were no less brutal. For instance, Otto Heess, the commander of subcamp Steyr, was spared the gallows and received instead a life sentence, despite implication in the deaths of the hundreds who perished there.[10] Christoph Pfaffenberger, who led a Gusen guard company, received a ten-year sentence for beating numerous inmates, some of whom succumbed to their injuries.[11] Gusen battalion commander Alois Obermeier likewise received ten years for leading executions at the camp.[12] Company commander Hans Vaessen received only three years for leading an execution detail at Gusen.[13] The minority who were condemned to death for their crimes often had their sentences reduced upon review.

These sentences, strikingly lenient when compared to those handed down at the Mauthausen parent trial, reflect a trend common to all proceedings at Dachau. Generally speaking, the later a trial occurred, the more lenient the sentences imposed. During 1945, for instance, 56 percent of convictions resulted in the death penalty; for 1947, only 21 percent. Not surprisingly, the acquittal rate, as well as the number of life sentences, grew.[14] This phenomenon sprang from several circumstances. First, as months and years passed since the end of hostilities in Europe, fewer and fewer of those assigned to judge these cases had directly experienced the war, seen sites of atrocity firsthand, or met camp survivors shortly after liberation. Judges may therefore have been less driven by the shock and passion felt by those first exposed to such crimes.[15] Second, far fewer witnesses were on hand to testify in the latter stages of the program. As memories faded with the passage of time, testimony tended to be less detailed and therefore likely less compelling to the judges.[16]

Uneven punishment was due also to the flexibility of trial procedure at Dachau, and in particular to the absence of sentencing guidelines. Because American army judges were not required to explain their verdicts, previous trials involving similar crimes did not provide a good source of precedent when sentencing.[17] Taking into consideration also that numerous courts operated simultaneously, it is not surprising that while defendants may have been tried for similar crimes, they nonetheless received dissimilar sentences. In order to remedy this situation, staff judge advocates used the "Review and Recommendations" they produced for each case tried at Dachau to determine whether sentences fit the crimes in question. As time passed, this led to more-lenient punishment, as the army reduced prison terms and commuted executions in order to guarantee equal sentencing.

Scandal and Mounting Political Pressures

At the beginning of September 1947, Deputy Judge Advocate for War Crimes Clio E. Straight convened a conference in Munich in order to discuss the future of the trial program at Dachau. When it began trying cases in the summer of 1945, the army had not set a time frame for the completion of war crimes prosecutions, planning instead to prosecute all cases involving crimes against Americans or mass atrocities committed within the U.S. zone of occupation.[18] Increasingly, however, the war crimes trial program was perceived as a hindrance to the reestablishment of a stable and democratic German state and to the securing of German goodwill in the wake of growing tensions between the United States and the Soviet Union. Though many Germans had viewed the International Military Tribunal at Nuremberg as just, Germans increasingly saw lesser perpetrators brought before American courts as victims of unfair proceedings rather than as war criminals.[19] The trials, many Germans felt, defamed the nation as a whole. As American occupation goals shifted in order to shore up diplomatic relations with the soon-to-be-independent West German state, public opinion in Germany was of ever-increasing importance. As a result of the cumulative pressures brought to bear by these circumstances, Colonel Straight announced at Munich that all trials needed to be completed by December 31, 1947.[20] In the final months of the trial program, therefore, priority shifted to those cases involving American victims. If necessary, Straight explained, remaining concentration camp cases could simply be dropped.

Though political and diplomatic considerations had prompted the army to draw the trial program at Dachau to a close, such pressures were slight compared with those generated by a series of scandals in 1948 and 1949 that threatened to undermine the legitimacy of the American war crimes program as a whole. The first major controversy prompted by the trials at Dachau concerned Ilse Koch, wife of Buchenwald commandant Karl Koch. Known as the "Bitch of Buchenwald," Koch had initially been sentenced to life in prison in August 1947, for her role in the abuse of inmates. Koch's case was widely reported on in the press, owing to the alleged depravity of her crimes, her physical beauty, and the fact that she had become pregnant in American custody under mysterious circumstances. During trial, camp survivors testified that she had selected tattooed prisoners for death, so as to collect their skins to make articles such as lampshades.[21] Owing in part to her pregnancy, as well as to the often circumstantial evidence linking her to crimes at the camp, Koch was spared the gallows and sentenced instead to life in prison. Following review of her case in September 1948, however, her sentence was reduced to only four years, reportedly owing to insufficient evidence.[22]

The decision to reduce Koch's sentence was met with shock, both in the American media and in government circles in Washington.

William Denson, who had prosecuted Koch in the original Buchenwald parent trial, voiced his outrage in a letter published in the *New York Times,* questioning the very wisdom of the army's review process. "The granting of clemency," Denson wrote, "is an act of grace that should be administered wisely and dispassionately. Improperly bestowed, it will undermine not only the faith of our own citizens in our institutions, but also the faith of those we have been trying to convert since May 7, 1945."[23] For Denson, evaluating the sufficiency of evidence in any given case was a task set for the court alone. Sharing Denson's frustration, a group of American senators and congressmen succeeded in establishing a Senate subcommittee under the leadership of Homer Ferguson to investigate the circumstances that had led to such a drastic reduction of sentence for such heinous crimes. Although the committee was of the opinion that trying Koch a second time was "undesirable," given legal principles that prohibited trying an individual for the same crime twice, it nonetheless concluded that the staff judge advocates charged with reviewing her case had overstepped their authority and that her sentence reduction had not been warranted.[24]

While the Koch controversy revealed major flaws in military trial and review procedure, as well as a stunning lack of commitment to the Dachau proceedings, the Malmédy trial scandal would prove to be by far the most damaging for the American war crimes program. In July 1946, a Dachau court had sentenced forty-three of seventy-four trial defendants to death for their role in the massacre of unarmed American POWs near the Belgian town of Malmédy in December 1944. Despite the fact that reviewing authorities commuted all but twelve of the death sentences in early 1948, Willis M. Everett Jr., the U.S.-appointed attorney who had defended the accused, petitioned the army for further examination of his case. According to Everett, his clients had not received a fair trial. The majority of confessions signed by his clients, Everett alleged, had been acquired through the use of physical abuse, mock trials, stool pigeons, or phony priests.[25] In May 1948, therefore, Everett petitioned the U.S. Supreme Court on behalf of his clients for writs of habeas corpus. Although Everett's petition failed, the judges' 4–4 vote prompted Secretary of the Army Kenneth C. Royall to appoint a commission under the leadership of Texas Supreme Court justice Gordon Simpson to investigate Everett's allegations and review 127 other death sentences handed down by the Dachau courts. In his own attempt to get to the bottom of Everett's allegations, U.S. military governor Lucius Clay set an independent investigation into motion, to be carried out by the Administration of Justice Review Board.

The Simpson Commission was the first to report, concluding in September 1948 that while "no general or systematic use of improper methods to secure prosecution evidence" had been used, the death sentences of the remaining Malmédy trial convicts should be commuted.[26] The conclusions of the Administration of Justice Review Board, however, which were reported to Clay in February 1949, were more disturbing. The board concluded that mock trials had occurred, during which prisoners forced to wear black hoods were brought before fake judges in order to gain confessions. Such activities, the board concluded, had "at times exceeded the bounds of propriety."[27] The board found further evidence that interrogators had threatened harm to the families of the accused, and "that undoubtedly in the heat of the moment . . . interrogators did use some physical force on a recalcitrant suspect."[28] The revelations of the reviews commissioned by both Royall and Clay heightened the crisis of confidence in the American military trial program—a crisis the Koch controversy had helped to unleash—and brought it to a fever pitch in both the United States and Germany.

The immediate result of the reports commissioned by both Royall and Clay was a temporary halt of all executions in Germany and the creation of an investigative Senate subcommittee in Washington in March 1949 chaired by Raymond E. Baldwin. Several Republican senators, most notably Joseph McCarthy, had grown highly critical of the trial program and were eager to call its overseers to account during committee hearings. Critics of the Dachau trials had found ammunition in remarks made by Judge Edward Van Roden, a member of the three-man Simpson Commission who had investigated allegations of abuse at Dachau on behalf of the secretary of the army. Although Van Roden had originally signed off on the commission report, which cleared military personnel at Dachau of any major wrongdoing, he soon changed his tune. In an interview given to the *Philadelphia Evening Bulletin,* Van Roden claimed that beatings and mock trials were in fact commonplace and that such activities had caused "permanent and irreparable damage" to "the prestige of America and American justice." Military authorities at Dachau, Van Roden insisted, had "abused the powers of victory and prostituted justice to vengeance."[29]

Drawing on such claims, McCarthy told the Baldwin Committee that Dachau investigators had employed "Gestapo tactics" in pursuit of their cases.[30] Despite charged rhetoric from such prominent detractors, the final report of the Baldwin Committee, published in October 1949, largely exonerated the American military trial program while at the same time acknowledging problems and recommending changes.[31] Nonetheless, the damage had been done. Domestic critics inside and outside of Congress latched onto claims made during the Malmédy hearings to discredit the American war crimes program as a whole. Further, the fiery oratory of McCarthy and other trial detractors made it abundantly clear to American military officials that support for the war crimes program at home was weakening by the day. Even Lucius Clay now appeared less resolute, exclaiming that he had grown tired of signing off on the hundreds of death sentences the Dachau trials produced.[32]

More damaging still, the Malmédy hearings reinforced growing perceptions within Germany that those convicted at Dachau were victims of a vengeful and unjust trial system. Though German discontent with the American trial program had existed prior to the

Malmédy scandal, it had never appeared so widespread or, for some, so well founded. Among the most vocal German opponents of the trials were a number of Catholic bishops and Evangelical church leaders who couched their criticism in stark moral terms. Previous claims that trials should be abolished in the interests of Germany's future were replaced with passionate protests aimed at undermining the legitimacy of the American program in Germany by revealing its ugliest excesses. Bishop August von Galen of Münster, who had taken a courageous stand against the Nazi euthanasia program in 1941, described the conditions suffered by German war criminals in Allied custody as akin to those endured by the victims of the concentration camps.[33] Bishop Theophil Wurm of Württemberg, chairman of the Council of the Evangelical Church in Germany, used equally extreme language to attack the legal processes that had led to the convictions of defendants at Dachau and Nuremberg. Even before the Malmédy scandal broke, he complained that "criminal methods and repellent tortures have been applied in order to extort statements and confessions" from those sentenced to death by American authorities.[34] Following the Baldwin Senate subcommittee hearings, Josef Frings, cardinal of Cologne, petitioned General Clay to revise court verdicts, similarly citing shoddy evidence and "unjust interrogation methods."[35] Munich auxiliary bishop Johannes Neuhäusler went above and beyond petitioning Clay, opting instead to write directly to members of the U.S. Congress, urging them to suspend executions at Landsberg Prison following the Malmédy defendants' charges of torture and mistreatment at the hands of Dachau interrogators.[36]

Ironically, one of the most extreme critics of the trial program was an American—Bishop Aloisius Muench of North Dakota—the Catholic liaison between the U.S. Office of Military Government and the German Catholic Church in the American zone. In the spring of 1947, a pastoral letter of Muench's entitled "One World in Charity" appeared in Germany, calling on U.S. authorities to end prosecutions of German war criminals labeled little more than exercises in vengeance. Muench referred to Allied authorities as "other Hitlers in disguise, who would make of the German nation a crawling [Bergen] Belsen." Advocating "Christ's law of love" over the "Mosaic idea of an eye for an eye," Muench's letter appeared to contrast what he saw as Christian virtue over Jewish vengeance.[37] Indeed, his deep anti-Semitism is revealed more explicitly in his diary, which repeatedly records his opinion that the American trials were conducted largely by Jews out for revenge.[38] Following revelations of detainee abuse at the Malmédy hearings, Muench expressed similar attitudes in a letter to Cardinal Frings, writing that "one should really be ashamed of the way the [interrogations] played out. The one satisfaction in this whole affair is the fact that true Americans did not conduct the pretrial interrogations, as evidenced by their names."[39] Muench also used his position to try to affect U.S. policy directly, passing on to General Clay a report penned by a Catholic pastor serving the Dachau detainees, which complained of "assembly-line trials" designed to punish Germans "simply because they were assigned guard duty in a concentration camp."[40] In the mind of Muench and many of Germany's church leaders, the Dachau trial program as a whole was corrupt and woefully unjust. Though U.S. authorities had initially hoped to work with the churches in reorienting the German public, protests of this kind prompted army intelligence to report the "unique role" church leaders played in "favoring the cause of interned Nazis."[41]

The protests spearheaded by the churches—and soon reiterated by veterans' groups—had far-reaching consequences. First and foremost, the new democratic West German government came to see championing the war crimes issue as an avenue to securing essential public support for the new Adenauer administration. Although the German Federal Republic had come into existence in May 1949, the United States retained custody of those individuals its military courts had convicted, and continued to decide all matters concerning parole and release. Dependent on public support and determined to retain the backing of the churches and former members of the armed forces, the Adenauer government declared its intention to champion the war criminal issue itself and seek the release of all those convicted by Allied military courts.[42] Not surprisingly, the United States therefore increasingly saw the war crimes trial program as a central obstacle to the close diplomatic relations it was so eager to foster with the emergent West German state.[43] With the United States dependent on Germany's participation in anti-Soviet defense plans for Western Europe, clemency and release became an effective bargaining chip in securing German goodwill.

Faced with pressures at home and dissent abroad, the army searched for a clemency program that could equalize or reduce sentences, avoid the pitfalls of the army's preexisting review process as highlighted by the Koch case, and take into account both American occupation goals and the political position of the new West German government.[44] The War Crimes Modification Review Board, created in November 1949, was to serve these purposes, guaranteeing that virtually all those serving sentences at Landsberg Prison for war crimes would see premature release. Composed of five senior officers, the board reviewed cases and recommended sentence modifications, taking into consideration factors such as membership in Nazi organizations, the severity of sentences when compared to those of others convicted for committing the same crime, good behavior while incarcerated, and health. Of the 512 cases the board reviewed, it recommended sentence modification in 392.[45] Among those who received the benefit of the board's review were the twelve defendants from the Mauthausen trial spared the gallows. Following appearances before the War Crimes Modification Review Board, all were released from Landsberg Prison between March 1950 and November 1951.[46] The further establishment of the Interim Parole and Clemency Board in 1952 and the Mixed Parole and Clemency Board in 1955 helped secure the release of the remaining prisoners tried by military courts at Dachau. The last Dachau trial defendant walked out of Landsberg Prison a free man in December 1957. Symbolic of the way German war criminals had come to be viewed by their countrymen and their government, those released from Landsberg were not stigmatized but instead rewarded with prisoner-of-war pensions, including tax benefits and compensation for the incarceration they had endured.[47] For many Germans, the Dachau defendants counted among the last victims of the war.[48]

Justice, Punishment, and History

As an exercise in expeditious justice, the Mauthausen trial was a great success for its American organizers. Between March 29 and May 13, 1946, Chief Prosecutor William Denson not only convinced the military commission court at Dachau that each of the sixty-one defendants was guilty of participating in a common design to commit war crimes, but also that Mauthausen and its many subcamps were inherently criminal institutions. Drawing on precedents from military law and making use of definitions of war crimes codified in the Geneva and Hague conventions, Denson did not have recourse to the novel legal charges in use at Nuremberg crafted to encompass the unprecedented nature of Nazi crimes. The preexisting mechanisms of military law were no hindrance to Denson and his team, however. To the contrary, lax rules of evidence and procedure, the nonexistence of an appellate process, and the absence of an independent reviewing authority facilitated the rapid conviction and punishment of the accused. Although Allied dedication to the war crimes issue waned in the months following the Mauthausen trial and led to sentence reductions for perpetrators of even the most heinous atrocities, forty-nine of the fifty-eight Mauthausen trial defendants sentenced to death by the court paid the ultimate price for their crimes. Fifty years later, Denson reflected with pride on those from Mauthausen who, owing to his efforts, were "pushing up flowers in the graveyards."[49] As a vehicle for punishment, the Mauthausen trial was staggeringly effective.

As with all the trials at Dachau, however, the American army had launched Mauthausen proceedings not only to punish Nazi perpetrators, but also to reorient Germans toward democracy and reveal to the German public and the world the true extent of Nazi criminality. In this regard, the Mauthausen trial was a resounding failure. Although testimony concerning the most horrific of atrocities defined trial proceedings, few outside the courtroom ever heard it. As the major surviving figures of the Third Reich garnered global attention at Nuremberg, the press had little interest in reporting on the fate of a group of unknown wrongdoers from a camp largely unfamiliar to its readership. Although Denson's preference for witness testimony over documentary evidence helped to create for the court a more tangible and powerful story of human suffering, rows of empty seats in the courtroom quickly demonstrated how slight was the trial's pedagogical impact. Further, the limitations of military law, coupled with the restricted jurisdiction of the court, meant that while Nazi atrocities may have stood front and center at the trial, prosecutors were unable to present such crimes within their proper historical context.

The pedagogical failings of the Mauthausen trial are also linked to the very peculiarities of the military commission court system that enabled the trial to function so efficiently. As Lawrence Douglas has argued, a trial cannot effectively convey a pedagogical message unless it is perceived to be fair by its intended audience.[50] Fairness, indeed, was in short supply at the Mauthausen trial. The average total of four hours that Mauthausen trial judges spent considering each defendant's case before handing down dozens of death sentences would have done little to assuage perceptions that the American war crimes program was anything more than an expression of "victor's justice." As evidenced by the Malmédy trial scandal, dubious interrogation techniques and improper treatment of war criminals in custody at Dachau prompted Germans to view trial defendants primarily as victims and therefore to avoid self-reflection on Nazi crimes. Although the trial program at Dachau conveyed the general message that even low-level Nazi perpetrators required substantial punishment, the Mauthausen trial did little to inspire the German public either to confront the reality of Nazi criminality or to embrace democracy as an alternative to dictatorship and terror.

Moreover, while the Mauthausen trial failed to prompt much self-reflection among the German public, it did even less to inspire Austrians to contemplate honestly the crimes that had occurred in their midst. The decision to conduct the Mauthausen trial in Germany rather than in the American-occupied zone of Austria inadvertently fortified the popular, self-serving, and erroneous contention that Austria was the "first victim" of German aggression and free of implication in Nazi crimes. Opting for the practicality of centralizing the war crimes trial program at Dachau, the American army allowed the Austrian public to avoid confronting crimes committed at an institution that now stands as the most dramatic symbol of Austria's Nazi past. Instead, those who had lived alongside Mauthausen and its dozens of subcamps could entertain the convenient and skewed perception that Mauthausen was intrinsically "un-Austrian," and something for which the Germans alone would have to atone.[51]

Despite the Mauthausen trial's shortcomings, however, it would be wrong to conclude that it failed to achieve a measure of justice. First, it held to account sixty-one "ordinary" perpetrators who may otherwise have escaped prosecution. Though atrocities such as those committed at Mauthausen can scarcely be matched with commensurate penalties, punishment for Holocaust crimes remains essential, as Hannah Arendt observed many years ago.[52] While the gallows lacks the power to undo past suffering, it stands as a powerful symbol of the moral condemnation by the collectivity of an individual's actions. Though capital punishment may legitimately raise moral questions of its own, it communicated a resounding rejection of the view that the lives of Mauthausen personnel were worth more than those of their victims. In hindsight, Dachau judges guaranteed that forty-nine of those responsible for the crimes at Mauthausen would not benefit from the weakening of Allied resolve, and later, from the intricacies of German law, which all too often allowed Holocaust perpetrators to "get away with murder."

Inadvertently, the Mauthausen trial also provided a means for victims of the camp to emerge from powerlessness in the immediate wake of their liberation. Arising for practical reasons, American dependence on camp survivors during the investigation phase enabled Holocaust victims to play a meaningful role in both bringing their former captors to justice and establishing what had occurred at Mauthausen in the preceding seven years. Whether employed as translators, clerks, or later as witnesses at trial, camp survivors informed the vision of Nazi crimes presented by war crimes investigators and by prosecutors in the courtroom. Court proceedings at Dachau provided a forum where survivors could tell their stories and ensure that despite the attempts of the camp's SS personnel, Mauthausen's intimate and horrific history would not be erased.

To contemplate the legacy of the Mauthausen trial is therefore to confront a disquieting paradox: the measure of justice won at Dachau was achieved by recourse to a legal system that denied the accused a full and fair trial. Fifty years after the Dachau proceedings had come to a close, Chief Prosecutor William Denson remained their staunch defender, insisting there was "no need for any apology for conducting these trials under the conditions then prevailing."[53] The fact that the Mauthausen trial defendants were clearly guilty of participating in some of the most hideous atrocities committed during the Second World War justified their rapid prosecution—prosecution that stretched the bounds of legal propriety and yet rendered the sort of expedient justice required to prevent perpetrators from slipping back into European society after the American occupation had come to an end. Recent debates concerning the establishment of American military commission courts at Guantánamo Bay, Cuba, however, reveal a deep discomfort with the idea that a system of law parallel to national criminal codes may be used in order to prosecute abroad perpetrators of historically significant crimes. Like the courts at Guantánamo Bay, the Mauthausen trial forces reflection on the implications of compromising legal ideals in the pursuit of justice.

Born of the exigent circumstances of its time, the Mauthausen trial leaves a legacy tainted by questionable legal practices, and yet fortified by the invaluable historical record the trial produced. As a result of the work of American war crimes investigators and prosecutors, as well as of the survivors who aided them, the trial generated a robust historical record detailing the everyday function of a major concentration camp. Further, the interrogations and testimony of the sixty-one accused provided early insight into the worldviews and motivations of lower-level Nazi perpetrators. Most important, the trial elicited the testimony of more that one hundred survivors who bravely faced their former captors in the courtroom and whose accounts—told less than a year after their liberation—form an indelible and detailed chronicle of suffering during the Second World War. If the gallows was a necessary answer to the sheer depravity of the crimes committed by the Mauthausen trial defendants, the production and preservation of a historical record stands as the most powerful tribute to the camp's 100,000 victims.

APPENDIX

NOTES

BIBLIOGRAPHY OF PRIMARY SOURCES

ACKNOWLEDGMENTS

INDEX

The Mauthausen Trial Charge Sheet

From *The United States v. Hans Altfuldisch et al.*, Case no. 000–50–5, William Dowdell Denson Papers, Manuscripts and Archives, Yale University Library, Manuscript Group 1832, Series 2—Trials, 1945–2001, box 8, folder 37.

Dachau, Germany
7 March, 1946

Names of the Accused

Hans Altfuldisch	Paul Kaiser
Stefan Barczay	Anton Kaufmann
Karl Billmann	Franz Kautny
August Blei	Kurt Keilwitz
Willy Brünning	Eduard Krebsbach
Michael Cserny	Ferdinand Lappert
Hans Diehl	Josef Leeb
Ludwig Dörr	Julius Ludolf
Otto Drabek	Wilhelm Mack
Willy Eckert	Josef Mayer
August Eigruber	Erich Miessner
Hans Eisenhöfer	Emil Müller
Friedrich Entress	Wilhelm Müller

Rudolf Fiegl
Heinrich Fitschok
Willy Frey
Heinrich Giese
Georg Gössl
Werner Grahn
Johannes Grimm
Herbert Grzybowski
Paul Gützlaff
Heinrich Häger
Hans Hegenscheidt
Wilhelm Henkel
Walter Höhler
Franz Huber
Willy Jobst
Kaspar Klimowitsch
Viktor Korger
Gustav Kreindl

Rudolf Mynzak
Josef Niedermayer
Vinzenz Nohel
Herman Pribyll
Theophil Priebel
Josef Riegler
Adolf Rutka
Thomas Sigmund
Hans Spatzenegger
Otto Striegel
Karl Struller
Leopold Trauner
Andreas Trum
Erich Wasicky
Waldemar Wolter
Viktor Zoller
Adolf Zutter

Are hereby charged with the following offenses:

CHARGE: Violation of the Laws and Usages of War.

Particulars: In that Hans Altfuldisch, Stefan Barczay, Karl Billmann, August Blei, Willy Brünning, Michael Cserny, Hans Diehl, Ludwig Dörr, Otto Drabek, Willy Eckert, August Eigruber, Hans Eisenhöfer, Friedrich Entress, Rudolf Fiegl, Heinrich Fitschok, Willy Frey, Heinrich Giese, Georg Gössl, Werner Grahn, Johannes Grimm, Herbert Grzybowski, Paul Gützlaff, Heinrich Häger, Hans Hegenscheidt, Wilhelm Henkel, Walter Höhler, Franz Huber, Willy Jobst, Kaspar Klimowitsch, Viktor Korger, Gustav Kreindl, Paul Kaiser, Anton Kaufmann, Franz Kautny, Kurt Keilwitz, Eduard Krebsbach, Ferdinand Lappert, Josef Leeb, Julius Ludolf, Wilhelm Mack, Josef Mayer, Erich Miessner, Emil Müller, Wilhelm Müller, Rudolf Mynzak,

Josef Niedermayer, Vinzenz Nohel, Herman Pribyll, Theophil Priebel, Josef Riegler, Adolf Rutka, Thomas Sigmund, Hans Spatzenegger, Otto Striegel, Karl Struller, Leopold Trauner, Andreas Trum, Erich Wasicky, Waldemar Wolter, Viktor Zoller, and Adolf Zutter, German nationals or persons acting with German nationals, acting in pursuance of a common design to subject the persons hereinafter described to killings, beatings, tortures, starvation, abuses, and indignities, did, at or in the vicinity of the Mauthausen Concentration Camp, at Castle Hartheim, and at or in the vicinity of the Mauthausen sub-camps—Ebensee, Gros-Raming, Gunskirchen, Gusen, Hinterbrühl, Lambach, Linz, Loiblpass, Melk, Schwechat, St. Georgen, St. Lambrecht, St. Valentin, Steyr, Vienna, Wiener-Neudorf, all in Austria—at various and sundry times between January 1, 1942 and May 15, 1945, wilfully, deliberately and wrongfully encourage, aid, abet, and participate in the subjection of Poles, Frenchmen, Greeks, Jugoslavs, Citizens of the Soviet Union, Norwegians, Danes, Belgians, Citizens of the Netherlands, Citizens of the Grand Duchy of Luxembourg, Turks, British Subjects, stateless persons, Czechs, Chinese, Citizens of the United States of America, and other non-German nationals who were then and there in the custody of the German Reich, and members of the armed forces of nations then at war with the then German Reich who were then and there surrendered and unarmed prisoners of war in the custody of the German Reich, to killings, beatings, tortures, starvation, abuses and indignities, the exact names and numbers of such persons being unknown, but aggregating many thousands.

Notes

Introduction

1. See for instance Ilsen About, Stephan Matyus, and Gabriele Pflug, eds., *Das Sichtbare Unfassbare: Fotografien vom Konzentrationslager Mauthausen* (Vienna: Mandelbaum Verlag, 2005); Andreas Baumgartner, *Die vergessenen Frauen von Mauthausen* (Vienna: Verlag Österreich, 1997); Christian Bernadac, *Mauthausen* (Geneva: Ferni Publishing House, 1978); Evelyn Le Chêne, *Mauthausen: The History of a Death Camp* (London: Methuen, 1971); Michel Fabréguet, *Mauthausen: Camp de concentration national-socialiste en Autriche rattachée, 1938–1945* (Paris: Honoré Champion, 1999); Gordon Horwitz, *In the Shadow of Death: Living Outside the Gates of Mauthausen* (New York: Free Press, 1990); Hans Marsalek, *The History of Mauthausen Concentration Camp*, 3rd ed. (Vienna: Austrian Society of Mauthausen Concentration Camp, 1995); David Wingeate Pike, *Spaniards in the Holocaust: Mauthausen, the Horror on the Danube* (New York: Routledge, 2000). For an exhaustive bibliography of all Mauthausen literature, including journal articles and memoirs published through 1998, see Karl Stuhlfarrer, Bertrand Perz, and Florian Freund, *Bibliographie zur Geschichte des Konzentrationslagers Mauthausen* (Vienna: Forschungsgemeinschaft zur Geschichte des Nationalsozialismus, 1998).

2. Florian Freund, "Der Dachauer Mauthausenprozess," in *Dokumentationsarchiv des Österreichischen Widerstandes: Jahrbuch 2001* (Vienna: Dokumentationsarchiv des österreichischen Widerstandes, 2001); Bertrand Perz, "Prozesse zum KZ Mauthausen," in *Dachauer Prozesse: NS-Verbrechen vor amerikanischen Militärgerichten in Dachau, 1945–1948,*

ed. Ludwig Eiber and Robert Sigel (Göttingen: Wallstein Verlag, 2007). Though Joshua Greene's sensationalized biography of Chief Prosecutor William Denson contains a chapter on the Mauthausen trial, court proceedings are summarized in a highly abridged narrative. Joshua Greene, *Justice at Dachau: The Trials of an American Prosecutor* (New York: Broadway Books, 2003).

3. Patricia Heberer and Jürgen Matthaus, "War Crimes Trials and the Historian," in *Atrocities on Trial: The Politics of Prosecuting War Crimes in Historical Perspective*, ed. Jürgen Matthäus and Patricia Heberer (Lincoln: University of Nebraska Press, 2008), xxi.

4. See for instance Omer Bartov, *Hitler's Army: Soldiers, Nazis, and War in the Third Reich* (New York: Oxford University Press, 1991); Christopher R. Browning, *Ordinary Men: Reserve Police Battalion 101 and the Final Solution in Poland* (New York: Harper Collins, 1992) and *Nazi Policy, Jewish Workers, German Killers* (New York: Cambridge University Press, 2000); Edward B. Westermann, *Hitler's Police Battalions: Enforcing Racial War in the East* (Lawrence: University Press of Kansas, 2010).

5. The only monograph on the Dachau trial system as a whole remains Robert Sigel's *Im Interesse der Gerechtigkeit: Die Dachauer Kreigsverbrecherprozesse, 1945–1948* (Frankfurt: Campus Verlag, 1992). Frank M. Buscher's *The U.S. War Crimes Trial Program in Germany, 1946–1955* (Westport, CT: Greenwood Press, 1989) also includes an excellent overview. Two lengthy doctoral dissertations on the Dachau trials, Lisa Yavnai's "Military Justice: The U.S. Army War Crimes Trials in Germany, 1944–1947" (London School of Economics and Political Science, 2007) and Wesley Hilton's "The Blackest Canvas: U.S. Army Courts and the Trial of War Criminals in Post–World War II Europe" (Texas Tech University, 2003), remain unpublished. Other works dealing with narrower aspects of the Dachau trial program include Michael S. Bryant, "Punishing the Excess: Sadism, Bureaucratized Atrocity, and the U.S. Army Concentration Camp Trials, 1945–1945," in *Nazi Crimes and the Law*, ed. Henry Friedlander and Nathan Stolzfus (Cambridge: Cambridge University Press, 2008); William Dowdell Denson, *Justice in Germany: Memories of the Chief Prosecutor* (Mineola, NY: Meltzer et al., 1995); Ludwig Eiber and Robert Sigel, eds., *Dachauer Prozesse: NS-Verbrechen vor amerikanischen Militärgerichten in Dachau, 1945–1948* (Göttingen: Wallstein Verlag, 2007); Patricia Heberer, "The American Commission Trials of 1945," in Friedlander and Stoltzfus, *Nazi Crimes;* Holger Less-

ing, *Der erste Dachauer Prozess, 1945–1946* (Baden Baden: Nomos Verlagsgesellschaft, 1993); Augusto Nigro, *Wolfsangel: A German City on Trial, 1945–48* (Washington, DC: Brasseys, 2000); James J. Weingartner, *Crossroads of Death: The Story of the Malmédy Massacre and Trial* (Los Angeles: University of California Press, 1979); Lisa Yavnai, "U.S. Army War Crimes Trials in Germany, 1945–1947," in Matthäus and Heberer, *Atrocities on Trial*.

1. War Crimes Trials and the U.S. Army

1. See Martin Gilbert, *Auschwitz and the Allies* (New York: Henry Holt, 1981), chapters 2–5.
2. On June 30, 1941, for instance, three major British papers published stories that described genocide. A headline in the *Times* read MASSACRE OF JEWS—OVER 1,000,000 DEAD SINCE THE WAR BEGAN; the *Daily Mail* reported GREATEST POGROM—ONE MILLION JEWS DIE; the *Manchester Guardian* read JEWISH WAR VICTIMS—MORE THAN A MILLION DEAD. Papers in the United States published equally alarming stories. See Gilbert, *Auschwitz and the Allies*, 43–44. For an in-depth study of reportage in the *New York Times*, see Laurel Leff, *Buried by "The Times": The Holocaust and America's Most Important Newspaper* (New York: Cambridge University Press, 2005).
3. Robert Sigel, *Im Interesse der Gerechtigkeit: Die Dachauer Kriegsverbrecherprozesse, 1945–1948* (Frankfurt: Campus, 1992), 12.
4. The term "United Nations" had been introduced January 1, 1942, to describe the alliance of the Big Three, China, and twenty-two other nations in the struggle against Germany, Italy, and Japan; "11 Allies Condemn Nazi War on Jews," *New York Times*, December 18, 1942.
5. Ibid.
6. Telford Taylor, *The Anatomy of the Nuremberg Trials* (New York: Little, Brown, 1992), 28.
7. Arieh J. Kochavi, *Prelude to Nuremberg: Allied War Crimes Policy and the Question of Punishment* (Chapel Hill: University of North Carolina Press, 1998), 133.
8. Ibid.
9. Winston Churchill, Franklin Roosevelt, and Joseph Stalin, "Moscow Declaration, November 1, 1943," in *The Nuremberg War Crimes Trial, 1945–46: A Documentary History*, ed. Michael Marrus (Boston: Bedford Books, 1997), 20–21.

10. Ibid.
11. Lisa Yavnai, "U.S. Army War Crimes Trials in Germany, 1945–1947," in *Atrocities on Trial: Historical Perspectives on the Politics of Prosecuting War Crimes,* ed. Jürgen Matthäus and Patricia Heberer (Lincoln: University of Nebraska Press, 2008), 50.
12. Frank M. Buscher contends that the Moscow Declaration was in fact "rhetoric over substance." See Buscher's *The U.S. War Crimes Trial Program in Germany, 1946–1955* (Westport, CT: Greenwood Press, 1989), 10.
13. Ibid., 9.
14. The Kharkov trial was held before the Military Tribunal of the Fourth Ukrainian Front and resulted in the hanging of four German soldiers for the killing of Soviet POWs and civilians.
15. Kochavi, *Prelude,* 66.
16. Donald Bloxham, *Genocide on Trial: War Crimes Trials and the Formation of Holocaust History and Memory* (New York: Oxford University Press, 2001), 8.
17. Ibid., 9.
18. The precedent refers specifically to Napoleon's forced exile on Saint Helena, which was imposed according to a political rather than judicial decision. See Taylor, *Anatomy,* 30.
19. Lieutenant Colonel Murray Bernays was put in charge of formulating a specific policy by Assistant Secretary of War John McCloy. Bernays proposed that major Nazi Party and state organizations be tried by an international court as essential parts of a *conspiracy* to commit war crimes. The trial of those considered to be the leaders of these organizations would illustrate the conspiratorial nature of the organization in question. The rank-and-file of these organizations could then be dealt with rapidly, their guilt already established by virtue of their membership alone. See Taylor, *Anatomy,* 35.
20. Yavnai, "U.S. Army," 50.
21. Ibid.
22. The command comprising the U.S. armed forces in Europe was known as "European Theater of Operations, United States Army" until July 1, 1945, and as "United States Forces, European Theater," until the spring of 1947; Theatre Judge Advocate, hereafter referred to as the Judge Advocate.
23. Bloxham, *Genocide,* 8.

24. Lieutenant Colonel C. E. Straight, *Report of the Deputy Judge Advocate for War Crimes, European Command, June 1944 to July 1948,* 247 pages, National Archives and Records Administration (hereafter NARA), Record Group 549, General Admin., box 13, pp. 3–4.

25. Ibid., 17.

26. Ibid., 4.

27. Ibid., 35.

28. Ibid.

29. Wesley Vincent Hilton, "The Blackest Canvas: U.S. Army Courts and the Trial of War Criminals in Post–World War II Europe" (PhD dissertation, Texas Tech University, 2003), 95–96.

30. James J. Weingartner, *Crossroads of Death: The Story of the Malmédy Massacre and Trial* (Los Angeles: University of California Press, 1979).

31. War Department letter; subject: Establishment of War Crimes Offices, December 25, 1944. Provided for the establishment of a branch in the Office of the Judge Advocate, European Theater, under the supervision of the Judge Advocate General—"its primary function being the investigation of alleged war crimes, and the collection of evidence relating thereto, including, for transmission to the governments concerned, evidence relating to war crimes committed against nationals of other United Nations." Quoted in Straight, *Report,* 18.

32. Ibid., 5.

33. Ibid., 3–4.

34. Ibid., 5.

35. George S. Patton, *War as I Knew It* (Cambridge, MA: Riverside Press, 1947), 294.

36. Dwight D. Eisenhower, *Crusade in Europe* (Garden City, NY: Doubleday, 1948), 409.

37. Letter, Headquarters, Euro Theatre of Operations—Subject: War Crimes Interrogation of US Military and Civilian Personnel, April 28, 1945. Quoted in Straight, *Report,* 19.

38. Yavnai, "U.S. Army," 54.

39. JCS 1023/10—Directive on the Identification and Apprehension of Persons Suspected of War Crimes or Other Offenses and Trial of Certain Offenders, July 8, 1945, NARA RG 549, General Admin., box 1.

40. Ibid.

41. Report—War Crimes Activities, August 17, 1949. Attached to document: Headquarters—United States Forces European Theatre—to

Commanding General—Third Army Area re. War Crimes Trial Cases, October 14, 1946, NARA RG 549, General Admin., box 9.

42. Lisa Yavnai, "Military Justice: The U.S. Army War Crimes Trials in Germany, 1944–1947" (PhD dissertation, London School of Economics and Political Science, 2007), 126.

43. Eisenhower to commanding generals, 25 August 1945. Quoted in Yavnai, "U.S. Army," 54.

44. Report—War Crimes Activities.

45. Report—War Crimes Activities.

46. International Military Tribunal, "Charter of the International Military Tribunal," in *Trial of the Major War Criminals before the International Military Tribunal, Nuremberg, 14 November 1945–1 October 1946,* vol. 1 (Nuremberg: International Military Tribunal, 1947), 11.

47. Under Control Council Law No. 10, the United States held twelve additional trials at Nuremberg, aimed at major institutions of the Nazi state. In total, these trials involved 185 defendants from the SS, police, judiciary, medical profession, industrial and financial concerns, the military, and the diplomatic service. The only other trial ultimately conducted under Control Council Law No. 10 was at Rastatt, where French prosecutors charged five German industrialists with contributing to Germany's war of aggression and making use of slave labor.

48. Yavnai, "Military Justice," 128. The International Military Tribunal at Nuremberg tried 22 of the most powerful figures of the Reich; the subsequent proceedings at Nuremberg involved an additional 185 defendants. Because the high-command case at Nuremberg did not finish until the spring of 1948, it is not included in the number cited. The Dachau trial series was brought to a close at the end of 1947.

49. Benjamin Ferencz, interview by the author, April 11, 2006.

50. Hilton, "Blackest," 11.

51. Yavnai, "Military Justice," 27–30; Hilton, "Blackest," 37.

52. Hilton, "Blackest," 11.

53. Ibid., 34.

54. Ovid L. Futch, *The History of Andersonville Prison* (Hialeah: University of Florida Press, 1968), 2.

55. Ibid., 117.

56. While the international movement to institutionalize laws of warfare was largely a product of the nineteenth century, the idea of codifying

the conduct of war was not new. For instance, the Chinese warrior Sun Tzu in the sixth century B.C. suggested limitations be created for the ways war could be waged. Other early examples include the Hindu code of Manu, from c. 200 B.C., which included within it the concept of war crimes. Society of Professional Journalists, *Reference Guide to the Geneva Conventions,* www.genevaconventions.org.

57. Hague Convention IV, Respecting the Laws and Customs of War on Land (1907), in *The Hague Conventions and Declarations of 1899 and 1907,* ed. James Brown Scott (New York: Oxford Press, 1915), 108.

58. Ibid.

59. William Denson, interview by Horace Hansen, June 14, 1984. Transcript, William Dowdell Denson Papers, Manuscripts and Archives, Yale University Library, Manuscript Group 1832 (hereafter cited as Denson Papers), Series 1—Personal, box 2, folder 10.

60. Hilton, "Blackest," 11.

61. Denson, interview by Hansen.

62. Allied and Associated Powers, *The Treaty of Peace between the Allied and Associated Powers and Germany, June 28, 1919,* Article 228 (London: H.M. Stationery Office, 1919), 100.

63. The Allied powers that submitted lists of persons to be tried did not include the United States, which by 1920 had taken a decidedly isolationist position in world politics. Further, President Woodrow Wilson was opposed to the idea of punishing individuals and was wary that such trials would appear to be nothing more than "victor's justice." Wilson feared that such trials might stir up considerable resentment and drive the Germans toward communism. See Kochavi, *Prelude,* 2–3.

64. Michael Marrus, "Historical Precedents," in *The Nuremberg War Crimes Trial, 1945–46: A Documentary History,* ed. Michael Marrus (Boston: Bedford Books, 1997), 3.

65. Ibid., 4.

66. Ibid.

67. Hilton, "Blackest," 57.

68. Marrus, "Historical Precedents," 12.

69. Ibid.

70. Valerie Hébert, "Hitler's Soldiers on Trial: The High Command Case in Historical Perspective" (PhD dissertation, University of Toronto, 2006), 79.

71. William Denson, interview by Joan Ringelheim, August 25, 1994, video, United States Holocaust Memorial Museum Film and Video Archive, RG-50.030*0268.
72. *Rules of Procedure in Military Government Courts,* June 1945. Reproduced in Holger Lessing, *Der Erste Dachauer Prozess, 1945–1946* (Baden Baden: Nomos, 1993), appendix 5.
73. Circular 132—Headquarters, U.S. Forces, European Theater: Definition of War Crimes—October 2, 1945. Reproduced in Straight, *Report,* appendix 8.
74. The preamble to the Fourth Hague Convention provides guidance on this issue. It states that "the High Contracting Parties think it expedient to declare that in cases not included in the regulations adopted by them, populations and belligerents remain under the protection and the rule of the principles of the Law of Nations, as they result from the usages established between civilized nations, from the laws of humanity and the requirements of the public conscience." See Manfred Lachs, *War Crimes: An Attempt to Define the Issues* (London: Stevens and Sons, 1945), 7.
75. The terms "military commission courts" and "military government courts" are for all intents and purposes interchangeable; the latter term was adopted once the U.S. Army had established military government in Germany.
76. *Rules of Procedure in Military Government Courts,* June 1945. Reproduced in Lessing, *Der Erste,* appendix 5.
77. Straight, *Report,* 71.
78. Ibid.
79. *Guide to Procedure in Military Courts,* June 1945. Reproduced in Lessing, *Der Erste,* appendix 6.
80. Hilton, "Blackest," 192.
81. *Guide to Procedure in Military Courts.*
82. Ibid.
83. Ibid., 13–14.
84. Ibid., 54.
85. Ibid., 13–14.
86. Alexandra-Eileen Wenck, *Zwischen Menschenhandel und "Endlösung": Das Konzentrationslager Bergen-Belsen* (Paderborn: Ferdinand Schöningh, 2000), 390.
87. Belsen trial details from http://www.stephen-stratford.co.uk/belsen_trial.htm, accessed 5/10/2011.

88. "Conspiracy is the agreement of two or more persons to effect any unlawful purpose whether as their aim, or only as a means to it." Courtney Stanhope Kenny, *Outline of Criminal Law*, 15th ed. (Cambridge: Cambridge University Press, 1936), 335.

89. Hilton, "Blackest," 275.

90. Ibid.

91. The Supreme Court of Leipzig had earlier ruled that "the subordinate obeying an order is liable to punishment, if it was known to him that the order of the superior involved the infringement of civil or military law." The Llandovery Castle case, *Annual Digest 1923–1924*, Case No. 235, Full Report, 1921 (CMD 1450), p. 45—Reproduced at www.icrc.org.

92. Hilton, "Blackest," 222.

93. Patricia Heberer, "The American Commission Trials of 1945," in *Nazi Crimes and the Law*, ed. Henry Friedlander and Nathan Stoltzfus (Cambridge: Cambridge University Press, 2008), 49.

94. Hilton, "Blackest," 224.

95. Ibid., 226.

96. See also discussion of *The United States v. Goebell et al.* in Straight, *Report,* 57. Like the Gerstenberg case, no lawyer was present during the trial. Nonetheless, the case review stated that "in view of the absence of any provision specifying the amount of legal training and experience of such member and in the absence of assignment of functions and responsibilities to him analogous to those of the law member of general courts-martial, it was held that the failure to appoint a legally trained officer did not result in injustice to the accused."

97. Earl W. Kintner, ed., *The Hadamar Trial* (London: William Hodge, 1949), xxiv.

98. Patricia Heberer, "Early Postwar Justice in the American Zone—The 'Hadamar Murder Factory' Trial," in Matthäus and Heberer, *Atrocities on Trial,* 28–30.

99. Kintner, *Hadamar,* xxv.

100. Ibid., 14.

101. Heberer, "American Commission Trials," 55.

102. This charge also bears resemblance to those used to bring members of the American Mafia to justice during the racketeering trials of the 1980s. See Hilton, "Blackest," 231.

103. Kintner, *Hadamar,* xxiv.

104. Hilton, "Blackest," 231.

105. Ibid.
106. Denson, interview by Ringelheim.
107. Yavnai, "U.S. Army," 56.
108. Straight, *Report,* 50.
109. Joshua Greene, *Justice at Dachau: The Trials of an American Prosecutor* (New York: Broadway Books, 2003), 35.
110. William Denson, Speech at North Shore Synagogue, Syosset, NY, April 12, 1991, transcript, Denson Papers, Series 1—Personal, box 3, folder 25.
111. Yavnai, "U.S. Army," 56.
112. Hans-Günther Richardi, *Schule der Gewalt: Das Konzentrationslager Dachau, 1933–34: Ein dokumentarischer Bericht* (Munich: C. H Beck, 1983), 248.
113. Ibid.
114. William Denson, Curriculum Vitae, Denson Papers, Series 1—Personal, box 1, folder 1.
115. Denson's maternal great-grandfather had been a lawyer and member of the Alabama State Congress and had fought as a colonel in the siege of Vicksburg during the Civil War. His grandfather was Chief Justice of the Supreme Court of Alabama. Denson's paternal grandfather had been an Alabama congressman, while his father was a respected Birmingham lawyer and politician. See Denson, interview by Ringelheim.
116. William Denson, interview by Mark Goldberg, March 12, 1996, USC Shoah Foundation Institute Visual History Archive, Interview 13079; Greene, *Justice,* 20.
117. For further biographical information on William Denson see Greene, *Justice.*
118. William Dowdell Denson, *Justice in Germany: Memories of the Chief Prosecutor* (Mineola, NY: Meltzer et al., 1995), 3.
119. Greene, *Justice,* 41.
120. Military Government Court—Charge Sheet, Dachau, Germany, November 2, 1945. In Lessing, *Der Erste,* appendix 11, 383–385.
121. Ibid.
122. It is likely that Denson borrowed the common-design strategy from prosecutor Leon Jaworski, who assisted in the preparation of the Dachau case for trial. During the Hartgen case, in which Jaworski tried eleven men for the killing of six American fliers, Jaworski in his closing arguments drew on the concept of a common design. Leon Jaworski, *After Fifteen Years* (Houston: Gulf Publishing, 1961).

123. "Charter of the International Military Tribunal," Article 6, in *Trial of the Major War Criminals,* 1:10.

124. United Nations War Crimes Commission, *Law Reports of Trials of War Criminals,* vol. 11 (London, 1949), Denson Papers, Series 2—Trials, 1945–2001, box 4, folder 4.

125. Ibid.

126. Ibid.

127. *The United States v. Martin Weiss et al.,* Case no. 000–50–2, NARA RG 549, War Crimes Case Files (Cases Tried).

128. Sigel, *Im Interesse,* 60; Greene, *Justice,* 36.

129. Headquarters, United States Forces, European Theater, AG 000.5 JAG-AGO; October 14, 1945, Subject: Trial of War Crimes Cases, To: Commanding General, Third US Army Area. Reproduced in Straight, *Report,* appendix 10, 119.

130. Denson, Speech to North Shore Synagogue.

131. Hilton, "Blackest," 297.

2. American Investigators at Mauthausen

1. See for instance Raul Hilberg, *The Destruction of the European Jews,* 3rd ed. (New Haven, CT: Yale University Press, 2003), chapter 9, "Killing Center Operations"; Lucy Dawidowicz, *The War against the Jews, 1933–1945* (New York: Bantam Books, 1981), 281.

2. "'Honor' for Upper Austria—A Concentration Camp," London *Times,* March 30, 1938. Archiv der KZ-Gedenkstätte Mauthausen (hereafter AMM), A/5/3.

3. The Wiener Graben was out of use when the city of Vienna officially turned it over to DEST on August 18, 1938. See Andreas Baumgartner, *Die vergessenen Frauen von Mauthausen* (Vienna: Verlag Österreich, 1997), 84.

4. Ilsen About, Stephan Matyus, and Gabriele Pflug, eds., *Das Sichtbare Unfassbare: Fotografien vom Konzentrationslager Mauthausen* (Vienna: Mandelbaum Verlag, 2005), 46.

5. There were 36 recorded deaths at Mauthausen in 1938 and 445 in 1939; a prisoner could expect to survive fifteen months during this time period. See Gordon Horwitz, *In the Shadow of Death: Living Outside the Gates of Mauthausen* (New York: Free Press, 1990), 12–13; Hans Marsalek, *The History of Mauthausen Concentration Camp,* 3rd ed. (Vienna: Austrian Society of Mauthausen Concentration Camp, 1995), 46.

6. Marsalek estimates that a nonworker required 2,300 calories/day; a worker required 3,000–4,000. At Mauthausen, workers got only 1,400–1,500 calories—and were receiving only 600–1,000 by 1945. Marsalek, *Mauthausen*, 59.

7. Bertrand Perz et al., *Die Krematorien von Mauthausen: Katalog zur Ausstellung in der KZ-Gedenkstätte Mauthausen* (Vienna: Bundesministerium für Inneres, 2008), 28.

8. Der Chef der Sicherheitspolizei und des SD, Berlin, January 2, 1941. G.J Nr. 120—Geheim. AMM A/7/5.

9. Michel Fabréguet, *Mauthausen: Camp de concentration national-socialiste en Autriche rattachée, 1938–1945* (Paris: Honoré Champion, 1999), 164; Marsalek, *Mauthausen*, 125.

10. Falk Pigel, *Häftlinge unter SS-Herrschaft: Widerstand, Selbstbehauptung und Vernichtung im Konzentrationslager* (Hamburg: Hoffmann und Campe, 1978), 81n73.

11. Ibid.

12. Horwitz, *In the Shadow of Death*, 17.

13. Marsalek, *Mauthausen*, 198, 200.

14. Pierre-Serge Choumoff states that a total of 3,455 victims of the gas chambers are counted in Mauthausen camp documents, yet the total is almost certainly higher. Marsalek concludes the total number of those who died in the gas chamber at Mauthausen stands between 4,000 and 5,000. Choumoff, *Nationalsozialistische Massentötungen durch Giftgas auf österreichischem gebiet, 1940–1945* (Vienna: Bundesministerium für Inneres, 2001), 105; Marsalek, *Mauthausen*, 201–202.

15. David Wingeate Pike, *Spaniards in the Holocaust: Mauthausen, the Horror on the Danube* (New York: Routledge, 2000), 18.

16. Memorandum of Agreement between Heinrich Himmler and Minister of Justice Thierack, September 1942, http://fcit.usf.edu/holocaust/resource/document/docsla13.htm (accessed March 2007). See also Marsalek, *Mauthausen*, 116n8.

17. Michel Fabréguet, "Entwicklung und Veränderung der Funktionen des Konzentrationslagers Mauthausen, 1938–1945," in *Die nationalsozialistischen Konzentrationslager: Entwicklung and Struktur—Band 1*, ed. Ulrich Herbert et al. (Göttingen: Wallstein, 1998), 202.

18. Aufstellung der Lagerschreibstube über Zu- und Abgänge von SV-Häftlingen, AMM O/2/1.

19. Bauleiter Naumann to Topf and Sons, "Betr.: Verbrennungsofen KL Mauthausen u. Gusen," July 9, 1941, AMM N/7/8.

20. Horwitz, *In the Shadow of Death,* 18.

21. Fabréguet, "Entwicklung und Veränderung," 202.

22. Florian Freund, *Concentration Camp Ebensee* (Vienna: Austrian Resistance Archives, 1990), 30.

23. Der Reichsführer SS an 1) Chef der Sicherheitspolizei und des SD, 2) Chef des WVHA. Geheim. 5.7.44. AMM A/7/4.

24. Marsalek, *Mauthausen,* 59.

25. Bertrand Perz, *Die KZ-Gedenkstätte Mauthausen 1945 bis zur Gegenwart* (Innsbruck: Studein Verlag, 2006), 166.

26. Fabréguet, *Mauthausen: Camp de concentration,* 163. According to Pierre-Serge Choumoff, 1,168 prisoners were murdered at Hartheim in 1941 and an additional 445 in 1942. Choumoff, *Nationalsozialistische Massentötungen,* 78.

27. Baumgartner, *Die vergessenen,* 86.

28. Gottfried Fliedl and Bertrand Perz, *Konzentrationslager Melk* (Freistadt: Plöchl-Druckgesellschaft, 1992), 52; Wesley Vincent Hilton, "The Blackest Canvas: U.S. Army Courts and the Trial of War Criminals in Post–World War II Europe" (PhD dissertation, Texas Tech University, 2003), 106.

29. Florian Freund, "Häftlingskategorien und Sterblichkeit in einem Außenlager des KZ Mauthausen," in Ulrich Herbert et al., *Die nationalsozialistischen Konzentrationslager,* 2:879.

30. Horwitz, *In the Shadow of Death,* 144.

31. The death books of Mauthausen and Gusen record 14,336 Jewish deaths. This number does not include the additional 10,000 unregistered Jewish deaths, made up predominately of those evacuated to Mauthausen in March/April 1945 from forced labor camps in eastern Austria. See Marsalek, *Mauthausen,* 148, 292.

32. Fabréguet, "Entwicklung und Veränderung," 202.

33. Marsalek, *Mauthausen,* 144.

34. Ibid., 201.

35. Fabréguet, *Mauthausen: Camp de concentration,* 163. The ultimate tally of the dead at Mauthausen is difficult to establish. The death books at Mauthausen and Gusen show a combined total of 71,856 dead. However, this statistic does not include the huge numbers of unregistered prisoners murdered at Mauthausen. This includes those gassed at Hart-

heim, the thousands of mostly Hungarian Jews who died in the tent camp, a large portion of Soviet prisoners of war, etc. See both Fabré-guet, *Mauthausen: Camp de concentration,* chapter 3, and Marsalek, *Mauthausen,* 132–144, for an in-depth analysis of the statistics and a discussion of the problems involved in arriving at a final number.

36. Pike, *Spaniards,* 233.
37. Ibid., 234.
38. Louis Cernjar, letter to wife, Austria, May 9, 1945. AMM U/1/14.
39. Bericht eines unbekannten Belgiers über das "Internationale Befreiung-skomitee des Konzentrationslagers Mauthausen" für das belgische Außenministerium, AMM St/07/01.
40. Ibid.
41. Ibid.
42. Hilton, "Blackest," 127.
43. Benjamin Ferencz, interview by the author, April 11, 2006.
44. Lisa Yavnai, "U.S. Army War Crimes Trials in Germany, 1945–1947," in *Atrocities on Trial: The Politics of Prosecuting War Crimes in Historical Perspective,* ed. Jürgen Matthäus and Patricia Heberer (Lincoln: University of Nebraska Press, 2008), 4; Ferencz, interview.
45. Ibid.
46. War Crimes Investigation Team 6836, Subject: "DAWES" and MAUTHAU-SEN cases, January 14, 1946, NARA RG 549, War Crimes Case Files (Cases Tried), box 334.
47. Ausweis von Heinrich Dürmayer, May 7, 1945, AMM V/05/01/02.
48. Ausweis von Dobias Premsyl, AMM U/04b/02.
49. Aufforderung zur Zeugenaussage an die ehemaligen Häftlinge des KLM, unterzeichnet von Ludwig Soswinski, AMM U/04a/08.
50. Quoted in Florian Freund, "Der Dachauer Mauthausenprozess," in *Jahrbuch 2001, Dokumentationsarchiv des österreichischen Widerstandes,* ed. Christine Schindler (Vienna: Dokumentationsarchiv des österreichischen Widerstandes, 2001), 43.
51. Ernst Martin, Lebenslauf—Mauthausen, May 7, 1945. AMM E/1a/13.
52. Ibid.
53. The Death Books of Mauthausen and Gusen, NARA RG 238, National Archives Collection of World War II War Crimes Records, United States Council for the Prosecution of Axis Criminality—United States Exhibits, 1933–46, boxes 14–15.
54. Mauthausen Death Book Number Six, January to March 1945, NARA RG 238, National Archives Collection of World War II War Crimes

Records, United States Council for the Prosecution of Axis Criminality—United States Exhibits, 1933–46, box 15.

55. See About, Matyus, and Pflug, *Das Sichtbare Unfassbare;* Benito Bermajo, *Francisco Boix, El Fotógrafo de Mauthausen* (Barcelona: RBA, 2002).

56. Stephan Matyus and Gabriele Pflug, "Fotographien vom Konzentrationslager Mauthausen—ein Überblick," in About, Matyus, and Pflug, *Das Sichtbare Unfassbare,* 29.

57. Benjamin B. Ferencz, *Less Than Slaves: Jewish Forced Labor and the Quest for Compensation* (Cambridge, MA: Harvard University Press, 1979), 53; Ferencz, interview.

58. Pike, *Spaniards,* 262.

59. The first commandant of Mauthausen was Albert Sauer, who had previously served at Sachsenhausen. He was relieved from his position in February 1939 for "laziness." He was killed in uncertain circumstances on May 3, 1945.

60. Pike, *Spaniards,* 52.

61. Various accounts of Ziereis's capture exist, though the one presented here was confirmed by Ziereis himself during his interrogation. For complete details, see Marsalek, letter to Emil Valley, General Secretary—Amicale Nationale des Déportés at Familles de Disparus de Mauthausen et ses Commandos, April 10, 1969. AMM P/18/10. Interestingly, the circumstances of Ziereis's shooting and death apparently remained obscure to Chief Prosecutor William Denson. Upon meeting war crimes investigator and Nuremberg prosecutor Benjamin Ferencz in the 1990s, Denson shocked him by reportedly asking if *he* had killed Ziereis. Ferencz, interview.

62. Bermajo, *El Fotógrafo de Mauthausen,* 167–169.

63. Marsalek, letter to Emil Valley.

64. There are a number of different records of Ziereis's interrogation, which contain overlapping information. According to Hans Marsalek, this does not reflect inconsistency, but rather the fact that a number of people took notes during the interrogation but were present at different times. The different manuscripts can therefore be used together to construct a more complete record of the interrogation. See Marsalek, letter to Emil Valley.

65. Niederschrift des Verhöres des SS-Standartenführers Ziereis, Franz, ehemaliger Lagerkommandant des Konzentrationslager Mauthausen, May 24, 1945. AMM P/18/2.

66. Aussage von Franz Ziereis, Übersetzung aus dem Englischen, May 24, 1945. AMM P/18/2/1.

67. Niederschrift des Verhöres des SS-Standartenführers Ziereis.

68. Aussage von Franz Ziereis.

69. Marsalek, letter to Emil Valley; Aussage von Franz Ziereis; Niederschrift des Verhöres des SS-Standartenführers Ziereis. See footnote 33 for accurate mortality statistics.

70. See for instance Eugene S. Cohen, HQ Third United States Army, Report of Investigation of Alleged War Crime, June 17, 1945, NARA RG 549, War Crimes Case Files (Cases Tried), box 334, 278 pages, 6–8. Also, William Denson, Opening Statement, *USA v. Hans Altfuldisch et al.*, Trial Transcript, 3,512 pages. Denson Papers, Series 2: Trials—box 8, folder 37, 89–90.

71. Cohen, Report.

72. Ibid., 6.

73. In a report later submitted to military officials at Dachau, Martin listed the total number of unregistered deaths to be 57,911, bringing the grand total of dead to 129,767. See Ernst Martin, Erklärung—Tatsächliche Totenzahlen im gesamten K.L. Mauthausen nach Nationen, February 25, 1946. AMM H/9/3. It should also be noted that the Cohen Report includes a careless translation of the summary of facts that Martin and Ulbrecht swore to. Though both their actual report (Exhibit 4) and the death books show 71,856 deaths, the Memorandum in Regard to Death List of Deceased and Murdered Prisoners, signed by Cohen, lists 171,856 dead. See Cohen, Report, 21.

74. Cohen, Report, 24.

75. Ibid., 34–43.

76. Ibid., 142, 259.

77. Ibid., 8.

78. Ibid., 6.

79. Ibid., 5.

80. Ibid., 8.

81. Debórah Dwork and Robert Jan van Pelt, *Auschwitz, 1270 to the Present* (New York: W. W. Norton, 1996), 343.

82. Fabréguet, *Mauthausen: Camp de concentration,* 163. See footnote 35 for further discussion of Mauthausen statistics.

83. Cohen, Report, 43; Report of Two U.S. Physicians, re. Inspection of Mauthausen Concentration Camp, May 24, 1945, NARA RG 549, War Crimes Case Files (Cases Tried), box 335.

84. Exhibit 213 is a brief report concerning Hartheim, which contains no statistics or discussions of overall mortality. According to Cohen's description of the exhibit in question, he was clearly referring to Exhibit 215—the death books. See Cohen, Report, 277.

85. War Crimes Investigating Team 6836, "DAWES" and MAUTHAUSEN, 4.

86. Similar extrapolation can be found in the report of War Crimes Investigating Team 6824, concerning gassing at Hartheim. The report cites 65,000 deaths, based on the fact that a book found there pointed to "18,269 deaths from the start in May, 1940 to the end of August, 1941." Because one witness claimed that "most came in 1942–43," investigators simply multiplied the number 18,269 by the remaining years that the facility operated. See War Crimes Investigating Team No. 6824, HQ, Third US Army, Report of Investigation of War Crime, to Commanding General, Third US Army, July 17, 1945. Denson Papers, Series 2—Trials, box 7, folder 34.

87. Cohen, Report, 6–7.

88. SS-Hauptsturmführer Georg Bachmayer was responsible for the Mauthausen garrison and in charge of security, discipline, and capital punishment in the camp. He fled with his wife and two children into the Schönwald in the area of Priehetsberg; there he shot them and killed himself. The following day the bodies were burned. See Die SS-Angehörigen nach der Befreiung: Chronik—Nachtrag re. Georg Bachmayer. AMM P/18/13.

89. Cohen, Report, 11–16.

90. Third Geneva Convention, Article V, http://www.yale.edu/lawweb/ava lon/lawofwar/geneva02.htm.

91. See Lieutenant Colonel C. E. Straight, Report of the Deputy Judge Advocate for War Crimes, European Command, June 1944 to July 1948. 247, NARA, RG 549, General Admin., box 13, 13–14.

92. Robert Sigel, *Im Interesse der Gerechtigkeit: Die Dachauer Kriegsverbrecherprozesse, 1945–1948* (Frankfurt: Campus Verlag, 1992), 32.

93. It should be noted that while Guth denies abusing the suspects he interrogated, he asks the interviewer to turn off the tape recorder on various occasions before providing details. See Paul Guth, interview by Joshua Greene, Lafayette, LA, February 24, 2001. Four cassette tapes, Denson Papers—Series 5—Audiovisual Materials, 1918–2004, boxes 46–49.

94. Ferencz, interview.

95. Ibid.

96. "Eigruber Trap Used U.S. Agent as Nazi's Driver," *New York Herald Tribune,* October 15, 1945, NARA RG 549, War Crimes Case Files (Cases Tried), box 336.

97. First Detailed Interrogation Report of August Eigruber, November 14, 1945, NARA RG 549, War Crimes Case Files (Cases Tried), box 336.

98. Report on Preliminary Interrogation of August Eigruber, Former Gauleiter of Upper Austria, United States Forces in Austria, NARA RG 549, War Crimes Case Files (Cases Tried), box 336.

99. Eigruber Protokoll, AMM P/9/11, 10.

100. Ibid., 8.

3. The Prosecution Crafts Its Case

1. Of 3,887 cases investigated, the Deputy Judge Advocate for War Crimes closed 3,029, often because of the relatively minor nature of the crimes in question, because of a lack of sufficient evidence, or because the accused remained at large. The 858 cases that remained were consolidated into 462 trials. Lisa Yavnai, "U.S. Army War Crimes Trials in Germany, 1945–1947," in *Atrocities on Trial: Historical Perspectives on the Politics of Prosecuting War Crimes,* ed. Jürgen Matthäus and Patricia Heberer (Lincoln: University of Nebraska Press, 2008), 55.

2. William Denson, interview by Joan Ringelheim, August 25, 1994, video, United States Holocaust Memorial Museum Film and Video Archive, RG-50.030*0268.

3. See Chapter 1.

4. Denson, interview by Ringelheim.

5. Ibid.

6. William Denson, Speech to North Shore Synagogue, April 12, 1991, Denson Papers, Series 1—Personal, box 2, folder 25.

7. Paul Guth, interview by Joshua Greene, Lafayette, LA, February 24, 2001, four cassette tapes, Denson Papers, Series 5—Audiovisual Materials, 1918–2004, boxes 46–49.

8. Ibid.

9. Joshua Greene, *Justice at Dachau: The Trials of an American Prosecutor* (New York: Broadway Books, 2003), 130.

10. Robert H. Jackson, Report to the President, 7 October, 1946, Papers of Robert Houghwout Jackson, Library of Congress Manuscripts

Division, box 108, file: Nuremberg War Crimes Trial—Official Files—United States Chief of Counsel—Reports.

11. Lieutenant Colonel C. E. Straight, *Report of the Deputy Judge Advocate for War Crimes, European Command, June 1944 to July 1948,* 247 pages, NARA RG 549, General Admin., box 13, 36.

12. Guth, interview.

13. Greene, *Justice,* 40.

14. In a bizarre twist, von Posern was later sentenced to life in prison in one of the subsequent proceedings spawned by the first Mauthausen trial—the very one he helped to organize. Various witnesses testified that von Posern had beaten a number of prisoners to death while working for the camp SS in St. Valentin, a subcamp of Mauthausen. Deputy Judge Advocate, 7708 War Crimes Group, Review and Recommendations, *United States v. Hanscarl von Posern* [*sic*], Case 000–50–5–46, February 26, 1948, NARA RG 549, War Crimes Case Files (Cases Tried), box 421.

15. Denson, interview by Ringelheim.

16. Ibid.

17. "Nuremberg Prosecutor [*sic*] Reflects on History's Judgment of Evil," *New York Times,* May 6, 1990.

18. Denson, interview by Ringelheim.

19. Ibid.

20. Ibid.

21. See Franz Josef Kohl, interview by Dr. Alexander Becker, WCIT 6836, January 18, 1946, Transcript, AMM V/3/9; August Kamhuber, interview by Dr. Alexander Becker, WCIT 6836, January 18, 1946, Transcript, AMM V/3/11.

22. War Crimes Investigation Team 6836—letter, June 17, 1945, NARA RG 549, War Crimes Case Files (Cases Tried), box 335.

23. Lieutenant Jack H. Taylor, Report on Concentration Camp Mauthausen, May 1945, NARA RG 549, War Crimes Case Files (Cases Tried), box 336.

24. Western Union telegram, Lieutenant Jack Taylor to judge advocate general, March 20, 1946, NARA RG 549, War Crimes Case Files (Cases Tried), box 336.

25. Yavnai, "U.S Army," 61.

26. Greene, *Justice,* 29.

27. Yavnai, "U.S Army," 61.

28. Guth, interview.

29. For further discussion of the parent trial system see Chapter 1.

30. William Denson, interview for *Dachau: Justice on Trial* (film transcript), Denson Papers, Series 1—Personal, box 1, folder 4, 14.

31. Guth, interview.

32. Ibid. It should also be noted that while Guth did share his opinions on this matter during his interview, he also repeatedly asked that the tape recorder be turned off as he explained other aspects of the selection process.

33. Ibid.

34. Ibid.

35. Denson, Speech to North Shore Synagogue.

36. "Eigruber Trap Used U.S Agent as Nazi's Driver," *New York Herald Tribune*, October 15, 1945, NARA RG 549, War Crimes Case Files (Cases Tried), box 336.

37. First Detailed Interrogation Report, November 14, 1945, August Eigruber, NARA RG 549, War Crimes Case Files (Cases Tried), box 336.

38. Denson, interview by Ringelheim.

39. The Dawes mission occurred in the fall and winter of 1944 and involved the secret deployment of Allied airmen behind enemy lines in Slovakia. The objective of the mission was to liaise with antifascist partisan groups, forward Allied intelligence, and evacuate Allied prisoners of war. Between November 6 and December 26, fifteen members of the mission were captured by German forces and sent to Mauthausen. After ruthless interrogation and torture, they were murdered there on January 26, 1945, on the orders of Ernst Kaltenbrunner, chief of the *Reichssicherheitshauptamt* (RSHA) in Berlin. See War Crimes Investigating Team 6836, subject: "DAWES" and MAUTHAUSEN cases, January 14, 1946, NARA RG 549, War Crimes Case Files (Cases Tried), box 334.

40. See Chapter 2 for a discussion of the Extermination through Work program.

41. Denson received numerous reports concerning the brutality of Spatzenegger as a detail leader in the Wiener Graben. Apparently as a result of his ruthlessness and ideological fanaticism, his comrades named him "The Nazi." Spatzenegger in fact became the sixty-first defendant, with his name added in pen after the initial charge sheet had been prepared. See Eugene S. Cohen, HQ Third United States Army, Report of Investigation of Alleged War Crime, June 17, 1945, NARA RG 549, War Crimes Case Files (Cases Tried), box 334; David Wingeate Pike, *Span-*

iards in the Holocaust: Mauthausen, the Horror on the Danube (New York: Routledge, 2000), 57.

42. Schulz reportedly fled to Czechoslovakia at war's end. In 1967, he was tried in Cologne and sentenced to fifteen years in prison. See Winfried R. Garscha, "Mauthausen und die Justiz (I)," *Justiz und Erinnerung,* Nr. 5, Verein zur Förderung justizgeschichtlicher Forschungen, January 2002, 8.

43. See for instance the statements of Ernst Martin and Dr. Busek, Cohen Report; Charles B. Deibel, War Crimes Investigation Team 6836, Report of Alleged War Crimes to Commanding General, Third US Army, August 8, 1945, NARA RG 549, War Crimes Case Files (Cases Tried), box 335. It should be noted that the name Deibel is also spelled Diebel in various army records.

44. Hans Marsalek, interview by the author, Vienna, October 27, 2007. The chief physicians who served at Mauthausen and its subcamps were also referred to as "chief post physicians." The meaning here is the same.

45. On the night of May 22, 1943, Krebsbach shot a drunken Wehrmacht lance corporal named Josef Breitenfellner, after he was heard making a disturbance in Krebsbach's garden. As punishment, Krebsbach was relieved of his duties as chief physician and sent to work at Warwara concentration camp. He later entered the army and served as chief staff doctor. Hans Marsalek, *The History of Mauthausen Concentration Camp,* 3rd ed. (Vienna: Austrian Society of Mauthausen Concentration Camp, 1995), 174.

46. Deibel, Report on Alleged War Crimes.

47. Strauss himself would be tried at Dachau, in one of the many subsequent proceedings spawned by the Mauthausen parent trial, and sentenced to life in prison.

48. Marsalek, *Mauthausen,* 183.

49. Ibid., 181.

50. Straight, *Report,* 61.

51. Report of War Crimes Investigation Team 6824 to the General of the Third Army. Denson Papers, Series 2—Trials, 1945–2001, box 7, folder 34.

52. For a brief survey of the sixty-one Mauthausen trial defendants, see Review and Recommendations of the Deputy Judge Advocate for War Crimes, Case no. 000–50–5, February 25, 1947. Denson Papers, Series 2—Trials, 1945–2001, box 7, folder 35.

53. Of the 1,030 selected as defendants in the mass-atrocity trials at Dachau, only 3 were women. None were prosecuted in subsequent trials of Mauthausen personnel. Yavnai, "U.S Army," 61.

54. A total of 4,065 female prisoners were registered at Mauthausen over the course of its existence. At least 271 died there. Andreas Baumgartner, *Die vergessenen Frauen von Mauthausen* (Vienna: Verlag Österreich, 1997), 219.

55. United States Army, Theater Judge Advocate's Office, War Crimes Branch, European Theater of Operations, *Suggestions to Investigators of War Crimes*, April 18, 1945, appendix 15, in Straight, *Report*, 141–149.

56. Ibid.

57. Ibid.

58. It should be noted that while Guth denies abusing the suspects he interrogated, he asks the interviewer to turn off the tape recorder on various occasions before providing details of his approach. See Guth, interview.

59. Guth, interview.

60. Willy Brünning, Protokollauszug, AMM P/19/11.

61. Hans Altfuldisch, Protokollauszug, AMM P/19/11.

62. Vinzenz Nohel, Protokollauszug, AMM P/19/11.

63. Dr. Krebsbach, Protokollauszug, AMM P/19/11.

64. First Detailed Interrogation Report of August Eigruber, November 14, 1945, NARA RG 549, War Crimes Case Files (Cases Tried), box 336.

65. Eigruber Protokoll, AMM P/9/11, 10.

66. Guth, interview.

67. Ironically, Eigruber's son later became the star salesman in the Guth family's Austrian carpet company. Paul Guth never let on that he had known the gauleiter, or that he had played a significant role in the senior Eigruber's trial. Guth, interview.

68. See Chapter 1.

69. See Chapter 1 for a discussion of the Dachau concentration camp case.

70. William Denson, interview by Horace R. Hanson, Mineola, NY, June 14, 1984, transcript, Denson Papers, Series 1—Personal, box 2, folder 10; Denson, interview by Ringelheim.

71. Denson, interview by Hanson.

72. Denson, interview by Ringelheim.

73. Wesley Vincent Hilton, "The Blackest Canvas: U.S. Army Courts and the Trial of War Criminals in Post–World War II Europe" (PhD dissertation, Texas Tech University, 2003), 69.

74. Military Government Court, Charge Sheet, March 7, 1946, *The United States v. Hans Altfuldisch et al.,* Case no. 000–50–5, Denson Papers, Series 2—Trials, 1945–2001, box 8.

75. Straight, *Report,* 63.

76. United Nations War Crimes Commission, *Law Reports of Trials of War Criminals,* vol. 11 (London, 1949), Denson Papers, Series 2—Trials, 1945–2001, box 4, folder 4.

4. The Defendants in the Dock

1. Benjamin Ferencz, interview by the author, April 11, 2006.

2. *Heute* magazine, May 1, 1946, AMM P/19/34.

3. Lieutenant Colonel Robert W. Wilson's defense team included deputies Major Ernst Oeding, Captain Francis McGuigan, Lieutenant Charles B. Deibel, First Lieutenant Patrick W. McMahon, and civilians David P. Hervey and Alexander Wolf.

4. Joshua Greene, *Justice at Dachau: The Trials of an American Prosecutor* (New York: Broadway Books, 2003), 135.

5. *The United States v. Hans Altfuldisch et al.,* Case no. 000–50–5, William Dowdell Denson Papers, Manuscripts and Archives, Yale University Library, Manuscript Group 1832, Series 2—Trials, 1945–2001, boxes 8–12 (3,511 pages), 55–56.

6. From October 8 to December 7, 1945, an American military commission tried Japanese general Tomoyuki Yamashita for war crimes relating to the massacre of civilians in the Philippines during February and March 1945 and sentenced him to death. The trial established a precedent concerning command responsibility for war crimes sometimes referred to as "the Yamashita standard." See Richard L. Lael, *The Yamashita Precedent: War Crimes and Command Responsibility* (Wilmington, DE: Scholarly Resources, 1982).

7. *U.S. v. Altfuldisch et al.,* 66.

8. Ibid.

9. *U.S. v. Altfuldisch et al.,* 74.

10. *Heute,* May 1, 1946.

11. *U.S. v. Altfuldisch et al.,* 84.

12. Ibid., 87–90.
13. "Austrian Gauleiter Accused in Atrocity at Dachau—Trial May Last 6 Weeks," *News of Germany,* Information Control Division, Office of Military Government (US Zone), April 2, 1946, NARA RG 549, War Crimes Case Files (Cases Tried), box 347.
14. "61 Mauthausen 'Camp' Officials Placed on Trial," *Washington Times-Herald,* March 30, 1946, NARA RG 549, War Crimes Case Files (Cases Tried), box 336; "Austrian Gauleiter Accused in Atrocity at Dachau," *News of Germany.*
15. Michel Fabréguet, *Mauthausen: Camp de concentration national-socialiste en Autriche rattachée, 1938–1945* (Paris: Honoré Champion, 1999), 661–662.
16. *U.S. v. Altfuldisch et al.,* 92–144.
17. Ibid., 104.
18. Ibid., 121.
19. "61 Mauthausen 'Camp' Officials Placed on Trial," *Washington Times-Herald,* March 30, 1946, NARA RG 549, War Crimes Case Files (Cases Tried), box 336.
20. *U.S. v. Altfuldisch et al.,* 119.
21. Ibid., 117.
22. Ibid., 135.
23. Ibid., 107.
24. Guide to Procedure in Military Courts, June, 1945. Reproduced in Holger Lessing, *Der Erste Dachauer Prozess, 1945–1946* (Baden Baden: Nomos, 1993), appendix 6. See also my discussion of rules and procedures in Chapter 1.
25. *U.S. v. Altfuldisch et al.,* 142.
26. Ibid., 134–135.
27. Ibid., 143.
28. William Denson, interview by Joan Ringelheim, August 25, 1994, video, United States Holocaust Memorial Museum Film and Video Archive, RG-50.030*0268.
29. See Chapter 2 for a discussion of Martin's contribution to the investigation of war crimes at Mauthausen.
30. *U.S. v. Altfuldisch et al.,* 153.
31. Ibid., 155.
32. Ibid., 160–162.
33. Ibid., 182, 186, 235–237, 239–240.

34. Ibid., 189–190.
35. Ibid., 228.
36. Ibid., 267.
37. Ibid., 266–267.
38. Ibid., 258.
39. Ibid., 257.
40. Ibid., 329.
41. Ibid.
42. Ibid., 333–334.
43. Ibid., 334.
44. Ibid., 338.
45. Ibid., 344.
46. Ibid., 396.
47. Ibid., 398.
48. Ibid., 436–437.
49. Ibid., 444–446.
50. Ibid., 439.
51. Ibid.
52. Ibid., 542. Marsalek remembered being aware of this plan even prior to liberation, and to his interrogation of Ziereis. A fellow prisoner reportedly told Marsalek that the camp SS had ordered him to survey a site north of Mauthausen and close to the railroad tracks for the purpose of a new gassing facility. Hans Marsalek, interview by Tomaz Jardim, Vienna, October 27, 2007. See also Bertrand Perz and Florian Freund, "Auschwitz Neu? Pläne und Massnahmen zur Wiedererrichtung der Krematorien von Auschwitz-Birkenau in der Umgebung des KZ Mauthausen im Februar 1945," *Dachauer Hefte,* Nr. 20, ed. Wolfgang Benz and Barbara Distel (Brussels: Comité International de Dachau, 2004).
53. *U.S. v. Altfuldisch et al.,* 610.
54. See Chapter 3.
55. *U.S. v. Altfuldisch et al.,* 786. An inspection of the actual Mauthausen site makes von Posern's story an unlikely one, given the distance from the kitchen to the bunker, and the sight lines involved.
56. *U.S. v. Altfuldisch et al.,* 788–789.
57. As a result of his testimony at the Mauthausen parent trial, at subsequent proceedings, and during his own trial for war crimes, von Posern would be labeled one of a number of "professional witnesses," officially declared unreliable by the deputy judge advocate in a directive

issued in 1948. See Memorandum for Colonel William H. Peters, Jr., Chief, War Crimes Branch, Subject: Unreliable Witnesses in War Crimes Trials, March 28, 1951, NARA RG 549, Pre-Trial Activities, box 1.

58. *U.S. v. Altfuldisch et al.*, 638.
59. Ibid., 673.
60. Ibid., 900.
61. Ibid., 1239–1240.
62. Ibid., 1251.
63. The prosecution did not introduce statements from defendants Grahn, Pribyll, Wolter, and Spatzenegger.
64. *U.S. v. Altfuldisch et al.*, 1292.
65. Ibid., 1296–1297.
66. See Chapter 3.
67. *U.S. v. Altfuldisch et al.*, 1302–1303.
68. Ibid., 1302.
69. Ibid., 1454.
70. Ibid., 1332.
71. Ibid., 1464–1466.
72. Ibid., 1404.
73. Ibid., 1334.
74. Ibid., 1385.
75. Ibid.
76. Ibid., 1450; 1428.
77. Ibid., 1421.
78. Ibid., 1321.
79. Ibid., 1503.
80. Ibid., 2329.
81. Ibid., 2131.
82. Ibid., 2148.
83. Ibid., 2956, 2964.
84. Ibid., 3018.
85. Ibid., 1623, 1671.
86. Ibid., 2084, 1632.
87. Ibid., 1507, 1580.
88. Ibid., 1578.
89. Ibid., 2672.
90. Ibid., 2179.
91. Ibid., 2178.
92. Ibid., 2808.

93. SS-Hauptsturmführer Georg Bachmayer, responsible for the Mauthausen garrison and in charge of security, discipline, and capital punishment in the camp, committed suicide at war's end. SS-Hauptsturmführer Karl Schulz, head of Mauthausen's Political Department, initially escaped capture but was finally sentenced to fifteen years in prison by a German court in 1967.

94. Ibid., 2002, 2009.

95. Ibid., 2041.

96. Ibid., 2724.

97. Ibid., 1975.

98. Ibid., 1561.

99. Ibid., 2688.

100. Lisa Yavnai, "Military Justice: The U.S. Army War Crimes Trials in Germany, 1944–1947" (PhD dissertation, London School of Economics and Political Science, 2007), 144.

101. *U.S. v. Altfuldisch et al.*, 2597.

102. Ibid., 2666.

103. Ibid., 1911.

104. Ibid., 2502.

105. Ibid., 2565, 1586.

106. Ibid., 2843.

107. Lieutenant Colonel C. E. Straight, *Report of the Deputy Judge Advocate for War Crimes, European Command, June 1944 to July 1948*, NARA, RG 549, General Admin., box 13, 65.

108. *U.S. v. Altfuldisch et al.*, 3212.

109. Yavnai, "Military Justice," 203.

110. *U.S. v. Altfuldisch et al.*, 2632.

111. Ibid., 2641.

112. Ibid., 2929.

113. Ibid., 3074.

114. Denson to Counsel Section, Flossenbürg Concentration Camp Case, "Status of Personnel in Concentration Camps," 15 November 1946, quoted in Yavnai, "Military Justice," 199.

115. *U.S. v. Altfuldisch et al.*, 1701.

116. Ibid., 3015.

117. Ibid., 2056.

118. William Dowdell Denson, *Justice in Germany: Memories of the Chief Prosecutor* (Mineola, NY: Meltzer et al., 1995), 15.

119. Denson, interview by Ringelheim.

120. *U.S. v. Altfuldisch et al.*, 1533–1544.
121. Ibid., 1731.
122. Ibid., 2778.
123. Ibid., 1839, 1898.
124. Ibid., 1793.
125. Ibid., 3028.
126. Ibid., 2143.
127. Ibid., 2461.
128. Ibid., 2500–2501.
129. Ibid., 2086.
130. Ibid., 2085.
131. Ibid., 2703.
132. Ibid., 2241.
133. Ibid., 1309.
134. Ibid., 1379.
135. Ibid., 1361.
136. Ibid., 1330.
137. Jürgen Matthäus, "Vernichtungslager," *Enzyklopädie des Nationalsozialismus*, ed. Wolfgang Benz, Hermann Graml, and Hermann Weiss (Stuttgart: Klet-Cotta, 1997), 779.
138. *U.S. v. Altfuldisch et al.*, 3267.

5. Judgment at Dachau

1. *The United States v. Hans Altfuldisch et al.*, Case no. 000–50–5, William Dowdell Denson Papers, Manuscripts and Archives, Yale University Library, Manuscript Group 1832, Series 2—Trials, 1945–2001, boxes 8–12 (3,511 pages), 3455.
2. Ibid., 3456–3457.
3. Ibid., 3457.
4. Ibid., 3458.
5. Ibid., 3459.
6. Ibid.
7. Ibid.
8. Ibid., 3460.
9. Ibid., 3463.
10. Ibid., 3461.
11. Ibid., 3458.

12. Ibid., 89. For a discussion of current estimates concerning the number of dead within the Mauthausen camp system, as well as of the Cohen Report, see Chapter 2.
13. *U.S. v. Altfuldisch et al.,* 3465.
14. Ibid., 3468.
15. Ibid.
16. Ibid., 3467.
17. Ibid., 3470.
18. Ibid., 3470–3471.
19. Ibid., 3472.
20. For a discussion of the modern, bureaucratic nature of the Nazi state and the Holocaust, see for instance Raul Hilberg, *The Destruction of the European Jews,* 3rd ed. (New Haven, CT: Yale University Press, 2003); Zygmunt Bauman, *Modernity and the Holocaust* (Ithaca, NY: Cornell University Press, 1989).
21. *U.S. v. Altfuldisch et al.,* 3474.
22. Ibid., 3473.
23. Ibid., 3475.
24. Ibid., 3476–77.
25. Ibid., 3477.
26. See Chapter 4, 34–39.
27. *U.S. v. Altfuldisch et al.,* 3480.
28. Ibid., 3483.
29. Ibid., 3484–85.
30. Ibid., 3488.
31. Ibid., 3493.
32. Ibid., 3494.
33. Ibid., 3495.
34. "Three Given Life Terms in Trial for War Crimes," *Washington Post,* May 14, 1946; "U.S Tribunal Sentences 58 Nazi Murderers to Gallows," *New York Daily News,* May 14, 1946; "58 Germans Doomed to Be Hanged for Mauthausen Mass Murders," *New York Times,* May 14, 1946; "58 Todesurteile wegen Mauthausen," *Berliner Zeitung,* May 14, 1946.
35. *U.S. v. Altfuldisch et al.,* 3509–3510.
36. Ibid., 1037–1041.
37. Ibid., 1941–1943.
38. Ibid., 735.

39. Ibid., 853–855, 2054–2065.
40. Ibid., 862, 3206, 3225–3226, 3288.
41. William Denson, interview by Joan Ringelheim, August 25, 1994, video, United States Holocaust Memorial Museum Film and Video Archive, RG-50.030*0268.
42. Ibid.
43. William Denson, Speech to North Shore Synagogue, Syosset, NY, April 12, 1991, Denson Papers Series 1—Personal, box 2, folder 25.
44. William Denson, interview by Mark Goldberg, March 12, 1996, USC Shoah Foundation Institute Visual History Archive, 13079.
45. It is interesting to note that while the judges confirmed the major elements of the prosecution's case, their special findings refer to the existence of a "deliberate conspiracy," rather than a "common design" to commit war crimes at Mauthausen. Denson insisted throughout the presentation of his case that proving the existence of conspiracy was not his goal, nor was it required to convict all sixty-one defendants. It is not clear why the court opted for conspiracy, given its irrelevance to the prosecution's case. Although the court may have chosen conspiracy in order to further ease the burden for prosecutors trying Mauthausen personnel in subsequent proceedings, it is more plausible that the inclusion of the term reflects instead the lack of nuance in the thinking of military judges without legal training.
46. Denson, interview by Goldberg.
47. Denson, Speech to North Shore Synagogue.
48. Telford Taylor, *The Anatomy of the Nuremberg Trials,* appendix A: "Charter of the International Tribunal" (Toronto: Little, Brown, 1992), 648.
49. Lisa Yavnai, "Military Justice: The U.S. Army War Crimes Trials in Germany, 1944–1947" (PhD dissertation, London School of Economics and Political Science, 2007), 204–205.
50. Ibid., 205.
51. Ibid., 207.
52. Donald Bloxham, *Genocide on Trial: War Crimes Trials and the Formation of Holocaust History and Memory* (New York: Oxford University Press, 2001), 66.
53. Reflecting on the trial years later, Chief Prosecutor Denson still saw Mauthausen, Auschwitz, and Treblinka as functionally the same. During a speech to the North Shore Synagogue, he commented, "[Maut-

hausen] never received the notoriety of Auschwitz or Treblinka, but it was an extermination camp serving the Nazis in the west the same way that Auschwitz and Treblinka operated in the east." William Denson, Speech to North Shore Synagogue.

54. United States Holocaust Memorial Museum Photo Archive, 12295 and 12296.

55. Lieutenant Colonel C. E. Straight, *Report of the Deputy Judge Advocate for War Crimes, European Command, June 1944 to July 1948*, NARA, RG 549, General Admin., box 13, 71.

56. By December 31, 1947, a backlog of 216 unreviewed cases had accumulated. According to the Deputy Judge Advocate for War Crimes, this had resulted from "the almost total absence of personnel assigned to the War Crimes Group who had any prior experience with similar work, the small number of lawyers assigned to the War Crimes Group . . . and the great urgency placed upon the early completion of the other aspects of the program, i.e., investigations, apprehensions, and the screening of those in detention." Straight, *Report*, 72.

57. Deputy Theater Judge Advocate's Office, 7708 War Crimes Group, Review and Recommendations of the Deputy Judge Advocate for War Crimes, Case no. 000–50–5, February 25, 1947. Denson Papers, Series 2—Trials, box 7, folder 35, 4–13.

58. Ibid., 14–21.

59. Ibid., 57.

60. Franz Xavier Bücherl, Annex to the Petition for Review in the Case of BILLMANN, Karl and GRZYBOWSKI, Herbert, July 1946, NARA RG 549, War Crimes Case Files (Cases Tried), box 349.

61. Bücherl, Annex, 17.

62. Charles B. Deibel, Petition for Review—Josef Mayer, Paul Gützlaff, Theophil Priebel, Rudolf Mynzak, Ferdinand Lappert, Viktor Korger, Ludwig Dörr, Wilhelm Mack, Thomas Sigmund and Adolf Rutka, May 22, 1946, NARA RG 549, War Crimes Case Files (Cases Tried), box 348.

63. Alexander Wolf, Petition for Review—Michael Cserny, May 1946, NARA RG 549, War Crimes Case Files (Cases Tried), box 349, 2.

64. See Review and Recommendations.

65. Review and Recommendations, 105.

66. Colonel J. L. Harbaugh Jr., Acting Judge Advocate, Case Review, 000–50–5 (Mauthausen Concentration Camp Case) *U.S. vs. Hans* altfuldisch

et al., April 17, 1947, NARA, RG 549, War Crimes Case Files (Cases Tried), box 347.

67. Col. J. L. Harbaugh Jr., Various Review Notes for *U.S. vs. Hans Altfuldisch et al.,* April 1947, NARA RG 549, War Crimes Case Files (Cases Tried), box 347.

68. Harbaugh, Case Review.

69. Harbaugh, Review Notes.

70. General Lucius D. Clay, Military Government Court—Order on Review, Case no. 000–50–5, April 30, 1947, NARA RG 549, War Crimes Case Files (Cases Tried), box 346.

71. "Army Executes 22 for Crimes in War," *New York Times,* May 28, 1947; "Sühne für Mauthausen," *Berliner Zeitung,* May 28, 1947.

72. Office of the Provost Marshal, First Military District, Report of Execution on 29 May, 1947, 3 June, 1947, NARA 549, War Crimes Case Files (Cases Tried), box 348.

73. Despite the stay of execution granted Striegel, he was nonetheless hanged at Landsberg three weeks later, on June 19, 1947. "26 More Executed by U.S in Germany," *New York Times,* May 29, 1947.

74. "22 Nazis Die on Gallows; More Today," *Washington Post,* May 28, 1947; "Army Executes 22 for Crimes in War," *New York Times,* May 28, 1947.

75. "26 More Executed By U.S in Germany," *New York Times,* May 29, 1947.

76. Willy Brünning, Statement of Last Words, NARA RG 549, War Crimes Case Files (Cases Tried), box 356.

77. Heinrich Fitschok, Statement of Last Words, NARA RG 549, War Crimes Case Files (Cases Tried), box 356.

78. Willy Frey and Waldemar Wolter, Statement of Last Words, NARA RG 549, War Crimes Case Files (Cases Tried), box 356.

79. August Eigruber, Statement of Last Words, NARA RG 549, War Crimes Case Files (Cases Tried), box 356.

80. Otto Striegel, Statement of Last Words, NARA RG 549, War Crimes Case Files (Cases Tried), box 356.

81. Willy Eckert, Statement of Last Words, NARA RG 549, War Crimes Case Files (Cases Tried), box 356.

82. Stefan Barczay, Statement of Last Words, NARA RG 549, War Crimes Case Files (Cases Tried), box 356.

83. "Doomsday at Landsberg," *New York Times*, May 29, 1947. As with other reports in the *New York Times*, *Washington Post*, and *Berliner Zeitung*, the author erroneously cites a figure of 700,000 dead at Mauthausen—a number that likely emerged from the confusing mortality statistics at trial, starting at over a million but reduced to 70,000 by the time proceedings came to a close.

Conclusion

1. William Denson, interview by Mark Goldberg, March 12, 1996, USC Shoah Foundation Institute Visual History Archive, 13079.
2. William Denson, interview by Joan Ringelheim, August 25, 1994, video, United States Holocaust Memorial Museum Film and Video Archive, RG-50.030*0268.
3. Denson, interview by Goldberg.
4. For discussion of the parent trial system see Chapter 1.
5. See Lieutenant Colonel C. E. Straight, *Report of the Deputy Judge Advocate for War Crimes, European Command, June 1944 to July 1948*, NARA, RG 549, General Admin., box 13, 50.
6. The first subsequent trial concerned eight Dachau concentration camp personnel and began on October 11, 1946; the last such trial was of Nordhausen block leader Willie Palko and concluded on December 12, 1947. See Lisa Yavnai, "Military Justice: The U.S. Army War Crimes Trials in Germany, 1944–1947" (PhD dissertation, London School of Economics and Political Science, 2007), addendum, 267–446.
7. William Denson, Speech to Shelter Rock Jewish Center (manuscript), Roslyn, NY, April 17, 1990. Denson Papers, Series 1—Personal, box 3, folder 26.
8. Yavnai, "Military Justice," addendum.
9. Florian Freund, "Der Dachauer Mauthausenprozess," in *Jahrbuch 2001, Dokumentationsarchiv des österreichischen Widerstandes*, ed. Christine Schindler (Vienna: Dokumentationsarchiv des österreichischen Widerstandes, 2001), 36.
10. Deputy Theater Judge Advocate's Office, 7708 War Crimes Group, Review and Recommendations of the Deputy Judge Advocate for War Crimes, Case no. 000–50–8, *United States v. Willi Auerswald et al.*,

January 23, 1948, NARA RG 549, War Crimes Case Files (Cases Tried), box 373.

11. Deputy Theater Judge Advocate's Office, 7708 War Crimes Group, Review and Recommendations of the Deputy Judge Advocate for War Crimes, Case no. 000–50–10, *United States v. Georg Bach et al.*, March 15, 1948, NARA RG 549, War Crimes Case Files (Cases Tried), box 374.

12. Ibid.

13. Ibid.

14. Yavnai, "Military Justice," 215.

15. Holger Lessing, *Die Erst Dachauer Prozess, 1945–1946* (Baden Baden: Nomos Verlagsgesellschaft, 1993), 311; Yavnai, "Military Justice," 216.

16. Yavnai, "Military Justice," 216.

17. Ibid.

18. Yavnai, "Military Justice," 211.

19. In surveys conducted by the Office of Military Government, United States (OMGUS) in Germany between October 1945 and August 1946, an average of 79 percent of those polled found the trials to have been fairly conducted. See Anna J. Merritt and Richard L. Merritt, eds., *Public Opinion in Occupied Germany: The OMGUS Surveys, 1945–1949* (Urbana: University of Illinois Press, 1970), 35.

20. Colonel Straight, Conference at Munich Respecting Alleged Irregularities in the operation at Dachau and Other Matters, September 6 and 7, 1947, NARA RG 549, Gen. Admin., box 1.

21. Arthur L. Smith Jr., *Die Hexe von Buchenwald: Der Fall Ilse Koch* (Vienna: Böhlau Verlag, 1995), 102–103.

22. Office of the Judge Advocate General, War Crimes Activities, 17 August, 1949, NARA RG 549, General Admin., box 9, 4.

23. William D. Denson, letter to the editor, *New York Times*, September 21, 1948.

24. Office of the Judge Advocate General, War Crimes Activities, 4.

25. Frank M. Buscher, *The U.S. War Crimes Trial Program in Germany, 1946–1955* (Westport, CT: Greenwood Press, 1989), 38.

26. Yavnai, "Military Justice," 222.

27. Headquarters European Command, Final Report of Proceedings of Administration of Justice Review Board, February 14, 1949, NARA RG 549, General Admin., box 13.

28. Ibid.
29. Buscher, *U.S. War Crimes Trial Program,* 41.
30. Ibid., 42.
31. Ibid.
32. Lucius D. Clay to the Department of the Army, September 27, 1948, in *The Papers of General Lucius D. Clay: Germany, 1945–1949,* vol. 1, ed. Jean Edward Smith (Bloomington: Indiana University Press, 1974), 881.
33. Valerie Hébert, *Hitler's Generals on Trial* (Lawrence: University Press of Kansas, 2010), 42.
34. Norbert Frei, *Adenauer's Germany and the Nazi Past: The Politics of Amnesty and Integration* (New York: Columbia University Press, 2002), 108.
35. "Clay Rejects Plea for War Criminals," *Stars and Stripes,* October 28, 1949, NARA RG 549, box 3.
36. Buscher, *U.S. War Crimes Trial Program,* 93.
37. Suzanne Brown-Fleming, *The Holocaust and the Catholic Conscience* (Notre Dame, IN: University of Notre Dame Press, 2006), 5.
38. Brown-Fleming, *Catholic Conscience,* 8.
39. Ibid., 7.
40. Frei, *Adenauer's Germany,* 99.
41. Hébert, *Hitler's Generals,* 42.
42. For a comprehensive study of the war crimes issue in the early West German state see Frei, *Adenauer's Germany.*
43. High Commissioner for Germany (HICOG), Political Brief No. 5—Political Aspects of the War Criminals Question, 1953, NARA RG 549, General Admin., box 12.
44. Yavnai, "Military Justice," 238.
45. Ibid., 239.
46. Freund, "Der Dachauer Mauthausenprozess," 65.
47. Yavnai, "Military Justice," 240.
48. A survey conducted by HICOG titled "Current West German Views on the War Criminals Issue" found that by September 1952, only 10 percent of the West German public supported the war crimes trials. See Buscher, *U.S. War Crimes Trial Program,* 91.
49. Denson, interview by Goldberg.
50. Lawrence Douglas, *The Memory of Judgment: Making Law and History in the Trials of the Holocaust* (New Haven, CT: Yale University Press, 2001), 3.

51. Bertrand Perz, "Prozesse zum KZ Mauthauen," in *Dachauer Prozesse: NS-Verbrechen vor amerikanischen Militärgerichten in Dachau, 1945–1948,* ed. Ludwig Eiber and Robert Sigel (Göttingen: Wallstein, 2007), 186.

52. Lotte Kohler and Hans Saner, eds., *Hannah Arendt–Karl Jaspers Correspondence, 1926–1969,* trans. Robert Kimber and Rita Kimber (New York: Harcourt Brace Jovanovich, 1992), 54.

53. William Denson, Speech to North Shore Synagogue, April 12, 1991, Denson Papers, Series 1—Personal, box 3, folder 25.

Bibliography of Primary Sources

Archival Collections

Archiv der KZ-Gedenkstätte Mauthausen, Bundesministerium für Inneres, Vienna

Library of Congress Manuscripts Division, Washington, DC

Papers of Robert Houghwout Jackson

Manuscripts and Archives, Yale University Library

William Dowdell Denson Papers, 1918–2004

National Archives and Records Administration, College Park, Maryland

RG 111, Records of the Office of the Chief Signal Officer
RG 153, Records of the Office of the Judge Advocate General (Army)
RG 165, Records of the War Department, General and Special Staffs
RG 226, Records of the Office of Strategic Services
RG 238, National Archives Collection of World War II War Crimes Records
RG 331, Records of Allied Operational and Occupational Headquarters, World War II
RG 549, Records of Headquarters, U.S. Army Europe (USAREUR)

United States Holocaust Memorial Museum

Benjamin B. Ferencz Collection
Oral History Interview—William D. Denson
Photo Archive
William Ornstein Papers

USC Shoah Foundation Institute Visual History Archive

Oral History Interview—William D. Denson

Interviews

Benjamin Ferencz, by phone, April 11, 2006
Whitney Harris, by phone, October 10, 2006
Hans Marsalek, Vienna, October 27, 2007

Published Materials

Newspapers

Berliner Zeitung
New York Herald Tribune
New York Times
Stars and Stripes
Washington Post

Books

Adenauer, Konrad. *Memoirs, 1945–1953*. Chicago: Henry Regnery, 1966.
Allied and Associated Powers. *The Treaty of Peace between the Allied and Associated Powers and Germany, June 28, 1919*. London: H. M. Stationery Office, 1919.
Arendt, Hannah. *Eichmann in Jerusalem: A Report on the Banality of Evil*. New York: Penguin Books, 1963.
Benton, Wilbourn, and Georg Grimm, eds. *Nuremberg: German Views of the War Trials*. Dallas: Southern Methodist University Press, 1955.
Blum, John Morton. *From the Morgenthau Diaries*. Vol. 3, *Years of War, 1941–1945*. Boston: Houghton Mifflin, 1967.

Chamberlin, Brewster, and Marcia Feldman, eds. *The Liberation of the Nazi Concentration Camps, 1945: Eyewitness Accounts of the Liberators*. Washington, DC: United States Holocaust Memorial Council, 1987.

Chandler, Alfred, ed. *The Papers of Dwight David Eisenhower: The War Years*. Baltimore: Johns Hopkins University Press, 1970.

Clay, Lucius D. *Decisions in Germany*. Westport, CT: Greenwood Press, 1970.

Denson, William Dowdell. *Justice in Germany: Memories of the Chief Prosecutor*. Mineola, NY: Meltzer et al., 1995.

Eisenhower, Dwight D. *Crusade in Europe*. Garden City, NY: Doubleday, 1948.

Gilbert, Gustav M. *Nuremberg Diary*. New York: Da Capo Press, 1995.

Goldensohn, Leon. *Die Nürnberger Interviews: Gespräche mit Angeklagten und Zeugen*. Düsseldorf: Artemis and Winkler, 2005.

International Military Tribunal. *Trial of the Major War Criminals before the International Military Tribunal, Nuremberg, 14 November 1945–1 October 1946*, 42 vols. Nuremberg: International Military Tribunal, 1947.

Jackson, Robert H. *Report of Robert H. Jackson, United States Representative to the International Conference on Military Trials, London, 1945*. Washington, DC: Department of State, 1949.

Jaworski, Leon. *After Fifteen Years*. Houston: Gulf Publishing, 1961.

Kintner, Earl W., ed. *The Hadamar Trial*. London: William Hodge, 1949.

Kohler, Lotte, and Hans Saner, eds. *Hannah Arendt–Karl Jaspers Correspondence, 1926–1969*. Translated by Robert Kimber and Rita Kimber. New York: Harcourt Brace Jovanovich, 1992.

Lemkin, Rafael. *Axis Rule in Occupied Europe: Laws of Occupation, Analysis of Government, Proposals for Redress*. Washington, DC: Carnegie Endowment for International Peace, Division of International Law, 1944.

Marrus, Michael R., ed. *The Nuremberg War Crimes Trial, 1945–1946: A Documentary History*. Boston: Bedford Books, 1997.

Merritt, Anna J., and Richard L. Merritt. *Public Opinion in Occupied Germany: The OMGUS Surveys, 1945–1949*. Urbana: University of Illinois Press, 1970.

———. *Public Opinion in Semisovereign Germany: The HICOG Surveys, 1949–1955*. Urbana: University of Illinois Press, 1980.

Overy, Richard. *Interrogations: The Nazi Elite in Allied Hands, 1945.* New York: Penguin Books, 2001.

Patton, George S. *War as I Knew It.* Cambridge, MA: Riverside Press, 1947.

Rückerl, Adalbert, ed. *The Investigation of Nazi Crimes, 1945–1978: A Documentation.* Hamden, CT: Archon Books, 1980.

Scott, James Brown, ed. *The Hague Conventions and Declarations on 1899 and 1907.* New York: Oxford University Press, 1915.

Smith, Bradley, ed. *The American Road to Nuremberg: The Documentary Record, 1944–1945.* Stanford, CA: Hoover Institution Press, 1982.

Smith, Jean Edward, ed. *The Papers of General Lucius D. Clay: Germany, 1945–1949.* 2 vols. Bloomington: Indiana University Press, 1974.

Taylor, Telford. *The Anatomy of the Nuremberg Trials.* New York: Little, Brown, 1992.

West, Rebecca. *A Train of Powder.* New York: Viking Press, 1955.

Wiesenthal, Simon. *Denn sie wußten, was sie tun: Zeichnungen und Aufzeichnungen aus dem KZ Mauthausen.* Vienna: Deuticke, 1995.

Acknowledgments

This book would not have been possible without the abundant intellectual, emotional, and financial support so generously extended to me throughout the course of my research and writing. First, I am deeply indebted to the various institutions that provided me with the funds necessary to travel, to research, and to write. Both an Ontario Graduate Scholarship and a grant from the Joint Initiative for German and European Studies at the University of Toronto allowed me to travel to archives in Austria and the United States and to complete major portions of my manuscript. In addition, receipt of both the Diane and Howard Wohl Fellowship and the Laurie and Andy Okun Fellowship at the Center for Advanced Holocaust Studies, United States Holocaust Memorial Museum, provided many productive months of both research and writing in Washington, D.C. I am particularly thankful to the knowledgeable staff at the Center for Advanced Holocaust Studies, and especially to Lisa Yavnai, whose suggestions helped inspire this project. I wish to express my gratitude also to the many people who assisted me at the National Archives in Washington, D.C., at Yale University Library (Manuscripts and Archives), and at the Mauthausen Memorial Archive. I owe particular thanks to my good friend Christian Dürr.

My greatest debt is owed to Michael Marrus, who could not have been more supportive or helpful throughout the course of my research and writing. In addition, the input of Doris Bergen, Christopher Browning, Jennifer Jenkins, and Derek Penslar was vital. I remain much obliged also to Hilary Earl, Devin Pendas, Richard Steigmann-Gall, and Rebecca Wittmann, whose advice at various junctures of this project was invaluable. Further, the support, encouragement, and thoughtful reflection from both Jacques Kornberg and Carolyn Kay helped make the process of writing both manageable and rewarding. The importance of the counsel of my friend Valerie Hébert cannot be overstated: Valerie's willingness to read draft chapters and to discuss with me the conclusions I reached along the way was nothing less than critical to the completion of this project. Many thanks also to Hugh Paisley, whose legal expertise was generously shared over a series of the most wonderful of meals. Thanks as well to Judy Cohen—survivor, activist, and humble hero—for inspiration and a treasured friendship. Finally, my utmost thanks to Benjamin Ferencz, Whitney Harris, and Hans Marsalek for agreeing to sit for interviews—it was an honor. In spite of the generous assistance received from so many individuals and institutions, however, the statements made and the ideas expressed herein are of course solely my responsibility.

Last but not least, I wish to thank my friends and family, too many to name, for their unwavering support and encouragement. There are no words . . .

Index